Nov. 1, 1992

Dad,

Happy Birthday

Love,

Wayne

A Biography by
Beach Leighton

MR. DUTCH
The Arkansas Traveler

Foreword by Bob Hope

SAGAMORE PUBLISHING INC.
Champaign, Illinois 61824-0673

© 1991 Sagamore Publishing, Inc.
P.O. Box 673
Champaign, IL 61824-0673

Book design: Brian J. Moore
Cover and photo insert design: Michelle R. Dressen
Cover photo: *St. Louis Globe-Democrat*
Editor: Lisa A. Busjahn
Proofreader: Phyllis L. Bannon

Printed in the United States of America

10 9 8 7 6 5 4 3 2 1

ISBN: 0-915611-44-9
Library of Congress Catalog Card Number: 91-60004

To Bob Hope

who has meant so much to golf,
and to Dutch Harrison,
and for that matter to all of us
who have followed his career as the
"Good Humor Man of America."

Contents

Foreword

Dutch Harrison was my kind of guy. He loved golf and people. I remember telling the press back in the 1970s I'd rather play a round of golf with Arnie Palmer or Dutch than anybody else in the world. With Dutch, I'd have a lot of laughs, get some tips on how to improve my game, and most of all, I'd feel comfortable. Dutch was special.

I remember a round I played with the "Dutchman" in Palm Springs. For three holes we laughed and swapped golf and race horse stories. On the fourth tee Dutch said, "Mr. Bob, if you would just keep your head down, slow down the talking and your back swing, you would have a bit more fun."

We continued playing with Dutch encouraging me and still smiling that easy grin. At the 12th hole he said, "Mr. Bob, if you par three straight holes, I'll carry your clubs the rest of the way."

Prodded by his wheedling and his earlier advice, I parred numbers 15, 16, and 17 — and Dutch kept his word. He toted my bag up the 18th fairway and onto the green. What an impression that made on the veranda crowd, especially when I told them why Dutch was carrying my bag. But just to let everybody know that he was still the boss, he knocked in a 20-footer on the last green for a bird—winning the hole and my money.

Dutch did for the two-dollar nassau what Lee Iacocca did for Chrysler. He invented more betting contests in golf than the big casinos have gaming tactics. In practice rounds Dutch was easy to spot. Look for the foursome with raw amateurs and the host pro and there was Dutch. He felt obliged to initiate the rookies. As he summed it up after accepting his winnings, "Well, I reckon they needed a bit of experience."

Even with their pockets emptied, everybody loved Dutch.

He may have ambled out of an Arkansas cotton patch with a corn pone accent, but he could outsmart anybody on a golf course. What a smooth sugar coater he was. I remember when he told me how good I was while he was giving me a lesson. It cost me $800. When I made a bad shot during a round, Dutch remarked, "Everything is all right, Mr. Bob. You're just limbering up."

That's what he told me on the 18th green once. And when I'd ask for help on a putt he'd say, "Just keep it low, Mr. Bob."

A politician was once playing a round with Dutch at Burning Tree in Washington, D.C. He lunged at the ball on an iron shot, took an enormous divot, and knocked it right in Dutch's face. Dutch wiped the ground out of his eyes and spit it out of his mouth.

At the end of the game the fellow asked Dutch, "How do you like the course here at Burning Tree?"

Dutch replied, "I like it. I've played all over the world and this is the finest course I've ever tasted."

I wouldn't have missed the dinner and pro-am we gave for Dutch in St. Louis in 1977. There was a lot of love for him that day from big turnouts at both events. I received the most courteous treatment possible playing with Dutch in the pro-am. I didn't mind his showing me how to hold my club or give me a line, but when he started to lift me in and out of the golf cart — well, that was ridiculous.

After the pro-am, Dutch and I celebrated by retreating to the second floor of the clubhouse. Tommy Bolt and T.D. Morris, host pro at Old Warson, were also there. We shared levity and libation over our golf and Army experiences. Tommy and Dutch were in rare form. I laughed so hard — for days my stomach thought it had been left at the 19th hole.

The movie moguls wanted to team Bing and me in a road picture titled, *Road to the Fountain of Youth.* Dutch should have been in that picture with us because as a senior golfer, he showed he had found it. It's hard to believe he won the U.S. National Seniors Open four times in a row. He'd be called "moneybags" if he were playing on the senior circuit today.

I knew Dutch for over 40 years and I played with the "Arkansas Traveler" around the world. We had so many fun times together. He was always a gorgeous, A-1 guy, and one of the most beloved figures in golf. He is truly a golf legend.

As great as he was in his professional field, I'll remember him as a marvelous human being. He brought a lot of sunshine to the course — always whistling and laughing along the fairways. Dutch had only one standard in choosing friends — that they be, in his words, "nice folks." What a privilege it was to be his friend.

Here's to you, Dutch... thanks for the memories.

Bob Hope

Preface

Dutch Harrison followed the sun to the far corners of the world for four decades carrying his magic touch with a golf club. Throughout his odyssey, he exuded a warmth and manner that was as easy-styled as an Ozark hoedown. Like a kid headed for the fishing or swimming hole, he always enjoyed himself.

Early on he was known as Ernie Joe, and in later years was commonly dubbed Pops. But to most of his friends he was just Dutch or Mr. Dutch. When the golf gods convene in the next millennium, the name Dutch Harrison will no doubt bring smiles and laughter as they remember his antics. This is a rags to riches story of a man who enjoyed life to its fullest and created fun wherever he traveled.

No matter if you were a pauper or king, youngster or oldster—Dutch was always the same Dutch of Arkansas, the crown prince of humor on the golf circuit. Norman Rockwell would have painted Dutch Harrison as the American Golfer. He had that "gee-gosh," foot-dragging, humble quality about him much like Gary Cooper. His heart was as big as his smile; his wit would light up a room. Arkansas has produced many famous people—William Fulbright, Douglas MacArthur, Paul (Bear) Bryant, Dizzy Dean, Glen Campbell—but few captured the hearts of people all over the world as did Dutch Harrison. The golf course was his stage and the whole world became his theater.

No one present at the Seminole Tournament in 1940 will ever forget the first meeting of Dutch with the

Duke of Windsor and no one tells the story better than Dutch: "My first meeting with the Duke of Windsor was at a pro-am tournament at Seminole near Palm Beach, Florida. There was a crowd around the first tee area of this swanky club as the announcer introduced the players. 'Ladies and gentlemen, in the next foursome we have Jimmy Demaret and Robert Young (Chairman of the Board of the C&O Railroad and New York Central Railroad who was often a host for the Duke and Duchess of Windsor when they were in Florida) and we are honored to have with us the Duke of Windsor and his partner, Dutch Harrison.' So I went over to the Duke of Windsor—you know he had been King of England—an' said, 'Dukie, ol' boy, it's nice to meet you. I'm the Dutch of Arkansas — and I patted him several times on the back. Now I guess this was sorta unheard of for royalty, an' some of those old fuddy duds were a-blinkin' like a bullfrog in a hailstorm, an' those secret servicemen were quiverin' in their boots. But the crowd seemed to love it. I always did like to loosen things up a bit. The Duke and I became good friends; in fact, after that first tourney he'd always ask me to be his partner. We sure had some good times. I remember he'd prance an' spread his tail feathers when I'd slap him on the back after a good shot an' say, 'Atta boy, Dukie!'"

Dutch was a golf artist from head to heel. He knew golf clubs the way Heifetz knew a Stradivarius. In his hands the golf club became a magic wand capable of changing impossible shots into brilliant approaches to the flagstick. He recovered from golf hazards as if they didn't exist. He called his shots like Willie Moscone at billiards, not merely the exact distance, but the trajectory and the spin of the ball required for the correct bounce and roll. Professional golfers admired his fluid swing and beautiful natural rhythm.

Spectators kept saying, "How can that fellow hit the ball that far with such a lazy swing?"

Dutch belonged to a group of golfers who shared a unique brotherhood. He was one of the final links, a vestige of an age gone by—the Jimmy Demarets, the Ben

Hogans, the Sam Sneads. They were a special breed fondly remembered as pioneers in building the golf tour. But they were more than that. They were a close-knit group with a communion maintained throughout their lifetimes. They developed a bond rarely found in the sportsworld of today.

Champion pro Doug Sanders spoke kindly of Dutch. "When people would ask me who was the best teacher in the world, I'd answer, 'For touch, feel and finesse, Dutch Harrison. He could do more with a golf ball than a monkey could with a coconut. He had that magic.'

"Dutch had the knack to tell a great story. His timing, his emotions, his expressions, his mannerisms—he was a charmer. He could tell you he got up in the morning and had breakfast and make it sound exciting. He was always king of the court.

"And Dutch would give you the shirt off his back. He always made you feel better after seeing him. In his humble way he'd ask, 'Doug, do you mind if I play with you?' Would I play with him? Whew—I'd caddie for him, I'd do anything to be with him. He's been called 'the Arkansas Traveler' and 'the Will Rogers of the fairways' but I think the greatest privilege of all who knew him was to be able to call him, *my friend.*"

Bob Hamilton, PGA Tournament Champion, knew Dutch as well as anybody. "Dutch had that knack of making a person feel good. He was a magician at massaging your spirits. By the time he'd get done, you'd think you were the greatest player in the world and that Dutch was learning from you. I'd say, 'Hey, Dutch, don't put all that grease under my feet. Man, I'm about to slide out, with you telling me how good I am. Don't give me all that romance.' Boy, he made you feel good. He was the greatest guy in the world, that's all there was to it. What a wonderful man—the most lovable person to ever walk a golf course. The world was fortunate to have a human being like that."

This writer understands those sentiments. Dutch almost made me think I was the best writer in the world, inspiring me to do this book.

Acknowledgments

There are so many friends to thank over the ten years of writing this book. First, I am grateful to Dutch and Shirley Harrison for the opportunity to write about Dutch. The Warren Van Normans furnished 53 tapes and abundant clippings and transcripts, and Bob Nuelle contributed data, publication ideas, and review time. Their ideas and warm support are much appreciated. The three living stepchildren, David, Martha, Kimo, and Raymond's widow, Helen, and two oldest daughters, Nalani and Kahala were particularly helpful in the data collection process, as were Shirley Harrison, Emma Harrison and Thelma's sister, Anne Kauaihilo. To Morris and Jean Leighton, Jane Leighton, and Mark Bracich, I am indebted for their research of the Australian and Philippine scenes, respectively, and extensive editing by the latter two.

Others who reviewed portions of the book (one or more chapters) were Jack Berkley, Rose Carnahan, Bob Crosby, Tim Crowley, Stan Grossman, Bob Hamilton, Phil Harris, Ben Hogan, Wilbur Johnson, Herman Keiser, Dick Kohlmann, Wanda Leighton, Margo Mateas, Chief Editor Karen Minckler, T.D. Morris, Robb Munson, Bob Nuelle and the Warren Van Normans.

Many of the people described in this book reviewed selected passages. I extend my deepest gratitude to all of these generous people, too numerous to mention. To the more than 300 interviewees, all of whom lit up when Dutch was mentioned, my grateful thanks. These people are listed in Sources and References along with the other credits for the book.

Huck Finn Days

Two drifters, off to see the world,
There's such a lot of world to see
We're after the same rainbow's end,
Waitin' round the bend -
My Huckleberry friend,
Moon River - and me.

from "Moon River" by Johnny Mercer

"I wasn't raised on a golf course...I was raised on farms near the Arkansas River. An' the swing I learned as a kid was the swing of an ax when I chopped wood. I did it the easiest way, an' for me the easiest way was left-handed, an' I jus' kep' swingin' left-handed."

Cornbread an' Milk

"I grew up in Little Rock, but was born on a plantation 30 miles north of Little Rock in Conway, Arkansas. Guess I never did rush through life — an' I began that way, eventually showin' up on March 29, 1910. I was named Earnest Joe after two Field brothers who were owners of the plantation where Daddy was a sharecropper — an' I later changed Earnest to Ernest. Maybe my parents were thinkin' the Fields would leave me some money, but that was jus' wishful thinkin'. I had

1

one younger brother, Walter, two older sisters, Isibell (Belle) an' Gertrude, an' three younger sisters, Ruby, Elsie Jean, an' Lena, an' a brother Jeff who passed on at an early age.

"When I was knee-high-to-a-grasshopper, I was pickin' cotton half-days an' weekends on the plantation an' helpin' Daddy with the chores. In them days you had to pick a hundred pounds of cotton to make fifty cents. That was hard work for me 'cause I picked slower than most an' that ol' gunny sack didn't want to fill up. Left to me, I'd dilly-dally gettin' the cotton planted in the first place.

"Mother never let the eight kids goof-off or get too rambunctious. She saw to it that we were always workin' an' doin' our chores. I'd slop hogs an' I learned to chop wood an' did that ever' day. Used to stoke the cast-iron stove. I was in school before I realized my name wasn't 'Fetch Wood.' We had a horse — Tim was his name — a nice gentle horse — an' he had his chores, too. He'd walk round an' round in circles to pump the water from the well an' churn the ice cream. We rode Tim two miles to school — my sister liked to get him goin' fast — too fast for me. Our school house was so small that some of us went mornins an' the rest went afternoons. I liked school an' quit only 'cause I was goin' to play pro baseball."

His sister, Lena, recalled Dutch riding with his father to deliver ice to the townsfolk in the summer, "At one home they were invited to see a newborn baby just christened. Dutch stubbornly refused, saying, 'Me'n don't want to; us'ns have plenty of those at home.'" In his boyhood environment, conventional rhetoric was uncommon. "I talk gooder now," Dutch would smile and say when reminded of that story.

"I'm made up of a half-dozen nationalities, but my nickname, 'Dutch,' came from my habit of twistin' words an' confusin' pals. They'd understand 'bout every third word. It was on the plantation that I learned to address elders an' others as 'Mistuh' and 'Missus.'

"When I was still in half-britches, my daddy joined the police force of Little Rock an' the family moved from Conway to Little Rock. Conway had been a poke an' plumb town. You poke your head out the window an' you're plumb outta town. Little Rock was a big city to us kids. We lived in a rented farmhouse near the Little Rock Country Club at the edge of town. The farmhouse stood in the middle of a large clearin' an' there was a fork of a crick in back. We didn't have air conditionin', heatin', refrigeration or indoor plumbin', but we did have a basement tornado shelter. On one side stood the barn n' stable n' pigsty, an' on the other side was the smokehouse with its cured hams. We had two work mules an' a cow, besides the horse.

"We'd fatten up the hogs until the first frosts in October an' then butcher 'em. I was agin' the killin' an' didn't take any part in axin' them. I could hear 'em hollerin' plumb to the road half mile away an' I'd shudder. I didn't like to clean 'em either — even when it came to curin' 'em with salt I just stayed a fer piece from the smokehouse area an' those ol' turkey buzzards circlin' overhead.

"We had a garden an' a apple orchard. In our garden we grew corn, taters 'n' peas 'n' beans 'n' sorghum for our molasses. I remember those sweet smellin' apple blossoms in the apple orchard in spring an' the harvest at the end of summer. That apple pickin' was a lot sweeter than cotton pickin'. I can hear the buzzin' of the locusts in the late summer, the rat-a-tat-tat an' the thump-thump of the woodhens, an' the coon dogs yelpin' through the hollers (hollows), the rustlin' of the dry cornstalks an' piles of golden leaves in the fall. I remember sneakin' under the tent to see the circus in summertime an' ridin' the trolley cars that had different sections for the white an' colored. The fairs an' ferris wheels were mighty big in Little Rock in summertime. Then the duck huntin' came right after football season.

"My mom doled out big platters of victuals, everythin' family style. For a big dinner we'd have baked ham, boiled taters an' country gravy, cabbage an' a mess o' greens an' cornbread an' biscuits. An' we'd have us several bowls of jelly an' a couple of kinds of pie. She baked the biggest an' lightest biscuit of anyone. Us kids harvested nuts an' berries in the woods, an' Mother used 'em in cakes an' pies an' jams an' jellies. For breakfast we sure had a lot of hominy grits an' bacon with our porridge. I remember Hoppin' John, a dish consistin' of black-eyed peas cooked with hog jowl. It was mighty tasty. Reckon we used everythin' from the hog 'cept the grunt an' squeal. We children were told, 'waste not, want not.'

"I went barefoot 'til I started to school an' by then my big feet were flat as pancakes. As a boy, I was always afraid of snakes — a lot of rattlers were in the area. I was barefoot when I saw my daddy get bit by a water moccasin. If we hadn't got him to a doctor as soon as we did, he'd a died.

"My daddy never had much to say, but my mother made me walk the straight an' narrow. She was strong an' resourceful — the real backbone of the family. I can remember that cold mornin' in January, 1930, when she woke me at three, an' asked me to saddle the mules to the rickety ol' wagon. She'd been awakened by a dream. I was to go to the bank at the corner of Main an' 2nd Streets in Little Rock an' withdraw our savin's — several hundred dollars. I pulled the wagon up behind the bank in that muddy alley an' waited an' waited. When I got home all I could say was, 'Mama, we don't have any money. That bank never opened.' That was the beginnin' of the Depression that could make a tater cry its eyes out. I'll never forget that day an' the anxiety on the faces of Daddy an' Mother. I felt as low as a mole's bellybutton at diggin' time.

"We almost lost what we owned. My mother had always set such a good table, but we had slim pickin's durin' those Depression years. I was raised on cornbread an' milk, but half the time it was corn pone 'cause we didn't have the milk when we had to sell the cow. Well, pardner, the key to us folks gettin' by during the Depression was hard work an' pullin' together — a frontier-type approach. There was no suckin' our hoe handles, I'll tell ya.' We mighta been poor but we weren't downtrodden.

"I was an Arkansawyer lowlander, not an Ozark hillbilly, but Little Rock was sorta at the crossroads, an' Harold Blaylock an' I had eyes for the girls from both directions, much like that son of the Little Rock woman-hater whose wife ran off with some other fellah. The man took his son up into the Ozark mountains to raise him an' didn't bring him down to town until he was about 14 years old. All the stores were new to the boy an' the crusty ol' man took delight in explainin' what was in the show windows of the general store. About then, a pretty teen-age girl comes sashaying down the street.

"'What's that, Pappy?,' asked the boy.

"'That's a devil red-hot from Hell,' growls the old man.

"Then he went on explainin' the things in the store an' the old man bought some new shirts an' overalls for both of them, an' said, 'Son, I want to buy you a nice present. How about a new pump shotgun?'

"When the boy told him that his old single barrel suited him fine, he asked if the boy would like a pony. But the son wasn't interested in that either. 'Son, I wanta get you somethin' special — what would you like?'

"'Pappy, there ain't but one thing in this town that I want.'

"'Speak up, Son.'

"'Well, Pappy, get me one of them devils red-hot from Hell!'

"Harold an' I indulged a bit in chasin' those devils red-hot from Hell — an' had a good time doin' it! Sometimes I stole out at night to go adventurin' with Harold. Girls were more than a passin' fanny to us."

"One time Harold an' I hitchhiked to Texarkana to visit friends. We slept under a bridge that first night an' were scared stiff in the middle of the night by a shout, 'Don't move or we'll shoot. You're under arrest.'

"My teeth was a rattlin' like hogs eatin' charcoal. Guess those State Police were expectin' a knock-down-drag-out fight. They handcuffed us an' took us to jail an' didn't get down to brass tacks until we got there. Then we learned the police mistook us for the two bankrobbers who had broken out of jail in Benton that day. What a hullabaloo! It was embarrassin' to be in jail, but even more to have 'em phone my Daddy on the Little Rock Police Force. He sure put 'em straight real quick an' we got to hit the road again. The police even helped us find a ride to Texarkana."

Ain't Outa Texas Yet

Stories of Texas fascinated Dutch and captured his imagination as a youth. Cowboys were heroes with skill and fortitude. Sagas of their individualism, love of open spaces and ranching on Longhorn-spreads intrigued him. To him Texas sounded like the promised land with its bright, sunny skies and beautiful bluebonnet country. His childhood dream was that he might visit Texas one day. As he grew older he became obsessed with fulfilling that dream.

"At age 15, when summer had come an' gone, I tied my clothes together, put on my extree set of bib overalls an' drifted west for a spell. Found out there were more outhouses than warmin' houses. An' I discovered how big Texas was. I used to recite the jingle:

> 'The sun is riz an' the sun is set
> An Dutch ain't outta Texas yet.'

"I didn't tell my folks where I was goin' or anybody. I hoboed a rumblin' freight train outta Little Rock with only a couple dollars in my pocket. When I was hungry, my first stop was Hope, Arkansas. Jumped off the train an' looked for a friendly farm family. I found when you're lookin' for a handout ya offer to chop wood or somethin'. An' one trick was to go to the farmhouse right after breakfast or right after dinner.

"I knocked at a farmhouse near Hope an' perchance they let me split wood for a meal. After a delicious chicken dinner I felt like a million dollars again an' hopped the next freight train to Texarkana. The brakeman discovered me an' I got plumb tossed off that train. Finally found one with a box car that had eight to ten other hobos. There was a knock at the door an' a guy wanted a dime from each of us or he'd report us to the brakeman. We came up with the money quicker'n a snake goin' through a holler log.

"At the Texas border outside Texarkana the hobos showed me their camp. There were some rough dudes there — some of 'em as ornery as a blood-suckin' hound. If they was too mean, I'd wait for a chance to slip away — sometimes with the excuse of lookin' for wood for the campfire. One mean hombre was Texas Slim, a big hobo who carried a big stick. I saw he could really pop ya with that stick. "I tried to mind my p's an' q's, but he chased me an' kep' yellin', 'You better stop or I'll get ya!'

"I was scared spitless! I ran an' hid behind a tree. He found me an' was ramsackin' me. When he saw how young I was an' learned I didn't have a bankroll, he befriended me an' helped me hitch a freight train goin' to Dallas. He showed me how to catch it at the top of the hill when it would be slowin' down. I jumped at his offer like a chicken on a June bug.

"Some of those hobo nights were mighty cold. I had a long coat an' I'd either sleep on top of it or cover with it, usually near the train tracks. I'd always try to find some branches an' leaves to lie on. I recollect wakin' up when there would be frost on the tracks an' I'd be wonderin' how I survived the night. A settin' round the campfire in the early mornin' felt mighty toasty. I sure consorted with a lot of different people — peddlers, horse traders, swampers, moonshiners. They was jus' poor-hoggin' along. I recollect sittin' round the fire with beans in the pot an' drinkin' that awful black coffee with 'em. Some of 'em had the smarts of a Solomon an' others the smarts of a tadpole. There always seemed to be a friendly philosopher in the bunch — with alotta gray matter between his ears. An' there were a few walkin' whisky vats with leaky mouths.

"I caught a few hitches an' at one train stop in Texas I thumbed a ride with a farmer on his wagon an' wound up pickin' cotton for him. I cain't fer sure remember when I ever hated anythin' as much as pickin' cotton. I had to go like the dickens with both hands to make any money. Never did make much, but it was a grubstake. I found out when you cut an egg several ways, it doesn't go very far. Sometimes I was so wore out I couldn't of yelled 'sooey' iffen the hogs had me down.

"From Dallas I went to Fort Worth an' San Antonio. Traveled all over Texas an' was gone several months. I sure knew what it was to take a slow freight. Sometimes I'd find a golf course to caddie at, or chop wood or load baled hay at a cattle ranch. Even helped with some threshin' an' recollect wipin' the chaff an' sweat off my neck afterwards. The fields of baled hay reminded me of giant biscuits of Shredded Wheat cereal. At one ranch, I got on as a cowhand, ridin' the ranch on an ornery ol' Spanish Mustang to check weak places in the fences, an' I helped mend fence an' string barbed wire. Listened to the cowpunchers spin yarns. I was really a greenhorn when it came to ridin' an' ropin' — guess I was throwed as much as I rode. Didn't exactly press my spurs as a wrangler runnin' herd, but they called me "Cowboy" after the trip.

"When I returned to Little Rock, I was wearin' a big Stetson creased in ol' Fort Worth style, a bright red shirt with a yellow rose emblem on it, an' Levis stuffed into cowboy boots. I had left Arkansas with jus' a cottonsack an' jug of gravy, but came back with a cowboy outfit an' some spendin' money. I was really bustin' my britches an' walkin' tall. Came home carryin' a big cake for my mother. She was pleased as a skunk in a churn."

Harold Blaylock remembers Dutch's colorful garb, that angular jaw jutting below the ten-gallon hat, an' that proud smile on his face when he returned home. "Dutch came back part-Wyatt Earp and part-Cowboy Ernie Joe. He had a bellyful of bullcorn to blow." There were some "stretchers" as Huck Finn would say.

The word "traveler" tasted great to Dutch. Although it was good to be back home, his newly acquired sense of adventure was a stimulus that would remain throughout his life's journey. Dutch would gently roll through it like notes in a lullaby; his temperament was in harmony with the mellow verses of Moon River — with a few meanderings in between.

Moon River, wider than a mile
I'm crossin' you in style
Wherever you're goin'
I'm goin' your way...

Caddie Days

C is for Caddie, who trudges the course
With a burden of clubs that would worry a horse.

"Golf is a Four Letter Word"
by Richard Armour

"Up the mountain 50 yards from our farm was Hole Number 3 of the Little Rock Country Club. Some of my school chums were caddies at the Club, an' I was eager to earn pocket money. I started caddyin' when I was 12. Caddyin' beat choppin' wood an' doin' the farm chores. Besides, by caddyin' on Sunday, I could skip Sunday School — those hellfire an' brimstone preachers never did make much of an impression on me.

"The beautiful Little Rock Country Club was situated above the bluffs of the Arkansas River. Its narrow fairways were surrounded by woods of pine, oak an' hickory. The facilities at the Club were some showcase of luxury 'cause golf came second to all the social activities of the club. Those wealthy members looked on the golf pro as more of a servant than an equal. The pro was in charge of the pro shop an' the course, but if he set foot in the clubhouse, that was trespassin'.

"Herman "Hack" Hackbarth was hired as golf professional (1907). He came south from Wisconsin an' was about 40 years old when I started caddyin'. He was fixin' to become my first an' only golf teacher."

School of Hard Knocks

"He looked me over, saw I was a pretty wiry kid for 12 years, had a wide pair of shoulders, an' he put me to work. I worked my first round of golf, was paid off, an' went home — not to do any more wood choppin' an' milkin', but to go out in the woods an' cut me a nice gnarled cypress branch. With my knife, I trimmed it smooth an' then started whittlin' the knot into the head of a golf club...it wasn't too long before I had three or four left-handed clubs of my own, an' right from the start, when I began usin' that old cypress root, I could lay my approaches close to the hole.

"We caddies generally hung out behind the clubhouse in the caddie pen (yard). While waitin' for a bag to tote, we'd swap stories, throw dice, play cards, or have puttin' an' chippin' contests. The caddiemaster in a shack right next to the caddie pen handed out tickets for each round we caddied, usually in order of seniority an' the check-in times.

"I watched Joe Houck, an older caddie at Little Rock become a favorite of the golfers. He hardly ever lost a ball, even if there was high weeds in the rough an' the woods. Joe explained his talent to me. He kept a pocketful of the same ball his golfer was playin' an' dropped one of those balls before the player reached the spot — if Joe couldn't locate the first ball fast enough. An' with that hole in his shoe, his golfer never had a bad lie an' Joe never missed an extree tip.

"My caddie earnin's of 50 cents a round didn't stay in my pocket long. In order that my money wouldn't be stolen by some of the other caddies, I put it in my high button shoes an' then gave most of it to my mother when I got home. Sometimes I'd win a little pocket money playin' dice — an' then I'd have to figger out a story for my mother 'cause she could frisk me pretty good. Once after caddyin' I got into a crap game with Don Murphy an' lost my money. When I got home an' tried to explain I didn't caddie that day, my Mother told me to bend over an' she gave me a good lickin'.

"Since 100 to 125 caddies competed for turns, I slept in the sand bunkers on Friday an' Saturday nights so's I'd be first out the next mornin' an' able to get in two rounds. How I survived the chigger season an' cold stormy weather I don't know.

"Every new caddie was introduced to the School of Hard Knocks. We went through some mighty rough times — with belt-strap whippin's an' bein' tumbled in a barrel down a hill. I injured my back when some bullies rolled me over a cliff at the sixth hole. Some of the older caddies were really mean ragamuffins, carryin' knives an' stealin' caddie earnin's. One ugly incident involved "Mexican Joe," the toughest an' roughest caddie at Little Rock Country Club. He would physically punish anyone who he thought was outta line. Once when his turn was taken by another caddie, he took out his knife an' cut the guy behind the ear in three places. Them days was tough. I'm tellin' ya, I almost quit caddyin' from fear."

Dutchisms

Dutch spent as much non-caddie time as possible away from the roughhousing, preferably looking for lost golf balls in the woods. Finding them seemed to be an innate ability of his. Ex-caddie Hugh Brown remembers meeting Dutch for the first time when he came out of the woods on Hole Three of the Little Rock Club carrying a blue bandanna full of golf balls, and ex-caddie Harold Blaylock recalls first meeting Dutch on the same hole, barefoot and in bib overalls, carrying a flour sack full of balls. Selling these balls to club members or the pro shop could bring an extra pocket full of nickels. Dutch carried his reputation of "The Greatest Ball Hunter" throughout his life.

William "Bill" McDonnell of McDonnell-Douglas fame was a member of the Little Rock Country Club and fondly recalled, "Every golfer sought Dutch as a caddie. We asked for 'Slim' Harrison, as we called him. He was thin as a rail. Give him a pink lemonade and he'd look like a thermometer. Having 'Slim' caddie for 18 holes was the equivalent, if not better, than a lesson from our pro."

Dutch was also known to express generous admiration for good shots, a tactic calculated to please the ego of the player—and perhaps produce a liberal tip at the end of the round.

"I never did see the likes of that shot ever before, Mr. Bill," he'd say. Or "I've seen all the pros play that shot an' none did it better, Mr. Bill." McDonnell added, "Talk about compliment overkill! His jubilation couldn't have been more had the golfer made a hole-in-one. His enthusiasm inspired some good shots from duffers, who felt Dutch treated them as a friend."

A good caddie can be invaluable to the pro golfer. "Let's put it this way," Dutch would say, "If I'da been caddyin' for Sam Snead, he'd a won a couple of U.S. Opens. I coulda helped him be aware of his options an' help him use the right club to keep the ball in play. Ya know, a caddie is the only person a pro can ask for advice in a tournament."

Dutch acquired his sense of humor early. When he was told that a game resembling golf was played in 1089 A.D., he suggested that this same game was still being played by some of those for whom he caddied.

"One doctor would pay me $10 for going to Harrison, Arkansas to caddie. Whenever I traveled there, I hitchhiked with a gypsy pack that included the head of my putter that I detached from the shaft 'cause I could always borrow a hickory shaft when reachin' the next golf course. The putter head was much more useful to me than a toothbrush. That ol' doctor tol' me that golf was not a game but a disease, an' he wished more of his patients would catch it so he might have more time for it.

"I did all I could to make my golfer look good. I made it a practice to know ever' inch of the golf course an' be able to tell the golfer the distance to the green. I certainly wouldn't get upset with a duffer an' recommend the evenin' train when he asked before a shot, 'What shall I take now?'

"The golfers always appreciate a caddie that knows what he's doin'. I've never forgotten the caddie I turned to durin' a tournament at Riviera Country Club in Los Angeles. On the ninth hole — I was ready to make my second shot an' it was a long way to the green. I asked the caddie, 'Can I get home from here?'

"The caddie didn't hesitate: 'Mr. Dutch, I don't even know where you live.'

"Needless to say, I didn't consult that caddie any further.

"I recollect a match when my caddie was also the caddie for Bob Considine, the journalist. The caddie was musclin' 22 clubs for Mr. Bob. In those days before 1938 players could carry more than 14 clubs in their bag — ol' Walter Hagen used to carry 28. Mr. Bob sliced twice into the woods on the first hole, then hooked into the woods on the second an' third holes. When Mr. Bob asked how far Hole Number 4 was, the caddie looked at him kinda funny an' replied, 'Mr. Considine, you don't want to know how far it is — you need to know how wide it is.'"

Although Dutch usually helped a golfer achieve and maintain self-confidence, there was an exception when he and Gibby Sellers, budding pro, hitchhiked to Texarkana to caddie. On their way they were drenched by a cold downpour.

"My new $9 suit shrank so much that my pant legs rose above my ankles, an' looked like knickers. Gibby an' I had one thin dime between us an' went to a diner where we could get donuts an' a cup of coffee for a dime. Gibby ordered an' when one waitress asked me what I wanted, I told her that I'd already eaten. When her back was turned, we divided the donuts, sipped the coffee through two straws, laid the dime on the counter an' walked out.

"Still shiverin', we met an old Scotsman pro at the Texarkana Country Club who saw the shape we were in an' tol' us that we could caddie that afternoon in a Class

C championship an' would receive 50 cents apiece. We drew two golfers who were fierce competitors. Gibby's player pulled him aside an' informed him, 'I've never beaten this man, but if I do, I'll give you five dollars.'

"Gibby immediately told me, knowin' I'd be able to help a bit while caddyin' for his player's opponent. Even though it was freezin' cold, I went barefoot so I could sly my player's ball between my toes an' give it a bad lie. I also helped Gibby by overclubbin' an' underclubbin' my player.

"At the end of the round, I said, 'Sir, you are the most unlucky man I've ever seen.'

"He bristled, 'Son, you're the worst caddie I've ever had!'

"That contest really saved us from starvin'."

A Real Hooker

"Golf was under my skin, right from when I played my first rounds — though before, baseball had been my main sport. I liked baseball an' my daddy really loved it. He had been a pitcher in the Texas league an' was fixin' for me to be a baseball player too. He'd drag me off to the pasture to play. I was a lefty an' got so I could switch-hit that ball purty good. But I didn't like the baseball people I knew. They used rough language. I wasn't much of a religious person, but I didn't care for all that cussin'. The baseball players really went at it — their language would make a longshoreman's parrot blush.

"Since I was a lefty an' maybe headed for pro baseball, Mr. Hack (Hackbarth) didn't wanna spend time with me. He favored helpin' Gene Rogers an' Don Murphy — they were also caddies. When I showed him I was determined, he started workin' with me, 'bout age 15. It took me over a year to switch from left to right-handed. I had been borrowin' left-handed clubs from Mr. Newcomb, the only left-hander in Little Rock. Mr. Hack gave me some wood-shafted right-handed clubs an' I practiced an' practiced. I would play in the middle of the woods, hittin' hickory nut after hickory nut. Later on, we caddies cleaned off a meadow just outside of ol' Hole 10 an' played there by the hour. I was always itchin' to get out to the real course an' play, an' sometimes I would start right early of a mornin' on Hole 3."

Dutch, like most caddies, dreamed of turning pro and having someone else carry his golf bag. Monday of each week was always eagerly anticipated, because that was the day when caddies could golf on the course. One foursome that played together frequently included Dutch, Hugh Brown, Harold Blaylock and Ed Ackerbloom. All came from poor to modest backgrounds and all later became successful golfers and close friends. They would borrow clubs from members and play for marbles or money. Hugh Brown remembers winning marbles from Dutch at school, and then losing them to him at golf. Caddie Don Murphy, who became a successful head pro at the Texarkana Country Club, remembers that Dutch lost to him in craps but "whupped me and the other caddies in golf."

When Dutch entered his first caddie tournament at the age of fourteen, he found himself in the championship match with Harold Blaylock, a long hitter who was known as the best of the caddie golfers.

"I had a sweeping hook that could spell trouble," said Harold. "After the second hole, Dutch was one hole down to me, but he told me that when we got to Number 17, a hole in which a hook severely penalizes the golfer, 'You're going to hook it out of bounds and I'll be able to win the match.'

"Approaching Number 17, I was still one up with two holes to go. Even though I played my drive a mile to the right, it still hooked out of bounds. So we were tied coming to the last hole, a par five. Both of us had good drives, but I pushed my second shot into the pine trees, then hit a tree twice coming out of the woods. I turned and looked at Dutch and he was laughing and slapping his thighs up and down. His psychology had really worked on me."

"From caddyin' I moved into the golf shop," said Dutch, "cleanin' an' mendin' clubs. I shagged (chased) a lot of golf balls for Mr. Hack in payment for some lessons. We'd talk 'bout Bobby Jones an' his lazy golf swing an' I kept thinkin' of this 'bout the same time I started playin' right-handed. I was on high throttle watchin' the exhibition ol' Walter Hagen an' Joe Kirkwood gave at the Club. They showed all kinda shots in the book an' Joe Kirkwood — Whew! What a trick artist. The first good one, too. He'd borrow some fellah's pocketwatch, put the ball on the watch with a little piece of gum, an' hit the devil out of the ball. Then he'd hand that watch back to the fellah who had held his breath, showin' him his watch was still tickin'. Hagen an' Kirkwood toured the country that year with two English golfers, George Duncan an' Abe Mitchell. They'd play 18 holes for the crowd besides holdin' quite a show. Must admit, I got some of my ideas for later exhibitions from them.

Titanic Thompson

"Guess my biggest thrill was the big bettin' match with the wondrous Titanic Thompson for $4,000. I was 19 years old, a real greenhorn, an' had just started as assistant to Mr. Ackerbloom, the pro at the Willow Beach Country Club — it used to be beside the Arkansas River south of Little Rock.

"Mr. Ti was a famous, big-league Arkansas golfer an' gambler whose life (1882-1974) was full of adventure. He was a tall, good-lookin' man. He never went on the professional tour, but pro Ed Dudley claimed that Mr. Ti was one stroke better as a left-handed golfer than any other pro player. If his opponent shot 78, Ti would shoot 77; if he shot 66, Mr. Ti would shoot 65. He was the beatin'est feller I ever saw. An' often the stakes were a king's ransom. His callin' cards were $100 bills.

"I remember the phone rang this bright summer day (in 1928 at Willow Beach Golf Club) an' I answered. 'Kid, this is Ti Thompson. I'm in town on business a little while. Could we have a game?' I said, 'Sure, Mr. Thompson, come down anytime.' After our golf game, he invited me to a chicken dinner at the apartment he rented from some belle who cooked mighty good Southern fried chicken.

"At dinner, Mr. Ti explained that he was arrangin' a golf match that would pit him an' me against the top rankin' professional golfers in Arkansas, Paul Runyan an' Julius Ackerbloom. Mr. Ti was bankrollin' the $4,000 himself an' some business people were stakin' Runyan an' Ackerbloom. If we won, I would receive $400. 'Course I knew he had a shadowy reputation — an' he sure had the sharpest, most penetratin' eyes I've ever seen. Them eyes jus' bored a hole right through ya.

"He was known to let the other opponent beat him the first few times, losin' maybe two or three hundred dollars to bait the hook for a real big bet. An' off the golf course he would dream up all sorts of big bets. Paul Runyan saw him take one of Mr. Paul's backers, Mr. Jack Vilas, for $5,000, a bet he arranged while sittin' on the veranda of this ol' hotel eatin' English walnuts. He bet he could throw an English walnut from the bunch he was shellin' clean over the eight-story buildin', which he did. Really amazin'! What Jack Vilas didn't know was that Mr. Ti had bored inside the shell of that walnut an' filled it with lead.

"An' I remember he snookered someone else for $2,000 on a bet he could throw a pumpkin on top of the roof of a three-story buildin'. He made the bet in front of a sidewalk fruit stand where the pumpkins were bigger'n basketballs. So, he walks down to the next fruit stand, gets a pumpkin the size of a softball an' throws it on top of the buildin'. What an arm he had! His schemes were as amazin' as they were right clever.

"Sam Snead called Mr. Ti the shrewdest juggler of odds he'd ever seen. We both remember Mr. Ti bettin' a rich pigeon $10,000 on a putt an' he lost. He grinned an' said, 'Double or nothin' I can hit a silver dollar with my revolver eight times out of eight from 20 feet.' An' he pulled that gun from his bag — bang, bang, bang an' he recouped his $10,000. He was a real expert.

"But as I was a-sayin', here I was, a gangly teenager still wet behind the ears, an' I was teamin' with probably the greatest match player of that time, against the two best golf pros in Arkansas. Little wonder I had alotta butterflies, 'especially when the whole town turned out for the match. It really shook me when Mr. Ti backed me up against a car in the parkin' lot beforehand an' poked a .45 revolver in my belly. He gave me that penetratin' eye an' told me he heard I'd been approached to throw the match. He asked who bought me off. I lost no time reassurin' him that I wasn't bought off, so then he said, 'C'mon boy, let's go play.' Mr. Ti was able to talk the opposition into givin' us a stroke an' a half when he agreed to play left-handed. What they didn't know was he played better left-handed.

"My hometown friends cheered me on an' I took the pressure okay. After 17 holes we had 'em by one stroke. On the last hole of 310 yards, Mr. Ackerbloom drove onto the front of the green, an' Mr. Ti, also a long hitter, drove close to the green an' then put his approach next to the pin for a sure three. Mr. Ackerbloom wasn't much of a putter, but he amazed everyone by holin' that 60-foot putt to square the match. What a potboiler we had! We were too exhausted to have a play-off. They claim that was the best Arkansawyer golf match ever.

"After the match Mr. Ti took me downtown an' bought me my first real suit. I thought the bright checkered outfit was a shade too loud, but I wore it anyway. I was mighty proud of that souvenir.

"Mr. Ti took me on a few of his little bettin' expeditions, but my good friend Herman Keiser, winner of the 1946 Masters Tournament, did more travelin' with Mr. Ti. They would go lookin' for two gamblin' opponents an' Mr. Ti would challenge them to a golf game. He'd encourage 'em by offerin' to play against them usin' a caddie from the caddie pen. Then he'd take those gentlemen over to the caddie pen an' sorta jus' pick out a caddie. Turned out the caddie was an ace golfer disguised in bib overalls by the name of Herman Keiser."

The Herman Keiser caddie story was always one of Dutch's favorites and did happen, with one slight variation. The caddie in bib overalls was actually Dutch Harrison.

The Boy with the Velvet Touch

"I had won my first amateur tournament in Little Rock as a left-hander but in 1929, the year of the big bust, I won the Arkansas Amateur Championship as a right-hander. As a left-hander I was wild as a March hare.

"I turned professional in 1930, the year Bobby Jones won the Grand Slam, an' moved to the Overton Park Municipal Course in Memphis. But when I turned 21, I was back in Little Rock as an unattached pro lookin' forward to the tournament circuit.

"Ol' Bob Harlow started tournament golf in 1930 for the PGA (Professional Golfers' Association). His daddy was a New England minister who hoped that his son would follow in his footsteps an' become an evangelist. Ya know, Mr. Bob did just that — he became the evangelist of tournament golf. He showed Chambers of Commerce an' big resorts how a golf tourney every year would be like a small Rose Bowl for 'em by generatin' revenue an' publicity. One sweet man, he was. The tournament circuit came to be known as the pro tour.

"Jack Delmar, a golfin' buddy, hitchhiked to tournaments with me. We couldn't afford caddies, so we flipped a coin. The winner played an' the loser caddied. We slept in the car at night an' shaved at gas stations. I had one change of clothes. We lived on half-rations — dividin' everythin' up equal. I was hangin' by my fingernails lookin' for a break."

In Dallas in 1933, Dutch introduced himself to Betty Jameson, national ladies' amateur and pro champion-to-be and Hall of Famer. Betty recalled, "Dutch was a human one-iron, he was so lanky and thin. He'd ride the rails to visit his sister in Dallas, my hometown. He was caddying at the Dallas Country Club where I was playing in the Dallas Women's Invitational. Dutch must have arranged from the caddie pen to carry my bag, knowing that I had won the Texas Publinx Championship the previous year when I was 13. In this crucial match I was the favorite. I'll never forget Dutch's trying to help me with my club selection.

"On a key hole where I thought I had a 6-iron shot over a water hazard, he said, 'Miss Betty, if I was you, I'd use a 5-iron, not a 6-iron.'

"I wish I had followed his advice. My shot fell short and caught the water hazard. It cost me the hole and the match.

"Dutch would later tease me, 'If you'd a jus' listened to me!'"

"Yep," said Dutch, "I was still caddyin' for pocket money. There were no new pro jobs an' it was tough pickin's on the hustlin' trail. Them that's poor must tote their saddle. It was jus' like chasin' a chigger round a stump.

"I spent alotta time in Texas. I drove my first car, a beat-up Pontiac with runnin' boards an' rumble seat, to San Antonio on my way to one of my first tournaments in Galveston. When I got to San Antonio, I sold my car for $15 so's I could pay the entrance fee — then I hitchhiked to Galveston and won $25. The Depression hung heavy — purses were small an' tournaments scarce—an' the competition was tough as bailin' wire."

The milestones in Dutch's career lay some years ahead of him as he would blossom late, but he was soon removed from the caddie ranks. He had already earned the nickname, "The Boy with the Velvet Touch," but his lean and trying times of youth continued during the Great Depression. His ambition to become a top professional golfer was no longer in question. The days following would change dreams to realities.

Wet Behind
the Ears

I see trees of green - red roses, too
I've seen them bloom - for me and you,
And I think to myself,
What a wonderful world.

from "What a Wonderful World"
by George Weiss and Bob Thiele

Emma Plunkett, a petite, shapely, young widow, was first mesmerized by Dutch in December, 1934. His sharp good looks, the smile in his voice, the twinkle in his blue eyes, and his entertaining storytelling captured her attention from the start. Emma was introduced to Dutch by her younger brother, Henry "Meany" Vopel, at the Fair Park Municipal Golf Course in Little Rock, Arkansas while she was playing golf.

Love and Practice

Try as she would, Emma couldn't get Dutch off her mind after that first meeting. Call it spontaneous affection. She later insisted it was not love at first sight. The moment she saw him in his well-worn clothes, she realized how poor he was. He may not have had silver in the bank, but he certainly had silver in his tongue.

She said about Dutch, "He always made me feel at ease. I knew he was buttering me up, but he did it in a way that made me want to hug him. He would go out of his way to help a person. And what a golfer he was — the best in Arkansas!"

Gradually she became convinced that all this 25-year-old eligible bachelor needed in order to be a success was self-esteem, and a supportive, caring wife to make it happen. However, Emma did not want to marry too quickly after her husband's death in 1932, from a sudden heart attack, at the age of 45.

"I wanted to make certain our relationship was right for both of us. Dutch was eager for the wooin' but not long in the doin'," Emma recalled.

After a courtship of over two years, long after his first proposal, they were married in Little Rock on August 7, 1937. The couple occupied a small home in the Pulaski Heights section of Little Rock, not far from the bluffs of the Arkansas River. The modest single-story, red brick house, trimmed with white wood siding, and fronted by a small yard of neatly cropped hedges, had been occupied by Emma and her late husband, and her brother, Henry, who she had helped raise following her mother's death.

Emma had moved from her hometown of Jonesboro to become a legal secretary, first for attorneys, then for the Lieutenant Governor of Arkansas, and later the Governor's private law firm. When the Governor was on the golf course, which was often, Emma handled many of the routine matters of his office. She met influential people in these positions, some of whom would be instrumental in furthering Dutch's career.

Though small in stature, Emma was tough as nails, both physically and constitutionally. Born in Germany, she had been raised in Jonesboro when her family immigrated in the early 1900s. Her father, William, was a filer in a heading factory in Jonesboro. He and wife, Minnie, had three children: William Jr., born in 1898; Emma born about 1900; and Henry born in 1908. Her father remarried some years after Minnie's death in 1915 and didn't stay in touch with Emma.

Her disposition embodied her stern German heritage. In fact, her attitudes were 180 degrees opposite of Dutch's easy-going style. She was high-strung, thin-skinned, compulsively neat, and a tough taskmaster. No grass could grow under her feet or his.

Emma, who was more than ten years older than her new husband, set out to help him build the self-confidence necessary for the demands of a golfing career. She saw that he practiced, persevered, and practiced some more.

Emma served as benefactor, housekeeper, cook, secretary, and bookkeeper, as well as mate and companion. With no children of her own, Emma exuded a mother-like concern for Dutch's well-being, seeing that he ate regularly, dressed properly, and rested sufficiently. She believed in his dream of becoming a champion and sympathized with his early struggles to finally shed the caddie ranks during the Great Depression.

Tournaments and Travel

Famed pro Johnny Bulla remembers when Dutch traveled to a midwest tournament in the mid 1930s, "He had barely enough money to reach his destination. In fact, he was so weak from hunger that he was having trouble taking a firm stance on the practice tee and meeting the ball squarely. I asked him if he was ill. Dutch told me that he and a square meal were total strangers. I came to his rescue and loaned him $25. That began a long friendship."

Emma also came to Dutch's rescue, financially and emotionally. Her contacts with legislators and businessmen proved helpful in bankrolling Dutch's early golf tours. Dutch recalled, "Henry Levy, North Little Rock businessman, staked me to my first trip on the professional tour in 1935.

"After it was over, I returned my winnin's in cash to Mr. Levy, who asked, 'How'd you travel, Dutch?'

"'I rode the rods, Mr. Levy.'

"'You hitched a ride on the freight train? That's crazy. Don't you know that if a hobo had seen your bankroll, he'd have opened your head and taken your money and golf clubs?'

"I recollected my teenage experiences and said, 'I reckon you're right, Mr. Levy. Guess, I was hopin' times had changed.'"

In 1936 Dutch finished out of the money at his first U.S. Open at Baltusrol Golf Club in Springfield, New Jersey, where he tied for 36th place, far below the first 18 money places. Although donors had sent Dutch to the tournament, the majority of the local golfing fraternity in Little Rock downplayed his chances of ever becoming a successful tour professional. It seemed his scores would soar on the last days of a big tournament. Many maintained he was a "choker" and would never make it. Newspaper critics tended to agree. That is, all but one local sportswriter, Wilbur Johnson, who often golfed with Dutch and followed him closely. In the *Arkansas Gazette*, Wilbur predicted: "Dutch Harrison will become one of the finest golfers of our time and soon will be eating steak instead of hamburger."

Dutch admitted that so much was expected of him in his first U.S. Open in New Jersey that when he stepped on the Number One tee, "My heart was in my mouth an' the ball looked the size of a grape. I was as nervous as a cat on a doghouse roof. One time the pro coaxed Club members into chippin' in to send me on a tour — an' I got stomach nausea and couldn't finish the first tournament. But I knew the sun don't shine on the same rooster's tail all the time."

Dutch began to blossom in 1937. He won four small tournaments, three in Mississippi on sand greens. The tournaments were the Arkansas Open, the Jackson Open, the Clarksdale Open, and the Tupelo Open.

"Mississippi was my lucky state in '37," chuckled Dutch.

After a 1937 exhibition match in Little Rock by

Horton Smith, Lawson Little, Jimmy Thomson, and Harry Cooper, Wilbur Johnson predicted: "Even with the class of this leading pro foursome you doubted any of them is better than Little Rock's own Ernest J. "Dutch" Harrison. His tee shots will travel as far as almost any professional and he has all the shots. When Mr. Harrison gets his break he will move to the top of the list."

Off the tee, Dutch would have been only a shade behind Jimmy Thomson, then recognized as the longest hitter by the PGA.

Dutch needed Emma's encouragement, faith, and support. Elsewhere he was full of good nature and handled stress with the placidity of a shepherd. He could sleep through a tornado and relax with a brass band blaring in the next room.

So happy-go-lucky was he that Emma had to fill the gaps with motivation and tenacity of purpose. She was the navigator, and although she didn't build or launch the ship, she certainly charted his course. She fine-tuned his biological clock so that it was synchronized with the rhythms of his golf life.

Dutch remembered, "I'd tell everyone what a good wife she was an' what a good husband she let me be. She helped me to think bigger than I had been doin' an' gave me a lot of good idee's. I told her I wanted her to be my toughest critic. At first I didn't know that was par for her course."

Everything was "satisfactual" to Dutch, even when Emma was a "sourpuss." He treated her deferentially, sometimes saying, "Here's the Boss," or "Momma, you're the one with the purse strings."

His homespun charm was like a big slice of Mom's apple pie. He believed that a teaspoon of kindness dissolved in a cupful of common sense could handle any personality conflict.

After they were married, Emma found little time to be an active golf participant, but she enjoyed walking the fairways rain or shine and leaving the golf to Dutch. At times she would be excused from her work or serve only part-time as a court recorder in order to be with Dutch at tournaments.

"He wanted me to be in the gallery. He was always light-hearted and humorous. Even in tournaments he was as full of good humor as could be. He was always just Dutch.

"If Dutch had a bad first nine holes, I might stop following him to change our luck, but if he had a good round, I would continue to walk with him the next day. At the putting greens, it was difficult for me to watch him, especially the short crucial putts. Often I would hide behind a tree until he finished. Dutch used to say, 'I saw you duck behind that tree,'" she recalled.

Emma told a news reporter, "That man is a golfing fool when he's playing for a new car. The fact is he is twice as tough than when he's playing for some household goods for me. Sometimes when I can't get to the first day of a nearby tournament, I don't follow him if he's going good. If he isn't doing well, I'll follow him, hoping to change his luck. You get powerful superstitious in this game."

Emma disliked having her picture taken on the golf course, and often insisted that Dutch pose alone. On one particular windy day, a photographer approached the Harrisons, but Emma begged off for another time when they would look less disheveled.

The photographer told her, "No matter how ya look, you're gonna get your picture took."

Emma retired into the shade, yielding to Dutch.

"Emma an' I drove out West several winters in a beat-up sedan. I figgered we drove 'bout 60,000 miles a year, sometimes four of us together. Usually we'd aim to be arrivin' at the tournament course in time for a practice round, but sometimes we'd be travelin' one day an' playin' a tournament the next. We'd play in a tournament four days, then drive to the next tournament. Some of them boardin' places became like family.

"In the summer of 1939 Emma an' I drove to New Brunswick for my first Canadian Open. I finished seventh and won only $77, but we put our car on a boat from Saint John to Boston, then drove home. It was a wonderful trip."

Emma and Dutch would travel often with Bob Hamilton and Herman Keiser, and sometimes their wives would join them.

Dutch remembered meeting Bob Hamilton, "He was a husky, jovial Hoosier, who I met at the North-South Open in 1938. I finished in the money an' Bob finished out of the money. After I was paid, Bob introduced himself an' told me he needed money to get back home to Evansville.

"He said, 'Mr. Harrison, I got busted and need $50 for the trip. I'll give you a check that'll be good in three days.'

"I didn't know Bob from a load of hay, but I said, 'Okay, but you keep the check. I'll see ya at the next tournament.'

"He said, 'Next tournament? I'll be lucky to get back to Indiana.'

"When he paid me back, we were on a first name basis an' have been close ever since. Bob didn't finish high up in the money until 1944, the year he became PGA Champion, but he was the best one-on-one money player I ever met.

"I met Herman Keiser in 1935 when he was changin' from amateur to pro. He was a former caddie from Springfield, Missouri. He worked awful hard an' became a Masters Champion."

Herman remembers driving with Bob and Dutch from Miami to Los Angeles practically nonstop and driving continuously from the Midwest to California and Nevada tournaments, "All that traveling and playing together earned us The Three Musketeers handle."

He described riding with the Harrisons: "We'd be driving along and Emma would say, 'Dutch, I haven't had my Postum' [a popular substitute for coffee during the 1930s and 1940s]. And Dutch would reply, 'I guess we'd better stop for the Boss at the first chance for refreshment.'"

According to Keiser, one time when Henry Ransom and his wife were along, Emma was told by the waitress that Postum was unavailable. She looked at Dutch and said, "Would you please go out and find me some?" Dutch obediently rose, ventured out, and finally returned with Postum in hand.

"We called Dutch 'a food destroyer.' He enjoyed good cooking, including Emma's.

"To Bob Hamilton's wife he'd say, 'Miss June, no one puts victuals on the table like you. I never tasted fried chicken that good.'

"He'd have a way with the waitresses too, saying, 'This little lady is going to take good care of us.' And she would do just that."

Keiser reported, "Emma's circle of confidants was small, but it did include Bob and me. She would ask our advice on many different issues. But she was generally a loner and not a good mixer like Dutch.

"Ol' Dutch was a great navigator, but he didn't relish driving except when he was alone with his wife. He logged as many snooze hours in the backseat as Bob and I did at the wheel. Bob and Dutch played a series of five to ten exhibitions between the long tournament intervals of the early 1940s. As you might guess, it was Bob driving most of the time and Dutch sawing wood in the back seat."

Dutch recalled, "We'd be sleepin' an' suitcasin' outta the car an' it was hard for me to do that longer than 'bout six weeks. But we had a good time travelin' together. We motored alotta miles — past Burma Shave signs, A&W root beer stands, red barns an' white picket fences. An' through desert hotter than love in the kitchen, carryin' our water bags an' thermos jugs.

"One time I was travelin' with Lloyd Mangrum an' another pro late at night from Phoenix to Los Angeles. Lloyd drove the first 200 miles while the two of us slept. He pulled into a gas station an' reversed directions so he could pull 'longside a pump. He wakes this other pro an' is sawin' wood in two shakes. After the car is gassed, the new driver pulls out. When we woke up, we're back in Phoenix. I'll tell ya, we didn't get our kicks on Route 66 that night."

During the 1940-1941 winter tour Dutch was driving with Emma from the Western Open in Phoenix to the Texas Open in San Antonio. Suddenly, on the lonely highway they noticed a smoke-black Lincoln Continental tailing them. When they increased their speed, the car followed suit and even gained ground. Then they heard honking as the car threatened to pull alongside.

"Hide the money, Emma," Dutch warned nervously, "We're being held up."

As Emma busied herself, Dutch glanced over and recognized Jack Grout, a fellow pro, shouting and waving frantically for them to stop. Henry Picard was at the wheel. Once both cars drew to a stop, Jack made clear his intentions.

"Dutch, at the beginning of our journey we discovered that neither one of us had any cash. Then we saw you pass us. Can you loan us $100 until San Antonio?"

"You can have all you want," laughed Dutch.

Depression and Money

The depression years taught Emma to keep a tight grip on the purse strings. She established a spartan budget that controlled the easy-come, easy-go nature of Dutch. She even monitored their "foolish money" at the race track. On trips Emma made certain that companions paid their share of expenses. Driving back from the Miami Open in 1939, Emma and Dutch were accompanied by sportswriter, Wilbur Johnson. At the time, Wilbur was flat broke and could not offer to pay the toll across the Mississippi River.

Emma lit into him. "You've come all this way and can't pay 50 cents?"

Dutch spoke up in his soft manner, "Emma, this guy is a friend of ours who has been good to us an' here you are quibblin' over 50 cents."

The golfers on tour squeezed every nickel and split expenses down to the penny. "Travel the road and share the load" was their motto. One time Herman Keiser and Dutch were riding in Sam Snead's car across country. When Sam stopped to get gas, Herman and Dutch went to the restroom and stayed until they thought the gas bill had been paid.

When they came out, Sam was loudly directing the gas attendant. "No, no, no! It's not $3.15 for me. Here's my $1.05. And you get $1.05 from that guy and $1.05 from the other guy."

Emma likened the tourist homes that she and Dutch preferred to the "bed and breakfast" offerings of today. "Sometimes Dutch would want to hit the road early in the morning. I'd say, 'Honey, if you want to move on, let's go!' We'd often get together with the other golfers and their wives in the evening. The womenfolk brought covered dishes for potluck, never knowing what the others might bring. Once we ended up with only pies and cakes. They liked the chocolate cakes I'd bake. We neither drank nor smoked, but we'd still get invited and go to the cocktail parties.

"I called him my angel even though he often lingered in the locker room to play cards with the pros. One day when I asked Porky Oliver if anyone had seen my angel, Porky laughed, pointed toward the basement locker room, and said, 'Your angel has shed his wings.'"

Dutch took a lot of kidding from the pros about Emma's choice of nickname, but he always came back with a humorous quip. "She's the one always up in the air—harpin'! Her tongue is always waggin' like the back end of a goose. I'll tell ya, escapin' her is like tryin' to slip sunrise past a rooster."

The camaraderie among the pros and their wives is fondly remembered. While a great deal of kidding went on, the spirit of friendship and individual support was there for everyone.

"We didn't make near the money these fellahs make today, but by golly we had a lot more fun," Dutch said.

"We were one big travelin' family in those days. You never had to introduce yourself to anybody 'cept some seldom-seen new pro comin' on tour. I remember all the wives an' players gettin' together one Thanksgiving before a Florida tournament. Bob Hamilton an' I went out an' got a couple of big turkeys."

Bob and Ellsworth Vines remembered that special Thanksgiving and how Dutch entertained the pros and their families with a lot of stories after dinner.

"He kept us in stitches," Ellsworth recalled.

Opportunity Knocks

Horton Smith won the first Masters Championship in 1934, repeated in 1936, and was the leading money winner in 1936 with $7,884. "A new door opened for me in 1937 when Horton Smith took me under his wing," Dutch claimed.

"He made me an assistant at the Oak Park Country Club in Illinois. I was with him for three years durin' the late 1930s. I got half the money I made givin' lessons — $3 a lesson an' I'd get $1.50. If I left Little Rock with $30 in the spring, I'd be lucky iffen I had that much left in the fall. Back in them days there was just no money 'round. Mr. Horton gave me the biggest check I'd ever seen, $400 of sunshine, to go out West on the1938-1939 winter tour. When I saw that check, my eyes liked t'have popped right out. But he had a good deal there, 'cause I was the leadin' money winner after four California tournaments. Yep, I not only paid him back, but split the winnin's with him.

"I placed fourth in the Los Angeles Open an' tied for first with that handsome dude, Dick Metz, in the Oakland Open. Then I lost in an 18-hole playoff by one stroke. Next I won the Bing Crosby tournament. That was the beginnin' of big business in pro-amateur (pro-am) golf, but it sure ended that California gold trail for me. I talked to Mr. Bing an' his pals at a barbecue followin' my win. I told 'em that I'd now be able to feed the hogs on the farm that winter an' was leavin' the next day for Little Rock to give 'em a good meal.

"Some of those tournaments had $5,000 purses divided into about ten prizes. In those days, 75 pros were playing for them ten prizes an' it was tough to break into the money circle. You either grew up early or went home early. But we had fun an' our health, if not the wealth. Lookin' back, if Horton Smith could come out of his grave today an' see what's happenin' with million dollar purses an' several different tours, he'd be happier than a pig in clover. For him it'd be like shootin' fish in a barrel."

Emma was outraged when Joe Dey, "Mr. Golf" and Executive Director of the United States Golf Association, disqualified Dutch and a group at the U.S. Open in 1940 at Canterbury, Ohio. It was common for golfers to be disqualified if they arrived even a few minutes late at the first tee, but this was probably the first time golfers were eliminated for starting early.

That last day of the tournament, Dutch, Johnny Bulla, and Porky Oliver had to play two rounds of 18 holes, one in the morning, the other in the afternoon. The three were having lunch between rounds when Johnny noted storm clouds gathering. He suggested that they tee off early before their official starting time. Joe Dey, the official starter, also happened to be at lunch and a young assistant was at the first tee when the group started their last 18 holes some 25 minutes early. When Joe returned and discovered two threesomes had started early, he walked out to the golfers and explained Rule 37-5: The player shall start at the time and in the order arranged by the committee. Penalty: *Disqualification.* The players continued play because they planned to appeal their case.

Emma had Canterbury Tales of woe for Joe Dey and crucified him for not being at the first tee to stop the golfers from starting early. Later, Johnny Bulla magnanimously shouldered the responsibility of starting early.

Dutch was disappointed at being disqualified. "Porky Oliver mighta won that U.S. Open since he was tied with the two leaders, Gene Sarazen an' Lawson Little. That roly-poly Irishman was one of the best friends I ever had. He was 'bout two axe handles wide an' walked like he had a corncob up his rear. His 'taters musta settled in one place, yet nothin' soured his disposition. He was the sweetest man. We were all pullin' for Porky to get a chance to enter the playoffs, but it was not to be."

(Lawson Little won the play-off with Gene Sarazen, who was not going to play unless Porky Oliver played also. However, Sarazen relented and the two-man, 18-hole play-off occurred the next day.)

Pro Duty and War Duty

During the winter of 1941-1942, Ben Hogan and Henry Picard recommended that Dutch be hired as club professional at the West Shore Country Club, Camp Hill, Pennsylvania. He signed a contract to serve as Pro-Greenskeeper until November when he expected to be inducted into the service. This was his first affiliation with a major club as head pro.

Dutch reported to West Shore in April after the Master's tournament. Fortunately, his salary of $1,800 could be supplemented by his winnings on the pro tour and golf lessons at the Club. Dutch also pocketed numerous friendly wagers made on varied courses in the area and profited from equipment sales in the pro shop, which was tended by Emma.

Dutch's dual assignment of professional and greenskeeper was an uncommon burden even in those days. When Dutch was asked at the end of the day what maintenance on the golf course had been accomplished by his crew, he invariably answered, "I don't rightly know."

Greenskeeping simply wasn't for Dutch. Consequently, a consultant was hired until the next professional came aboard.

Emma didn't endear herself to club officials from the beginning. Upon arrival she told them she had been misled and expected a swankier club and more mature landscaping. Heatedly, she told everyone within earshot what she had expected.

Dutch tried to calm her down, but as he often said, "Her adrenalin was pumpin'. Nothin' in tarnation can stop her when she's dishin' out how the hog ate the cabbage."

An official recalled that Emma served as caddie master, "The caddies were afraid of her and really hustled for her. Once when two of them kept getting into fights, Emma sternly dressed them down and told them she'd kick their rear ends and dismiss them if the fighting happened again. Days later she heard a fracas way out in the caddie shack and found the two caddies at it again. Grabbing each boy by the scruff of the neck, she banged their heads together with such force that the knees of one buckled and he fell to the floor. The other boy ran outside. I doubt that those caddies ever fought again while Emma was there. She was tougher than any mountain woman I ever met."

Members of the club enjoyed Dutch and spoke of him as everybody's favorite pro.

Harold B. Miller, a club champion and Chairman of the Greens Committee, related, "Dutch added prestige to the club, but he was always generous with his opponents. He would give me two strokes on each nine holes, yet always beat me by one stroke."

Bob Shaw, another club champion, said, "Dutch really blistered this course. He always beat me no matter how many strokes he gave me. His handling of golfers in a betting game was something to behold. He would nose out Charlie Wipperman, the assistant professional, by one stroke. If Dutch were ahead of Charlie by two strokes, he would usually let him win the last hole.

"Charlie kept saying, 'I almost beat him the last time. I know he can't outdo me all the time.'

"One day Dutch approached me to play a round with him," Shaw recalled. 'Let's go to the Colonial Club today an' slice a melon.'

"'Aw, Dutch, my golf can't help you very much.'

"'Don't worry, Mr. Shaw, you won't have to.'

"Well, a fivesome played at Colonial that day. We got to the last hole all tied. Dutch moseys to the tee for his drive and says to us, 'I'm gonna fry this one up nice an' brown.'

"He hits it down the middle out of sight. The round is completed with Dutch holing the winning putt.

"He raised his putter in triumph and smilingly drawled, 'The cake's all dough.'

"Dutch and I walked off with the whole melon."

While at West Shore, Dutch placed among the top ten prize winners in eight tournaments, all he entered except possibly one that is not on record. He additionally tied the course record during an exhibition with Lloyd Mangrum, Jack Grout, and a Mr. Coffey.

With the reluctant consent of Board members, Dutch and Emma left West Shore early in the fall of 1942 to spend time in Little Rock before Dutch had to leave for the service.

Storm Clouds

Although differences between Dutch and Emma occurred early in their marriage, one incident in the late 1930s would establish a frightening pattern. Dutch was scheduled to play a prestigious and widely advertised exhibition match with Sam Snead, Harry Cooper, and Jimmy Thomson at the Riverside public course, which was later known as Riverdale Country Club. However, unresolved conflicts with Emma provoked her brother, Henry "Meany," who threatened to shoot Dutch on the spot if he showed up for the match. Fearing that Meany would at least embarrass him, Dutch withdrew and brought in Gibby Sellers as his replacement. After quietly slipping away to Little Rock Country Club, he encountered Wilbur Johnson and shared the gun incident, which was to be just one of many.

In golf, when storm clouds threaten, umbrellas have to be popped open, bag covers snapped on, and rain gear pulled out. When storm clouds brew in a marriage, similar adjustments have to be made if one is to play on through.

 # The Will Rogers
of the Fairway

"You must be the storyteller," the little boy said.
"Yes, how'd ya know?" the smiling man responded.
"Well, look at you. You're three stories tall."

From Tia Gindick

The attack by the Japanese on Pearl Harbor, December 7, 1941, not only marked the beginning of World War II, but the end of the recently established professional golf tournament trail.

"I was 31 years old at the time of Pearl Harbor. Uncle Sam beckoned an' I made plans to enter the Army. Because I never went to any ivy-covered halls with ivy-covered walls — fact was I didn't complete 6th grade — I was made a buck private at Camp Robinson, which was just outside Little Rock," Dutch recalled.

Victory Gardens Replace Golf Fairways

Dutch's farewell gesture to the civilian world was to set a new course record of 59, six under par at the Fair Park Municipal Course, now known as War Memorial Park. This feat was accomplished in a cold, drizzling rain before a group of admirers. At that point, Dutch held the scoring records at all Little Rock golf courses.

Tournament golf suffered great uncertainty in 1942.

The picture looked bleak when many renowned golfers entered the service. Golf became viewed as unpatriotic and portions of some golf courses were converted to *victory gardens* for the war effort. It wasn't until some time later, when the United States went on the offensive in the war, that federal officials began to put their stamp of approval on golf as a national recreational diversion.

After basic training, Dutch traveled to Fort Ord, California where he was to prepare for overseas duty with an amphibious division. However, he applied for and received a transfer to the Army Air Force. Emma's help in the background, politically-aided, hit its mark. When he received new orders, Private First Class E. J. Harrison reported to the Air Force Center at Greensboro, North Carolina. He was lugging his cherished golf clubs over his shoulder, not having allowed them out of sight during his cross-country trek. That his orders were missing was incidental.

The government began encouraging the PGA to have its star players give exhibitions at hospitals and play in as many tournaments as possible for war relief and war bond drives. Tournament professionals that were rejected for the military joined with the pros in service who remained in the United States to bring golf to the threshold of a new era. Elated galleries welcomed golf back on the trail where spectators once again were allowed to mingle and converse with the pro golfers, led by Byron Nelson and Jug McSpaden.

Dutch credited Boston Irishman, Fred Corcoran, "the Persian rug dealer of golf tournaments," as the man who really promoted the pro tour in the 1940s. By the time he left his position as manager of the tour, purses had increased from $5,000 to $13,000 and tournaments from 22 to 45 per year.

The Flying Dutchman

Dutch was permitted to play in professional golf tournaments during furloughs and quickly regained his touch. He had not yet established himself in the public eye on the East Coast, but his opportunity was to come. At the Charlotte Open in March, 1944, a large gallery identified with his friendly chatter and sense of humor. Wearing GI pants, white T-shirt, and a garrison cap set at a rakish angle, he attracted the bulk of the crowd. There were no roped-off areas for the spectators and they were free to follow in the footsteps of the players. Nor were there restrictions on camera use or media noise. To Dutch all the hoopla was part of the tournament and he loved to banter and exchange quips with fans, even as he swung the golf club during the heat of competition. His flashes of wit relieved some of the tension down the home stretch on each day of this tournament. Audience response was enthusiastic.

He'd discuss life with anybody in the gallery, joke with his opponents and unleash a running barrage of anecdotes like, "The time an ol' huntin' dog ran through George Shafer's bowed legs when he was on the green goin' to putt," or, "The time my golfin' partner putted the ball into the hole an' the ball pops out — followed by a big toad frog."

It was a picnic for Dutch and his followers. On the other hand, his opponents rapidly quit laughing and got down to work after they realized he had birdied the last four holes. The newspapers dubbed him "The Flying Dutchman of the Air Corps." Most experts had favored the renowned Byron Nelson or the hot-streaking Jug McSpaden, but Dutch, with the help of the crowd, stormed from behind and beat McSpaden on the fourth and final day by one stroke.

Fans went crazy. They swarmed "a la Sinatra" and autograph hounds almost tore Dutch apart as he attempted to sign scorecards at the 18th green. Photographers and newspaper men surrounded the winner who had brought so much excitement and charisma to the tournament. Then the flash of cameras, the cheers and smiles — a scene to be repeated for Dutch many times in the coming years.

Dutch related, "I decided it was safer to collect the remaining scorecards an' asked the crowd's permission to sign 'em in the clubhouse. Squirmin' through 'em was like a boll weevil borin' through cheese. Later I met with the press an' told 'em how lucky I was 'cause Mista McSpaden was murdah on those greens.

"Gentlemens, there's flowers bloomin' today that won't be bloomin' tomorrow. I told 'em I never felt younger in my life than at age 34 an' never as strong, 'cause now I had 190 pounds on my 6' 3" frame compared to 165 pounds when I entered the army. I figured that for each pound I gained, I added a yard to my wood shots. Now I was drivin' 275 to 300 yards, about 30 yards more than before. Those bananas, grits, an' 'taters did it. I stowed more food than a mess hall sergeant.

"What a good feelin' it was to lay claim to those two $1,000 war bonds — I never had that much money all at one time. That was more than I could earn in two years as army sergeant at $78 a month."

Overnight Dutch had become a folk hero. He was the first serviceman to win a major golf tournament. Veteran pro golfers such as Craig Wood called his victory the best thing that ever happened in golf. With gate receipts going to War Relief, Dutch was proud that he had helped raise part of the money for that great cause.

Dutch was remembered as the grinning sergeant who won the first Charlotte Open in 1944, a feat described in the Open's 1946 official program: "Never was there a more popular victory in Charlotte. Dutch was the darling of the galleries, the fair-haired lad with the crowd, a soldier, nonchalant and jaunty, but even-tempered. He looked like just a big country kid who enjoyed playing golf."

The Storyteller

The cheers followed him back to his barracks where his soldier pals gave him a rousing welcome. They hoisted him on their shoulders and paraded him through the barracks. After evening mess, they wanted him to hold court, hoping to hear more details of his great victory. Then came the inevitable request for Dutch to tell a story. Dutch rarely needed encouragement as stories came out easily in his friendly Deep South drawl, enhanced by his expressive hands.

"Y'all probably remember Bob Hamilton of Evansville, Indiana, who won the North-South Open this year an' placed seventh this afternoon in Charlotte. Well, Mr. Bob an' I are great pals an' hustler partners. Back in the 1930s we'd recruited a couple of schoolteachers to play for 50 cents a hole in Pinehurst [North Carolina] an' they'd been donatin' about nine dollars a day to us. On about the fourth day, as Bob an' I an' the schoolteachers approached the first hole, there was a well-dressed stranger sittin' on the bench wearing a tie.

"He asked, 'You fellas got a game?'

"I said, 'Yes, Sir.'

"He said, 'Do you have four?'

"I said, 'Yes, Sir.'

"He said, can we play five?'

"An I said, 'Well, I don't think so.'

"About that time Bob looked over an' saw me talkin' to him an' called me aside.

"He asked me, 'Who is this guy?'

"I said, 'I don't know, Bob. I've never seen him before.'

"'Well, does he have any money?'

"'I don't know, Bob, I didn't look in his pocket.'

"'Well, bring him along. If he's got any, we'll get it.'

"Mr. Bob ever eager with the loot in sight, approached the stranger an' said somethin' subtle like, 'How much do you want to play for?'

"The man looked at him and said, 'I don't know much about betting.'

"Well, Mr. Bob invited him right along. At the first tee I explained we were playing 50 cent syndicates (skins) with carry-overs. That meant if we tied three holes, the winner of the fourth hole gets two dollars. If you lose 18 holes, you lose nine dollars. I explained all that to him.

"And the stranger says to me, 'Y'all play any side bets?'

"Well, that kinda' shook me a bit, an' then when this new guy took a practice swing, I knew we had our work cut out for us. Well, I coulda won the first hole an' again the third hole, but Bob wouldn't let me so we could have another carry-over.

"When we got to the par-5 sixth hole, Bob calls me aside an' says, 'You've been milkin' the syndicate all morning. Go ahead an' win this one.'

"So I hit a good drive for me. About 260 yards. An' Bob an' the schoolteachers hooked into the high rough. Goin' down the fairway, I see a ball about 40 yards ahead of me an' I figured it was one of the schoolteacher's second shots. I asked whose ball it was.

"The stranger says, 'It's mine. It must have hit a rock.'

"Well, I knew the only rocks were in the 19th hole covered with bourbon. I lined up my second shot an' hit probably the finest 3-wood I ever hit in my life. I put the ball 'bout 12 feet from the hole, relaxed a bit, an' figured, 'Now, we'll separate the men from the boys.'

"He took a 4-iron an' you could almost feel the electricity before he hit that shot. Would you believe it? He put the ball six inches from the hole. I knew we had a bear by the tail! Mr. Bob an' I really took after him, but at the end of the day the guy had 12 syndicates an' no one else had any.

"So he comes up to me afterwards an' says, 'I can play in the morning or afternoon tomorrow. What time can you play?'

"I looked him right in the eye an' said, 'Look, Mister, you work your side of the road an' we'll work ours.'

"And that's how I met Sam Snead. What a golfer! He an Jimmy Demaret robbed me so much I could never forget 'em."

As a storyteller, Dutch was unequaled. He spun his

tales with stunning impact. With his folksy manner, his aura of intrigue, and a unique style that set him apart, he entertained crowds for hours. Young or old, they often became convulsed in laughter. He did not spin far-fetched yarns or off-color tales, or indulge in folklore. His stories were based on fact, no matter how much they might be embellished. He had that rare facility of being able to take a humorless event and inject a chuckle into it — using those rolling eyes, drawling twang and talking hands.

In the Army Air Force his opportunities increased for storytelling. Dutch got better and better as he practiced and gained confidence. It was natural for him to treat commissioned officers with respect, but he went out of his way to give special consideration to rookies, the naive newcomers. They'd never get taken down a peg by Dutch. He'd sit with them in the mess hall and good naturedly counsel them in the evenings.

"See ol' Dutch if you've got a problem," was common advice and his popularity as a friend accelerated along with his self-confidence.

"I was really swingin' through the Eastern tournaments — finished no worse than sixth in the next five. Competed with little or no practice durin' the hurried furloughs when I'd spend most of my time on the train. My golf game became steadier because my nerves were steadier," Dutch said.

A Champion

Dutch was nominated by other golfers as the favorite in most of the tournaments that year. Sam Byrd, Byron Nelson, Henry Picard, and Jug McSpaden were particularly keen on Dutch. On short courses, Byron would tell reporters that he favored Dutch because, "He's long off that tee and his short game is good."

Henry was impressed with his balanced game and consistency. Jug and Sam were impressed with his putting and handling of pressure situations. Jug told reporters, "That man must have ice water trickling through his veins."

Dutch was so successful during the 1944 Eastern tour that he was invited to play many exhibitions, one with the renowned Gene Sarazen at the Greensboro Country Club.

Fans gradually changed from asking, "Who is Dutch Harrison?" to asking, "Where is Dutch Harrison?"

Although not always victorious, he always laughed and exchanged one-liners with the press and spectators. His thrilling victory in the Miami Open of December, 1944 was clearly as popular with the huge gallery as any finish in the Open's history. He survived a brilliant home-stretch battle with Henry Picard for a one-stroke triumph. Spectators were pulling for him all the way.

"Come on, Dutch; put it up there, Sarge," they shouted.

The crowd surged close to him all the way down the stretch. They whooped and hollered as Dutch edged ahead. At the close of his victory, he spoke about how much the cheering helped his confidence and how lucky he got on the greens. "The ball jus' kept findin' that hole," he quipped.

Not since Bobby Jones had the public responded as enthusiastically to a tournament golfer. Displaying a swashbuckling style, a sensitivity to fan communication, and a new confidence born of experience and acclaim, Dutch wore the mantle of a champion well. He had fun with his opponents, as well as the crowd.

"C'mon, Mr. Henry," he'd drawl, "Step up there an' hit one. You jus' been buntin' 'em all day."

Many in the large galleries had not seen golf played before, especially young women. Dutch had a contingent of WACS and WAVES that were captivated by him and his low-key Southern charm. Sporting size 11 shoes and boyish good looks, he was the 'Lil Abner' of the golf circuit. Dutch took kindly to all of the attention in the absence of Emma.

"I'll tell ya, it was a relief not to run into a buzz saw

out there on the golf course. I breathed easier. An' I slept sounder in the barracks at night knowin' she could never get past the guard at the gate. Whew! Man, I laid back."

About the middle of 1944 Dutch was transferred to Wright Field in Dayton, Ohio and assigned to the physical training program as Staff Sergeant under Major McCallister.

Dutch recalled, "He had me playin' exhibition matches all 'round Ohio — for 'morale buildin' he called it. They'd decided I could use a golf club a lot better than a rifle or bayonet. Major McCallister had organized such a wonderful physical training program an' introduced golf activities into it. I became Mr. Supple doin' all them calisthenics.

"One mornin' after a big steak breakfast in the quartermaster's area, I was restin' in my shorts on a cot with my feet up, lettin' that steak digest, an' tellin' the boys an' Major McCallister about my latest golf escapades when suddenly Commanding General Meyers surprised everyone by walkin' into the barracks.

"Major McCallister immediately recognized the importance of yellin', 'Attention!'

"As everyone came rigidly to attention, the Major motioned to me to stay in the cot. After the salute, General Meyers said, 'What have you got over there in the cot?'

"Major McCallister answered, 'I have a sick soldier, sir.'

"The general said, 'Well, get him to the hospital right away.'

"So they called an ambulance, put me on a stretcher an' loaded me in the back of the ambulance. I was worried about the syndicate golf game I had that afternoon with some high-falutin' officers. I raised up an' said, 'For God's sake, what are you doin — get me outta here!'

"They said, 'See you later, Dutch.'

"They closed the door an' off I went to the hospital.

If it wasn't for one of them doctor's bein' booked to play with me that week, I'd probably have been there overnight.

"That same year I was sent to New York for a secret assignment. I arrived at some Army Air Force offices an' there was Horton Smith, the golf legend of our time. Ol' Horton had become a Captain in the Air Force. He was organizin' a special group of athletes an' celebrities to visit service camps — guys like Billy Conn, the boxer, an' George Lott, the tennis player. He had requested General Meyers to let me go an' he had my orders all ready.

"When I saw him I said, 'Hi, Mr. Smitty.'

"I was casual 'cause I had worked with him in Oak Park an' knew him well.

"He said, 'It's Captain Smith to you, Sergeant.'

"I said, 'Where are we goin,' Captain Smith?'

"He said, 'To Rome.'

"I asked, 'Rome, Georgia — the tournament down there?'

"He answered, 'No, Rome, Italy. You need some overseas duty.'

"Well, I told him I wanted to check with the Wright Field people 'bout that. I didn't want to go to any Rome, Italy.

"So, I went back an' the General at Wright Field arranged other overseas duty. I wound up at Nassau in the Bahamas the next year for a couple of months. I remember playin' golf one day with a general, an admiral, an' a lord. The Wright Field people were mighty good to me. They even flew me in a B-17 to my tournaments an' had some of my golf pals flown in for exhibitions an' tournaments in Dayton. I reckon it was the General's personal plane. Whew! I was in hog heaven tourin' with the Air Force."

One pro elaborated on Dutch's sojourn in the Bahamas, "Dutch played a series of exhibitions with other sports figures such as Man Mountain Dean. There was one Bermuda golfer, a Turk, who kept challenging

Dutch in betting matches. Dutch pursued him and won a little, but never gave him a sudden sting.

"The last day that they were playing, Dutch told him, 'I've benefited by $100 from you. I'll give you a chance to get even. We'll play for $100.'

"The Turk upped the ante and Dutch rolled his eyes. After carefully keeping his winnings down over the past months, Dutch turned it on in this last match and won $900."

Feeling sentimental, Dutch dispatched a letter from Dayton, dateline December, 1944, to his friend, Orville Henry, sportswriter for the *Arkansas Gazette* in Little Rock. The letter that Orville published read, "You know, Orville, when it gets near Christmas, a fellow can't help but think of the things that make life worth living. I'm just wondering if sometime when you have a little space in your column you could put in a few words sort of dedicated to my wife by me. I just don't feel right taking all the glory this time when she is the one who really deserves it. If it hadn't been for her, I would still be in the same old rut of running around amounting to nothing. She is the only person who really ever encouraged me to make something of myself, and when I think of all the obstacles I knew, it was no easy job for her. All this, and I still have my first time to ever hear her take the credit for all that she has done. She's always been my good luck charm, and at this Christmastime, I am very thankful for the inspiration she had given me..."

Bob Hamilton marveled at Dutch being flown to every tournament by the Air Force. "Dutch and Herman, and I used to drive 3,300 miles without a motel break to reach California. Then the Air Force starts flying Dutch in the General's B-17 and the pilots are asking him how many thousands of miles he has logged. The general started getting a lot of flack from Congressmen. I heard that they told him the publicity wouldn't square with the other Armed Services if Dutch won the Los Angeles Open after winning the Miami Open. I don't know how true that is, but he led until the last day, then placed second."

The pinnacle of Dutch's career while in service came a month before World War II ended and two months before his discharge. In "the greatest finishing round of golf that the St. Paul Open has ever known," Dutch scored a spectacular 64 to wrap up first place in the four-day tournament held at the Keller course.

"Playin' that game on a course as tricky as this one is the grandest thing that ever happened to me," Dutch told the media after the tournament.

The most heart-warming incident occurred when Dutch walked off the final green a winner that Sunday in July. He doffed his cap from his sweaty brow and picked up a two-year-old girl. Planting a big kiss on her cheek in front of the crowd he exclaimed, "This is for the wonderful lucky ball an' hug you gave me at the start of today."

The little girl was the granddaughter of Tom Laser of Minneapolis who Dutch used to caddie for in Little Rock.

"It's old home week," said Dutch, "An' I plan to send my winnin's to my wife in Little Rock."

Dutch won $2,000 in war bonds. He had tied for first place in the previous St. Paul Open held in 1942 before tournament golf was suspended. (Chick Harbert won the play-off.)

Orville Henry of the *Arkansas Gazette* spoke of the poise Dutch gained from his association with the generals, dukes, and earls that he joined during those World War II golf outings, "Dutch acquired a new confidence in himself. He'd amble onto the golf course either loose or looser. Even in the face of adversity, he maintained his cheerfulness."

Dutch would downplay his coolness in tournaments during the war. "If I got steamed I'd talk to the lil' golf ball 'bout where I was airmailin' him. Sometimes it helps to give 'em an address an' a special talkin' to. Ya know, I'm twice the golfer I was before joinin' the Army."

In the war days Dutch Harrison became a living example of Americana. The tempo of his life was a far cry from the early 1930s when, still wet behind the ears, he picked up his first tournament paycheck for the princely sum of $25. Now he had become an authentic folk hero with his share of fan mail to prove it. In the days to come, he would lead and he would falter, but always with a smile. He graced the golf world and a wider world with a humorous and humanitarian spirit that made him a legend, the "Will Rogers of the Fairway."

Playing in the Roughs

You've got to give a little,
Take a little and let your poor heart break a little:
That's the story of, That's the glory of — Love.

from "The Glory of Love" by Billy Hill

Following Dutch's military discharge in September 1945, Emma insisted on accompanying him on the winter tour, which began that year in November at Richmond, Virginia. There Dutch tied for 13th place, followed by a 7th-place tie in Durham, North Carolina. Emma told the press at the Mobile Open that she was going to get her man back on his game.

Sure enough, Dutch and Sam Byrd wound up tied for first place. In an 18-hole playoff, Byrd won by one stroke. This success was followed by fifth- and fourth-place finishes at the Miami and Ft. Worth Opens in December. Dutch and Emma returned to Little Rock, but inclement weather and a severe cold kept him off the links until he and Emma attended the Los Angeles Open in early January 1946. Despite the ongoing struggle with his cold, he finished in a tie for sixth, followed by sixth, eighth, fourth and fifth place finishes at San Francisco and Richmond in California, and Phoenix and Tucson in Arizona.

That's My Wife

Signs of a strained relationship between Dutch and Emma surfaced at the San Francisco Open. Dutch was working hard for second spot to Byron Nelson who had already finished far ahead of the field. On the long 16th hole of the famed Olympic Club Lake Course, Dutch gambled with a wood shot from the rough. His ball didn't travel nearly as far as planned. Emma caught up with Wilbur Johnson, who was caddying for Dutch, and asked what happened on the hole. When Wilbur told her that he had gambled with a 3-wood despite the ball's poor lie, Emma stormed, "You always stick up for Dutch. That SOB looked up and it cost us $1,000."

At the 1946 Tucson Open, Colonel French, a good golfing friend of Dutch's, was following Dutch down the first fairway as a spectator and asked, "Who is that old gray-haired lady walking in the rough and following you?"

"That's my wife," smiled Dutch.

Colonel French remembers being embarrassed. "But it didn't seem to bother Dutch. He was used to hearing worse aspersions cast on his wife. He knew Emma would never win any beauty contests among the pro's wives, but he was never outwardly disrespectful."

Recalling accounts of the Tucson Open, Colonel French said, "On the eighth hole, Dutch missed a short putt and nearly kicked his putter off the green, a rare display of temper for Dutch. Emma admonished him in front of everybody and told him to behave himself. Red-faced, Dutch completed one of his poorest rounds."

Dutch returned to Little Rock on February 10, 1946, exhausted after eleven straight weeks of travel and tournaments. "I missed the next four tournaments an' didn't get back into the tour swing until the Miami Four-Ball Tournament in March," remarked Dutch.

After the Tucson Open, Emma never again accompanied Dutch on tour.

During the pro tour of World War II, Dutch struck

up a conversation with a pretty member of the gallery, a young brown-eyed country girl named Jeannie Weiss.

As Dutch would say, "She had a figure that would open a dead man's eyes." It became a struggle to keep his eye on the ball and his mind on golf.

After Dutch was discharged, Jeannie went on tour with him periodically during the declining years of his marriage, 1945 through 1949. Although she traveled extensively with Dutch and some of his pals, he introduced her to only a few of his friends. Jeannie was well-liked and Dutch's close friends were sympathetic to the relationship in light of his faltering marriage.

It was not by an accident of geography that Emma found herself in Portland, Oregon in August 1946 at the same time as Jeannie and Dutch, although Dutch had discouraged Emma from making the trip. Emma's suspicions of Dutch's other female companion forced her to contact some of his fellow servicemen.

She told how after receiving some disquieting reports from them, she hired a detective to follow him on tour. According to Emma, the detective phoned her from Portland where the PGA Championship tournament was being held, and reported that Dutch and another woman were sharing a room together.

Distraught, Emma quickly packed and flew there via Denver. On her stopover, she encountered golf pro, Harry Todd, and declared that she was going to shoot Dutch. Upon arriving in Portland, she met the detective and both proceeded to the motel where Dutch was staying.

Emma's story was that the detective forced his way into the motel room and ordered Jeannie out so that Emma could take her place. Emma claimed later she did throw Jeannie out, but other golfers in nearby rooms believed that Emma did not succeed in ousting Jeannie, although she was successful in causing quite a commotion.

In fact, one couple reported the detective knocked at the door, and when the door opened slightly, wedged his foot in and said, "I have your wife here to see you, Mr. Harrison."

Dutch roared, "She's the last person I want to see."

The detective gained entrance for Emma who then whipped the pistol from her purse, to everyone's surprise, and pointed it at Jeannie. "I'd shoot you but you're not worth the powder," she reportedly threatened.

Dutch responded, "Aw, Emma. Don't get careless now. That gun's mighty easy on the trigger."

The detective interceded and escorted Emma away. Emma spent the next two or three nights in Portland bending the ear of mutual friends. The golfers were sympathetic with Dutch. One couple left a note under the door the morning after the confrontation offering their assistance. The following day a phalanx of Pinkerton detectives and officials was posted to protect Dutch throughout the remainder of the tournament.

The first day of the tournament Dutch played with Sam Snead who remembered Emma had approached Dutch and threatened to call Ed Dudley, popular PGA president. Finally, she was taken off the golf course. Dutch had a remarkable 65 to take the lead in that qualifying round of the match-play tournament.

After his round, Dutch commented to the press, "I didn't play golf today, but Mr. Sam did. I was all over the course, but the ol' putter sure was workin'. I'm takin' it to bed with me tonight."

That evening, while Dutch was in the dining room of the Portland Golf Club, Emma entered. Still fearing her wrath, he scrambled and started to run for safety toward the locker room. As he did, her outstretched hands caught his coattails. He stumbled and fell, causing Emma to lose her grip. Jumping up, he leap-frogged several empty tables, and beat her to the locker room door. Once safely inside, he had the pros check from time to time to see if she was still outside. With their help, and that of the Pinkerton contingent, he escaped unscathed and not too badly shaken. Despite the concern for his life and Jeannie's, he was able to make a Herculean effort for the title and advanced to the third round. Emma was not allowed near Dutch again while he was playing in the tournament.

His golf friends would not let him forget those incidents. He had shared with them the cruel threat by Emma to shoot him someday at a tournament when he was attempting a critical short putt. One time, during a practice round putt, a well-known pro popped a paper bag and Dutch reportedly slithered on the ground like a snake as he retrieved his ball.

The next few months were rough ones for him and Emma. "She really laid the whip to me an' I was out practicin' at Riverside early every day 'til dark. She was always racin' her motor an' could really jaw up a patch. I'll tell ya— she could chew the gate off its hinges. I had to pull some Houdini's to escape her. Del Webb used to help me out."

Dutch explained his friendship with Webb, former co-owner of the New York Yankees and a wealthy developer. "We had a similar problem. We both drove our ducks to a poor market."

Return to Pennsylvania

In February of 1947, Otto Kohl, who often worked and caddied for Dutch, received a phone call from him. "Pack your bags, Otto. We're headin' for Pennsylvania. Humpy is already there an' we got a good deal."

Harold "Humpy" Blaylock, Dutch's close friend since boyhood, was a well-known golf pro with tours of duty at Duncan Air Field, San Antonio (1931-1942); the Country Club of York (1942-1948); Willow Springs, San Antonio (1949-1962); and Pecan Valley, San Antonio since 1963.

"But Dutch, Johnny Bulla and Gus Moreland want me to go to Pittsburgh and that's where I plan to go," Otto replied.

"The race tracks are closer here. Change your plans an' get that Model-A in shape for a long trip. See ya in

York, Pennsylvania."

This was the beginning of Dutch's attachment as head golf professional to the Country Club of York near Jeannie's home. When Dutch was not on tour, he stayed with her. Although Dutch considered himself separated, Emma didn't share that view.

Dutch and Harold Blaylock, assistant pro to Dutch, made the first visit to York in February to inspect the facilities. They planned to spend a month there, but got sidetracked by the races in New Orleans for several weeks. Upon reaching York, they drove up a winding road through the heavily wooded terrain of the Appalachian ridges to a stately clubhouse at the top of a knoll. There they admired the broad overview of the course, but turned to enter a vintage 1899 clubhouse and pro shop in bad repair. Dutch had phoned Otto to have him come out as an assistant to clean, paint, and make necessary repairs in readiness for play in the spring.

The annals of the Country Club of York, where President Eisenhower became an honorary member, record the following: "In 1947, the Country Club of York hired one of the most promising golf professionals of his day, Dutch Harrison. During his stay here he spent much time on the PGA Circuit and won three major tournaments. He attained membership on the Ryder Cup Team, a dream of all golf professionals."

Harold Blaylock handled the club professional duties while Dutch was on tour. Dutch liked York because it offered the balance between rural and urban living to which he was accustomed, and it was close to racetracks. Dutch barely missed winning the U.S. Open, which he led for three rounds, then won four quick tournaments, three in the space of five weeks. Jeannie accompanied Dutch chiefly on the eastern area tours.

Bob Hamilton recalled Dutch's lodging rituals on their western tours together, "When Dutch would reach his place of lodging the first thing he would do was go to a market and buy food. He always had to have food on his night stand — canned sausages, cold cuts, sandwich food. Anytime he wanted something to eat, it was there. Then he'd sprawl on the bed in his shorts and read the sports page and his *Wall Street Journal*, the Daily Racing Form.

"He'd say, 'Gentlemens, get your feet up!' Dutch was a great believer in resting and relaxing. He'd go to bed early and he was an early riser. At night if we were having a jaw session and it kept going he'd likely say he was going to rest his eyes a bit. That meant he was retiring."

Reno Open

"My biggest thrill in 1947 came at the Reno Open," Dutch happily remembered.

Bob Hamilton recalled that experience with one of his favorite stories. "Dutch would come through Evansville (Indiana) in August so we could go to the races together. You know I live only five miles from Kentucky. We'd play golf every morning at Evansville Country Club with my good friends, Jimmy Stevens and sports editor, Dan Scism. They loved old Dutch. Then we'd go to the races in the afternoon. That August, Dutch was winning $50 every morning. His golf was outstanding. He shot the first nine holes in 30 every day — I don't mean 31 or 32, but *30*—and he did this about eight straight days. Amazing!

"Now the race track was something else. He'd lose about $100 every day and before long, he was busted. He wanted to go back to York, Pennsylvania, but I talked him into accompanying me to the Reno Open.

"I told him, 'The way you're playing, Dutch, you'll terrify them. I never saw you play better.'

"I had a brand new car, so I said, 'We'll use my car, but I'm going to drive 100 miles, then you're going to drive 100 miles. It's 2,000 miles and I'm not going to drive you clear across the country. We'll start next Saturday and that will give us plenty of time the following week to practice before the tournament.'

"Dutch says, 'Oh, that's fine, Mr. Bob.'

"What he means is that it's okay because I loaned him $500 and it's my new car. So the trip begins. After we get 100 miles toward Reno, I stop and get out of the car.

"'What's the matter with the car, Mr. Bob?'

"'Dutch, if I have to get back under the wheel, we're heading for Evansville.'

"'Man, have we gone 100 miles already?'

"Well, we get to Washoe Country Club, now a public course, and I'm beginning a practice round with Herman Keiser. We notice Dutch is not practicing, just sitting under a tree talking to Porky Oliver. I'm concerned, so I check.

"Dutch says, 'Mr. Bob, with this high altitude I can't be hittin' no balls today.'

"As soon as Herman and I tee off, we look back and Porky and Dutch had disappeared from under that tree. When we complete our round, I find that Dutch and Porky went downtown to those bookies to play the horses. Before the tournament starts, Dutch hasn't played more than a few holes. Gulp! I look over and the big parimutuel sign has Dutch at 25 to 1. Herman and I want to bet $100 on Dutch, but we come down to $50 because Dutch hasn't been practicing. We both know that Dutch usually plays his best golf when he's busted, but we're worried. The tournament begins and Dutch is in contention with Ben Hogan, Jimmy Demaret, Herman Keiser, Lloyd Mangrum, and Ellsworth Vines."

Dutch completed the story, recalling his stretch drive. "I'm playin' with Jimmy Demaret an' Herman Keiser in that last round, my best in the tournament. You know how dusty-lookin' it gets out there? Well, when I got to that last hole, the desert turned green. I knew I was back in the big bucks again an' tears came to my eyes. I knew I had me a 66, 16 under par for the tournament. I was in a daze, really enjoyin' it before my last putt.

"Finally, Herman, who had a bad round after he hit his caddie in the head with the ball while practicin', says, 'Aren't you gonna putt? Let's get this thing over.' My winnin's for first place was $2,500, but with the $100 bet on myself an' those final 30-1 odds, I had no trouble payin' Bob back. I was in green heaven."

The following October, Jeannie accompanied Dutch to the Reading Open in Pennsylvania, where he emerged the winner by three strokes over Bobby Locke. She followed him as he played the fourth and final day, head-to-head with his frequent exhibition partner who was beaten soundly. During the contest, Dutch kept lauding Locke's talents in front of the large gallery.

He kidded his other partner, wealthy amateur Frank Stranahan, "Frank, you gonna win me a watch at the Crosby? Mine hasn't been runnin' for a week."

Hawaiian Open

Winning the Hawaiian Open in November, 1947 was high on Dutch's list of top accomplishments. This was the first Hawaiian Open to attract a multitude of PGA pros from the Mainland and it was the first $10,000 purse that attracted them. Dutch flew to Hawaii, without Jeannie or Emma, following his victories in the Ryder Cup in Oregon. He and most of the other pros stayed at the Royal Hawaiian Hotel in Honolulu and were royally entertained. Dutch raked in the pro-am first prize before he played the grueling 72 holes the next four days at Waialae Country Club in Kahala.

Charlie Isom, a Little Rock native on leave from the Navy, watched the Open. "Lloyd Mangrum was the favorite, but I followed Dutch the first seven holes. He was two-over-par, so I was about to transfer to Mangrum's group when Dutch birdied the eighth hole, then made an eagle on the ninth. I stuck with Dutch as he got hotter than fireworks and had a record 66 that first day. He lost the lead when the tradewinds started to blow, but wound up edging out Johnny Bulla for first place."

Dutch scored a 13-under-par 275 to achieve his victory.

At the presentation ceremonies, Dai Rees, British Ryder Cup golfer, told the cheering throng of 5,000 fans, "I've had the pleasure of playing with one of the greatest golfers of my career, the Dutchman."

Dutch thanked Rees and told his avid golf followers, "I've never played before a finer gallery in all of my golfing career."

The 1947 Hawaiian Open had established golf as a spectator sport in Hawaii.

Separations

In July of 1948 at the Reading, Pennsylvania Open, Emma showed up during a practice round. Ed Tabor and Clayton Heafner were conferring on the first tee when she approached.

"Clayt," she said, "I understand Dutch is playing in this tournament. I'm looking for that SOB — and if I find him, I'll shoot him."

Clayton knew she carried a revolver in her purse. After she left, both golfers decided they'd better locate Dutch out on the course. They were told by a couple of amateurs who had been playing with Dutch that he left suddenly in his car. Obviously, he had gotten the message and rushed to see that Jeannie changed motels.

In August Dutch traveled alone to Chicago for the World Championship of Golf at Tam O'Shanter Country Club. Concentrating more on golf than nearby Sportsman's Park Race Track, he tied for first place with Sam Snead and Lloyd Mangrum.

This tournament was part of the George S. May series in which some pros refused to participate because they were required to wear identification numbers on their posterior.

Dutch's response to the requirement was, "I'd wear Scottish kilts for that kinda money."

Lloyd Mangrum won the play-off, during which Dutch noticed a young boy in the large gallery straining to watch. Dutch sauntered over and said, "Come on an' let my little buddy through the ropes so he can see," as he helped bring the boy out front.

"I'll never forget that nice gesture," recalled the boy, who went on to become a Ryder Cup Champion. His name is Gardner Dickinson.

Emma's long-time wish to accompany Dutch to the Hawaiian Islands on a golf outing came true in November of that year when Dutch defended his Hawaiian Open championship. Close friends were surprised and found it hard to believe that Dutch would allow it, because Dutch and Emma were separated, but somehow Emma had her way.

Upon arrival, she was quoted by the *Honolulu Star Bulletin*: "I've always wished that someone would put one of these leis around my neck and here I have more than I can handle."

Emma and Dutch stayed first at the recently re-opened Royal Hawaiian Hotel, touted as "The World's Most Beautiful Hotel." Then they switched to a less expensive hotel nearby. Friends directly above them reported that they were shouting and arguing most of the time. Despite the early- and late-hour skirmishes, Dutch finished fourth in the tournament.

At the Waialae golf course, a photograph was taken of the "golf widows" who enjoyed jaunts together while their husbands played. Kitty Alexander, honeymooning with Skip, one of Dutch's best golfing friends, was as astonished as the other wives when Emma performed an entertaining whirling dervish ballet in her undies on an isolated sand beach in northern Oahu. She disrobed behind a large trash container, then twirled and danced with complete abandon and joy along her sandy stage.

Kitty recalled, "We never laughed so hard in our lives."

Here was a normally prudish wife behaving like an enthusiastic child. The Hawaiian trip, the sand, ocean, and all-encompassing beauty formed a dream come true. With joy in her heart and music in her mind, a part of her soul previously hidden had been revealed.

In April, 1949 Dutch and Jeannie checked in at a hotel in Virginia Beach, Virginia where the Cavalier Specialist Golf Tournament was being held. Emma had surreptitiously followed. When she tried to go to his room, she was told that Mr. and Mrs. Harrison had registered. She was not permitted access upstairs. Sighting Kitty Alexander in the lobby, Emma vented her anger and displayed the gun in her purse.

"You may think this tournament has already generated a lot of publicity, but that's a mere shade of what there will be when I shoot Dutch," she told her.

Kitty, pregnant at the time, experienced both terror and panic.

She recalled, "It was nightmarish. Skip was to play with Dutch the following day."

When told of Emma's appearance and threats, Dutch once again tried to be a calming influence, "Don't worry. She's just a mean howler. Barking dogs don't bite."

As quickly as Emma had appeared on the scene, she disappeared, much to the relief of those in the know. Feeling expressive afterward, Bob Hamilton, and Dutch came down the stairs to the lobby dressed in red blazers, only to see that all of the hotel attendants were also in red blazers. The two golfers made a hurried exit upstairs to change. The quips and laughs afterward restored levity to the Virginia Beach scene.

In May, Jeannie and Dutch traveled to the Sam Snead Festival Tournament, held in Greenbriar, West Virginia. Emma followed, looking for Dutch. When she found him on the fairway, she was pointing a gun.

Dutch said, "Looka' here...just a minute, you can't shoot that thing...don't you pull that trigger."

The other pros, shocked and frightened, scattered quickly.

Dutch played his golf shot and Emma stashed the

revolver back in her purse while shouting, "I picked you up from the gutter, Dutch — and brought you to where you are — and now I'm going to break you and return you to where you came from."

She was unceremoniously escorted off the course as she protested to anyone within hearing range. Not one to brood and worry about what might happen tomorrow, Dutch continued playing and tied for second place with a score of 124 in the pro-am event.

Later, when asked where Emma was, Dutch casually replied, "Ol' Emma's gone south on a load of logs."

Following Dutch's win in the Canadian Open that June, Dutch told the other players, "Now I reckon I can settle down, get me a li'l ol' Club and work at bein' a family man."

Although their relationship was not quite over, according to friends he never married Jeannie because she was not the mother-type of wife that he needed.

Another encounter with Emma pointing a gun is reported to have occurred the following July at the Washington Star Open, near Washington, D.C., where Dutch placed sixth. However, the eternal and infernal triangle would soon change its configuration, including a fading relationship with Jeannie.

Hustling

"Work consists of whatever a body
is obliged to do...
Play consists of whatever a body
is not obliged to do."

from "The Adventures of Tom Sawyer"
by Mark Twain

Most legends of golf retired to the 19th hole regularly, but not Dutch. His shots were on the golf course, his spirits were free, not bottled. He enjoyed timely tee-offs and hangover-free golf. He never learned to mix a drink, and for most of his life was a soft drink fan and non-smoker, determined to keep his accomplished hands steady and his eagle eyes clear.

This penchant was well expressed by his bromide, "A good player drives for show an' putts for dough."

Though he cashed in around the greens, Dutch was not infallible.

Dutch's Stock Market

Two facets of gambling permeated Dutch's blood: golf hustling and pony hustling. Hustling on the course represented his stock market. He studied the odds in the same way as the bettors on Wall Street. With pony

67

hustling, he had a one-track mind — the race track. He loved to bet on "my ponies," using the Daily Racing Form as his *Wall Street Journal.*

Bob Hamilton and Dutch Harrison probably made the greatest pair of hustlers that golf has yet to see. They operated in tandem, beginning with locating their quarry (called pigeons) and inviting the pigeons to a "friendly game" with a small stake. Generally, the first objective was to assess the victim-to-be and let him win the first holes, or win the first match. Dutch called this "saltin' the pigeon," always building the interest and enthusiasm for a return match. At the proper moment, he'd raise the ante and the trap was set.

Dutch explained the bets. "We give the other fellahs a fair handicap of so many strokes on each hole. The usual bet was the "nassau" which came from the Nassau Country Club on Long Island where the bettin' games first became popular. Two-dollar nassau means I'll play ya for two dollars on the front nine holes, two dollars on the back nine, an' two dollars for the total match, a stake of six dollars. But there are all sorts a side bets that can run the stakes sky high. Generally, the losin' side can suggest a press. That's a new bet to try to get even.

"After the stock market crash in 1929, half the 6,000 golf courses went broke. Who'd want to become a pro golfer? Ya had to love the game to play it. Shucks, we pros woulda played whether there was money or not — if the stakes was a Confederate bill we'd go after it.

"The hustler was born durin' the Great Depression when tournament purses were so small the tourin' pros could hardly survive. In the 1930s mosta our pocket money for reachin' the next tournament town came from wagin' friendly, li'l games. It was the day of the hustlers hustlin' the hustlers, an' anyone else. There was always alotta side action amongst us. Bettin' amounts weren't much, 'cause the pros in those days didn't have much money. But the bookmakers began advertisin' bettin' odds at tournaments on big Calcutta signboards — like at the Masters, Seminole, and Greenbriar."

Hustling had royal beginnings. The Duke of York, later to become King James II, in 1681 hustled two English noblemen. When he and his partner, a shoe-maker, won the match, the Duke gave the winnings to his partner to build a home. Hustling and large auction pools were supported by such distinguished gentlemen as John D. Rockefeller, the Duke of Windsor, Bobby Jones, and Walter Hagen.

It took little to whet Dutch's gambling spirit on the golf course, and he always seemed to have a psychologi-cal advantage over opponents. Most believed the key was his sweet-talk, which came easy for him because of his good nature. In 1939 this conversation was recorded with Horton Smith, leading pro, on the first tee in the quarter finals of the PGA Championship. At the time, Horton Smith was Dutch's boss.

Dutch: "I hope you play good today."

Horton: "Well, we'll have a good match."

Dutch: "I hope you don't beat me too bad."

Horton: "Well, I'm not going to beat you too bad."

In that match, Dutch skinned Horton 4 and 3 (four holes ahead with three to play.)

Henry Ransom called Dutch a real oil artist and recalled, "He'd grease you up one side and down the other, saying, 'This course is built for your game, Mr. Henry — fits you perfect. Wish I had a swing like that. I know you're goin' to play wonderful golf this week,' — and later in the game, 'You're such a great putter, Mr. Henry, I probably should concede that short putt, 'cause its a lead-pipe cinch you'll make it.' Even during the most crucial rounds, his wise-cracking, nonchalance and sympathy could be enough to unnerve the most hardened veteran."

To the opponents he hustled, Dutch could be even more magnanimous, "Man, can you massage that ball. How'd that feel? Didn't that feel gooood? I haven't seen a swing that good since Mac Smith. What a pair of hands! If you don't like your grip, you don't like home cookin'. My hands feel like they've been pickin' cotton."

Or he'd say, "That sure looked like a perfect stroked putt to me. You won't miss any more with that stroke."

Other times Dutch would distract with this approach, "That li'l ol' sandtrap hidin' over there won't bother you none — you cut your eye-teeth on escapin' those hazards. I've got 'bout as much chance against you with that handicap as a one-legged man in a butt-kickin' contest."

Herman Keiser remembers well Dutch's light-hearted approach, "One tournament round I was playing with Dutch and he'd keep sweet-talking me.

"Before I putted, he'd say, 'C'mon, Mr. Herman, now knock it in.'

"I was about to use the putter on him! Afterward I said, 'Dutch, I've never played a good round with you in a tournament. You jinx me. Now you and I are good friends, right?'

"Dutch says, 'Oh Mr. Herman, you know we are. I always try to help you.'

"I said, 'Well, if you want to help me, next time don't open your mouth. If I ask you something, okay. But don't say one word about my wonderful shot, knocking it in, or anything. You're going to brag me broke!

"Dutch kept nodding his head. 'Okay, Mr. Herman, okay.'"

Herman spoke about Dutch's love of playing with amateur golfers. "He did a lot for the amateur golfers. He was popular with all of them because he'd kid them, build them up, and often put their golf game ahead of his own. When we other pros were playing practice rounds together before tournaments, we'd look over in the next fairway and one of us might say, 'Oh, there's Dutch. Bet we don't know who the other three guys are who are playing two-dollar nassaus with Dutch!'

"And sure enough, we couldn't recognize any of them. Afterwards, I'd ask Dutch, 'Well, Dutch what did you do to those guys?'

"He'd say, 'Oh Mr. Herm, they really cleaned my clock. You should see that man brutalize the ball. He can outdrive Sam Snead.'

"In actuality, Dutch had probably won five or six dollars from each of them."

Before the 1939 Miami Open, Dutch and Wilbur Johnson entered the tournament locker room where Sam Snead and Henry Picard were planning practice rounds.

Sam said, "Dutchman, I've got a game for you."

"Mr. Sam, I've been there before. No thanks."

"What are you going to do — wait for some pigeons and then pluck their feathers good?"

"No, Mr. Sam, I brought one with me," and he smiled at his good friend Wilbur.

Dutch took his "pigeon" with him as a partner that day against Clayton Heafner and Henry Picard, two tour champions. Wilbur Johnson, who had a true four handicap, was given a stroke on each nine holes. The match lasted only two holes when Wilbur birdied both holes, sinking a 15-foot putt on the second hole.

Heafner reached into his pocket and threw two dollars on the green as he cut loose a barrage of expletives aimed at Dutch, "So this guy is a sportswriter from Little Rock? Well, this is the last time you're going to fleece me. Last year it was Leonard Dodson you brought, and he did the same thing to us!"

Dutch's reputation was established.

Leading Money Winner

Dutch and Clayton Heafner, the General Patton of the pro ranks, were recognized in 1947 as unofficial leading money winners, counting tournament wagers as well as prize earnings. They were close friends who would play exhibitions and swap Army stories when Dutch would visit the Heafners in their North Carolina home.

The lighter side of the hustling circuit came second nature to Dutch. In 1941 Dutch was scheduled to play an exhibition in Dallas with Ralph Guldahl, Cary

Middlecoff, and Byron Nelson. The previous day he practiced at the municipal course, where he saw big-band leader Glenn Miller preparing to play. To make his practice interesting, Dutch found an old golf bag, put a few of his clubs in it, and introduced himself as Ernie Joe. Glenn had a 12 handicap and Dutch bet him that he'd beat him by one stroke at the end of 18 holes. On the first 17 holes Dutch matched him shot for shot, then seized an opportunity on the 18th hole and won the match by a stroke. Dutch invited his victim to the exhibition the next day. One can imagine Glenn's surprise when he discovered who his opponent had been.

Johnny Reynolds, San Antonio golfing ace, recalls Dutch "taking me to the cleaners in 1932, when he was wearing scruffy, white street shoes with spikes screwed into the soles. I decided I'd rather join him than play against him, and we ended up being pretty good hustlers together. One day after a match, our victim was totaling his scorecard when a mockingbird in the tree above him soiled his card.

"'For anyone else he'd sing,' we heard him lament."

While riding to California with Bob Hamilton and Herman Keiser, Dutch took a lot of ribbing from the two about all the amateurs that had been relieved of nassaus.

"Your hustling talents are known country-wide, Dutch, and you used to tell us, 'Oh, those schoolteachers ruined me, they carved me up,'" Bob Hamilton recalled teasing.

"We drove into the wee hours without stopping, but finally decided on some breakfast when we came to a little diner in a desolate section of Texas, 15 to 25 miles from El Paso.

"After we ordered at the counter, a tall bearded man entered wearing cowboy garb and immediately exclaimed, 'My God! It's Dutch Harrison. Do you remember me?'

"Dutch had that nice way of saying that he did, even though he was stuck for the name.

"'Well, Dutch, we played in St. Paul, Minnesota.'

"Dutch says, 'Yeah, an' you beat the devil out of me.'

"The man smiled, 'No, Dutch, you've got it backwards. You took *my* money!'

"Here out in the middle of no place at four a.m. and this cowboy knew Dutch Harrison. Did we ever kid him about that. It seemed someone knew Dutch any place in the world.

"Even though he took them to the cleaners, they all loved him. Dutch won almost every two-dollar nassau he touched and every heart with it. When he indulged with amateur pigeons, they wound up eating out of his hand. He helped so many of them with their golf game. But he was about as country as J.P. Morgan when it came to fattening his bankroll.

"Nobody was a better strategist at hustling than Dutch. He'd say to his partner, 'Take it easy now, Mr. Jack. You only have to win by one. Don't beat 'em too bad or you'll never get 'em back.'

"His philosophy was, 'Never extend yourself more than 85 percent in hustlin', cause you may need the other 15 percent any time.'"

Just before World War II, Dutch had some friendly games with the brass at Duncan Field, now Kelly Air Force Base, San Antonio.

These games included General Nathan Twining who later became Chairman of the Joint Chiefs of Staff. The General, realizing that Dutch never wanted to overwhelm an opponent, even when playing 25 cent or 50 cent nassaus, told Dutch, "I'm going to pay you anyway, so shoot your game all the time with me."

But Dutch rarely would unless pressed.

Together, Dutch and Bob Hamilton also concentrated on certain pro golfers, sometimes betting more than $1,500 in an 18-hole match. Charles "Monk" Wade, a former bank teller in Little Rock, remembers Dutch cashing five or six checks of $200 to $500 every time he returned from an outing on the pro tour — all signed by famous pros.

Once Bob Hamilton arranged a match in Arizona

with Jimmy Demaret and his brother. The stakes were high. Bob wasn't sure he could get Dutch to play, so he lined up Herman Keiser who told Bob, "Okay, I'll play, but Dutch will play better than me." Herman reached the club 30 minutes before the match and learned that Dutch had reluctantly agreed to play and post half of the bet with Bob.

Herman recapped the match, "Dutch buried them on the first three holes and the game was really over at that point. What a money player!"

Losses were minuscule with Bob and Dutch when they played against name pros, Sam Snead excepted.

There was one fellow that Dutch believed could play right along with Sam Snead. That was Bobby Locke from South Africa. After Bobby had beaten Sam 12 to 16 matches in South Africa in 1945, he asked Snead, "D'you think I could come to America and make a bean or two?"

"With that putter," Snead told him, "You could get rich."

After Bobby came over in 1947, many golfers wished Sam had been less candid.

Bobby Locke Stories

Dutch's stories of Bobby Locke and his first series of exhibition trips with him in 1947 are immortal.

"Arthur D'Arcy 'Bobby' Locke was a big, ruddy-faced, heavy jowled, jovial man who normally wore knickers an' tie on the golf course. He may have dressed old-fashioned, but he sure didn't address golf old-fashioned. He musta aged a lot from flyin' missions for the South African Air Force, 'cause he looked ten years older than he really was — which was about 30. He drove this big English-style car, an' when I first went to drivin' it an' found the steerin' wheel on the wrong side, I jumped out an' changed places with Mr. Bobby real quick. Even though he mighta indulged too much at the bar, it was a lot better for him to do the drivin'.

"Our fourth of 13 exhibitions was at the Tulsa Country Club, an' we had to drive all night from St. Louis after the U.S. Open. We arrived in Tulsa 'bout six in the mornin', slept a couple hours, an' headed for the Tulsa Country Club. Bobby, bein' quite attached to the moose milk, had a couple of 'wrist looseners' with his lunch. There were 'bout 12 people havin' lunch with us.

"Bobby asked, 'What's the course record?'

"When he learned that the lowest score was a 64, he said, 'What are the odds that I don't shoot a 64 or better?'

"I was wonderin' about him . . . drivin' all night an' havin' a little toddy or two, but the others said, 'We'll give you 5 to 1, Bobby.'

"He said, 'I'll bet $200 that I shoot 64 or better.'

"About that time I noticed some of the club group scattered an' I knew they were headed to put the flagsticks in tough places an' move the tee markers way back.

"As we started out to the course, Bobby turned an' said, 'Dutch, you've got $100 of this bet.'

"I said, 'I haven't got any.' He said I was wrong, so since he was gettin' $500 for the exhibition, an' I was gettin' $300, I reluctantly said, 'Okay.'

"He played well an' at the 17th hole, had about a 12-foot putt to go eight-under-par, which with a par on the 18th hole would have given him a score of 64. Now when Bobby would putt, if he knew the putt was goin' in the hole, he would take his cap off an' hold it. When he knew it had a chance to miss, he would sort of tip his cap but he wouldn't take it off. I was always watchin' that cap more than anythin' else while he was puttin'. When he hit this 12-footer, he didn't pull that cap off an' the ball lipped the hole. The crowd moaned. So he has to birdie that last hole, an' it's a long par-5, 'bout 580 yards to the green, an' Bobby's third shot wound up 'bout 42 feet away. Now he's got a curvin' downhill putt for all the cash. He stroked the putt in his hookin' fashion an' then took that cap off an' didn't put it back on. I knew we hit the jackpot before that ball went right in the middle of the hole.

"Our next exhibition was at the famous Tenison Park course in Dallas. There we were sittin' 'round the lunch table again with a dozen people.

"Over his drinks Bobby asks, 'What is the course record?'

"Tom Stockwell told him, 'Harry Cooper shot 30-30 for a 60 once.'

"Bobby Locke looked at him an' said, 'My word, that was some score, wasn't it.'

"Bobby was a smooth cookie. No bettin' on that score."

It was legal in those days to bet on other tournament players or share earnings with another entrant. There were few rules. Players who traveled together commonly split purses in order to subsist. Often when they found themselves in an enviable betting position, they extended or sold their bets.

Jerry Barber remembered one example with Dutch, "I was in tenth position in this tournament with one round to go. I kidded some golfers that I would take $200 for my tenth position because I expected that my purse prize would be about $200.

"Dutch heard this and suggested, 'Okay, Mr. Jerry, I'll take you in the bettin' an' give you $200.'

"I said, 'Dutch, I was just kidding.' I shot 65 on the final round in a windstorm and won $1,400.

"Dutch would have made $1,200 on me. If he had taken me and won, he was the type of guy that would have given me an extra couple of hundred dollars. That's the kind of person he was. He was such a gentle guy. Why, if a pigeon fell out of a tree, he'd pick it up and take care of it. That's the way he had fun. He always gave opponents a good chance to win, then beat them at their own game. He wouldn't take advantage of people, but if you came along and wanted to spend some money, he'd accommodate you. On the other hand, if you were down and out, and Dutch had money, it was yours. Everybody liked Dutch, and there was no better golf handicapper.

He's supposed to have won $1,000 11 times straight betting on Bobby Locke."

Favorite Hustlers

A favorite hustling partner of Dutch's was Gibby Sellers, a rotund professional hustler who was perhaps best known for dusting off the top pros and amateurs that came through Arkansas on exhibitions. Dubbed "Arkansas Fats," he reigned at the Number three course of the Hot Springs Country Club in the 1930s, 1940s, and 1950s, and was recognized as one of the greatest wedge players and putters in the country.

Former caddie partner Dutch said, "Mr. Gibby referred to his pigeons as clients. When he started on the pro tour he had a hard time learnin' that drinkin' an' golfin' don't mix. He emptied as many Seagram bottles as clients' pockets. He'd be shootin' a 62 an' leadin' some of those big tournaments after the first or second day, then open a case of Seagrams.

"One tournament mornin' he phoned fellow pro Andy Anderson who was stayin' at his hotel an' says: 'How 'bout a little toddy?'

"Mr. Andy asks, 'Isn't it a bit early for a toddy?' 'Hell,' says Gibby, 'toddies don't know what time it is.'"

In 1955 Dutch met Doug Sanders, a Georgia amateur who was to become his protegé and later a leading tour player. Impressed with Doug's play and his self-confidence under fire, Dutch invited him to be his partner in a pro-am tournament in Odessa, Texas.

"I told him, 'Son, I'll meet you in Dallas an' we'll drive to Odessa. Each team entered will have one professional an' one amateur — no handicaps. There's parimutuel bettin' an' I want to make a generous bet on ourselves,'" related Dutch.

"Well, we were at the golf course the day before the tournament. I told him, 'Son, go out to the practice tee an' show nothin'. Most of those people won't think you can play well because of that short swing, but I want you to shank the ball an' hit a few worm-killers. When I nod at you, hit it off the toe or heel. We want those parimutuel odds as high as we can get 'em.'

"An' Doug says, 'Well, if we don't get 'em tomorrow, Big Daddy, we sure will the next day.'

"I said, 'Son, if we don't get them tomorrow, there'll not be a second one. We'll look funny with those golf bags on our backs hitchhikin' home. You'd better come out of the chute like a greyhound. I didn't bring much green with me an' I left none at home. I'm bettin' the whole bankroll today.'

"The next day that boy came outta the chute like he had springs on his behind. He was hotter than a hen layin' a goose egg. He birdied five of the first six holes.

"I said, 'Son, Big Daddy can take over from here.'

"Ya know, we did all right at that parimutuel in Odessa."

The Ponies

Those who played tour golf with Dutch noted a unique characteristic. When they bemoaned an early assigned tee-off time, Dutch would chuckle, "Oh, that's perfect! We can be at Tropical Park Race Track at one p.m."

That was often the partner's introduction to Dutch's racing world, where the courses are for horses. As his golf score mounted, Dutch might say, "I think I belong with the ponies."

If Dutch were asked the date of Easter any year, he'd likely answer, "The two weekends before the Kentucky Derby."

Commonly, he was at the horse races in the afternoon and the dog races at night while on tour in Arizona, Florida, and Louisiana.

Dutch found that Fred Corcoran, accommodating official on the PGA tour, could provide preferred starting times.

"I was a 'dew-sweeper'. I wanted to tee off early

between seven and eight an' he generally saw to it that I could," Dutch remembered.

On the golf tour his trips to the track meant staying from the first post parade to the last homestretch drive. These trips were as traditional as the playing of "My Old Kentucky Home" or the sipping of mint juleps at the Kentucky Derby.

Thoroughbred racing made Dutch the king at the Sport of Kings. However, he conceded, "On occasion, I went from king to pauper. My favorite track was one where I could pick a winnah.

"I learned early 'bout bettin' on the ponies. When I was 17, Harold Blaylock an' I visited a bookie shop in North Little Rock. The bookie explained the operations an' offered to help us bet on a nag named Gallahadion whose odds at that time were 85 to 1. We decided to bet the eight dollars in our pockets to win. Unbeknownst to me, Harold got cold feet an' bet four dollars to win, two dollars to place an' two dollars to show. When Gallahadion came in a winner an' I feasted my eyes on our sudden stroke of luck, Harold had some explainin' to do.

"Emma an' I went to the races at Hot Springs, 55 miles from Little Rock, once or twice a week durin' racin' season. Emma saw to it that my investments didn't exceed the "foolish money" limits that we set, but she left the bettin' to me. She'd tell others how lucky I was when she was along.

"I followed the Daily Racing Form an' charted the outstanding daily workouts of all the tracks. I'd record anything unusual about a horse, such as the horse gettin' blocked out or a horse tryin' to run out of his path. It was wonderful havin' a streak of pickin' seven winners in eight races, but then I'd get my feet back on the ground an' go zero for eight. When I found a horse I really liked, I'd let the purse strings out a little bit.

"Johnny Bulla once tried to talk me out of gamblin' on the horses. 'Dutch, you might as well bet on the sun settin' in the east or the moon collidin' with the sun. Take me out to Hialeah Race Track with you and I'll bet you fifty dollars that you can't go in the track gate and come out with as much money as when you entered.'

"I took the bet, entered the Miami grandstands with fifty dollars, an' then sat out each race without goin' to the bettin' window. After the races, I showed Johnny the $50 in hand an' said, 'You owe me fifty dollars.'

"Johnny wouldn't buy that. 'It cost you fifty cents to get into the racetrack so you've come out with less than you took in. You owe me fifty dollars!'"

One time after a golf exhibition in Baltimore with Sam Snead and Herman Keiser, Dutch and Bob Hamilton had to drive to Detroit.

"We drove all night and, of course, Dutch wanted me to drive," said Bob. 'Oh, Mr. Bob, you're a whale of a driver,' he charmed.

"And then he'd put those long slender fingers on my back and say, 'You're doing a marvelous job.'

"The more he bragged the farther I'd drive — knowing he was conning me, but I went right along. So I'm driving all night while Dutch is sleeping and now it's about mid-morning and we're close to Pittsburgh.

"Suddenly, Dutch says, 'Mr. Bob, do you want me to drive a while?'

"I thought — there's something wrong here. This is the first time Dutch has ever said, 'Let me drive.'

"Well, I'm tired and sleepy, so I let Dutch take over. I'm lost in sleep for what seems like eight hours, but it couldn't have been more than a couple of hours. When I open my eyes I'm staring up at the sky. Dutch had my Cadillac going straight up a steep slope near Steubensville, Ohio. There on top of the mountain is a race track he frequented while in the Army. Horse racing fever had struck again. We made it to the races and didn't get to Detroit until late that night."

"One time Dutch invited Dick Shaiper and me to the track," said Doug Sanders. "Dutch studied the race sheet in the grandstand while Dick and I supported the bar. When we returned to the stands, Dutch had selected four or five horses for us. Every horse turned out to be a winner, and I remember walking away with a couple of thousand dollars in winnings that night. Dutch was an expert handicapper. He seemed to know everyone at the racetracks, especially the jockeys like Eddie Arcaro.

"He'd say, 'Mr. Doug, I got this from Mr. Jockey. This is from the horse's mouth.'

"He'd sit down on a stool, pushing that pencil and handicapping those horses. He had this knack of finding excuses to land himself in the vicinity of the racetrack. He would offer to take his friends to the greatest diner or restaurant in the world for chili or pork chops. We would accept his suggestion only to discover later that we were eating next to the racetrack. One night Dutch lost all of his spending money at the track and waited to meet us for dinner. We went to another place knowing Dutch would go ahead and order and eat. When we came in, we pretended we didn't even know him. Ol' Dutch thought he was going to have to wash dishes."

Herman Keiser tells about the time he and Dutch were driving east through the mountains of Pennsylvania and Dutch asked if Herman would like to go to the race track that day. "'Dutch, there isn't any track around here. What are you talking about?' he replied.

"So Dutch drives around and down some mountains and comes out at a trotter place. It didn't matter where he was, he knew every track or he'd always find one."

Dutch even allowed the races to hold up a professional golf tournament in 1958. The Tijuana Open Tournament, a major PGA event, was played at a golf course bordering the Agua Caliente Race Track in Tijuana, Mexico. The last day of this tournament Dutch had sent across a bet to the track on one of the long shots. When Dutch reached the tee closest to the track, he held up play so he could hear the loudspeaker for the big race.

"I stopped to hear the horses an' see how my money was doin'," he would explain.

The race didn't distract Dutch from his golf game one bit, and he was in seventh heaven when he and his horse were both first place finishers.

"I was hotter than Mexican chili. The mariachis played for me that day."

The byword was that when Dutch won a tournament, you shouldn't bet on him the following week, because he'd be playing the horses and not practicing. Moreover, he wasn't as hungry to win.

Golfers found Dutch a soft touch when they were losers. On the other hand, Harold Blaylock produced a receipt for $300 that he wired Dutch in Baltimore when the horses let him down.

"You never had to worry about Dutch repaying," related Harold. "We helped each other."

Early in Dutch's career, he and Wilbur Johnson were at Oaklawn Park in Hot Springs, Arkansas. By the last race, Dutch had run out of money.

"Wilbur, could you give me two dollars?"

"Sure, Dutch."

"Thanks. Who are you bettin' on?"

"I like Spring Mill, Dutch."

"Naw, I'll take another horse."

Spring Mill won and paid $12 to win. The next week Wilbur returned from lunch and received an envelope from Henry Loesch, the news editor and a longtime friend of Dutch's.

"Here's two dollars that Dutch left for you at the front office," he said. "He claimed you'd know the right horse to put it on."

Dutch remained a true gambling optimist. He is remembered for talking about what a wonderful race card he had lined up that racing day, and even though his horses faltered, he would pick up the next day's racing form and talk about what a wonderful card it was. Walter Hagen, preeminent pro, is said to have looked at the world through the hole in the doughnut, but kept his hands on the dough (*Golf World*, 1952); Dutch Harrison, preeminent golf artist, and generous to a fault, looked at the world through the doughnut and gave away most of the dough.

Dutch loved the thoroughbreds so much that he purchased three: Bo-Co, a seven-year-old bay gelding; Calico-Sis, a two-year-old filly; and Count Mattier, a stud. In the three years that Dutch and his trainer-jockey, Bill Skidmore, had Bo-Co, the horse won 17 of 54 races, never placing lower than fourth.

"Bo-Co entered the winnah's circle at many tracks like Churchill Downs, Fairmount Park an' Oaklawn Park," Dutch recalled. "He had lots of early speed, but with his bad right leg, every time Bo-Co hit the last turn, he'd go to the outside rail to look the gallery over. I was lucky to win so many races with him. His best friend was the weather man who predicted rain. He made other mudders look like pikers with Mr. Willy aboard."

Dutch would bet on any race, whether it was horses, mules, or dogs, but he made it a practice to never bet on a stud horse. His conclusion was based on a stud horse that cost him dearly. Count Mattier once surged to the front past a filly, then realizing that he was leaving her, the stud slowed for the filly and was nosed out at the wire.

"Thereafter, I never bet a stud again. I reckoned they don't have their minds on racin'," Dutch said.

When asked if he was too sentimental to have Count Mattier gelded, Dutch replied, "I tended to put myself in the horse's position, so I sold him."

When the bell at the starting gate rings and the gate opens, and the horses thunder away, one understands the excitement in the heart of the racing crowd. No one would be more pleased to hear those sounds than Dutch Harrison. How Dutch would have loved Vienna, Austria where a golf course lies within the confines of a race track.

Although, there was a 9-hole golf course at Oaklawn Park Race Track in Hot Springs, Arkansas, Dutch spent his mornings at the Hot Springs Country Club or the Belvedere Course where he derived his loot for the afternoon races.

Manila Crossroads

Moon over (Manila), Shine on as we begin,
A dream or two — that may come true,
When the tide comes in.

From the song, "Moon over Miami"
by Edgar Leslie

THELMA AKANA, MORTICIAN, read one entry on the sign boldly displayed in front of the Philippine Airline's plane bound for Manila. It was November 16, 1949. Other entries on the sign of this special flight included U.S. heads of state and a contingent of professional golfers, who were invited to play in the Philippine World Open Championship in Manila. The passengers would attend a fiesta celebration for Philippine Independence and President Quirino's reelection. Dutch, Johnny Bulla, Marty Furgol, Dick Metz, and Porky Oliver were among the golfers aboard who were to spend several weeks at the celebration in exhibitions and tournament play.

The Senator

As the heavy plane lumbered down the Honolulu runway and finally soared into darkening skies, the golfers made a number of irreverent cracks about an undertaker being aboard. When it was announced that a typhoon was raging in the Pacific and an unscheduled stop might have to be made, it was suggested by one golfer that Mortician Akana was bound and determined to get the passengers in the end.

In deference to this "sweet-looking lady," Dutch approached her to apologize for the remarks of his peers that had raised laughter in the cabin. Dutch's good friend Johnny Bulla was seated next to Thelma Akana. He introduced her as Senator Akana from Hawaii, explaining that she had taken over her late husband's mortuary business, as well as succeeding him as Territorial Senator.

She was born in 1905 as Thelma Alice Kalaokona Moore, daughter of Pennsylvanian William Charles Moore, of English-Irish-Norwegian descent and Eulalie "Lalla" Liftee of Hawaiian-English-Chinese lineage.

She laughed at her name prominently posted on the guest list as Thelma Akana, Mortician. Dutch made his apologies and returned to his seat, charmed by the Senator.

Johnny Bulla learned that Senator Akana was to be given special recognition by President Quirino for developing the modern nursing program in the Philippines and was invited to speak before a federation in Manila. Small talk between Bulla and the Senator centered on airplanes: President Quirino's large financial interest in the Philippine Airlines; the Senator's trips with Quirino on his flagship plane, the Mindoro; her flights between Hawaiian Islands on territorial business; and Bulla's own personal experiences as a pilot. President of Arizona Airways, Bulla had flown for Eastern Airlines during World War II and was the first pro golfer to fly golfers from tournament to tournament.

After Dutch returned to his seat, Bulla recalled for Thelma how Dutch had won the Hawaiian Open, "He barely edged me out in 1947. The next year I placed second again, this time to Jimmy Ukauka who all of you

Hawaiians were cheering for. Dutch and I are close, not only on the golf course. He introduced me to my wife, Polly (Pauline Chambers), on a blind date arranged by his wife, Emma. Polly and Emma were legal secretaries in the same building in Little Rock. When I learned about the blind date, I resisted because I was so tired from driving all night and day from a golf tournament in North Carolina. Dutch talked me into doing all the driving while he did all the sleeping.

"When we got back to Little Rock he told me, 'You can't stand up this girl, an' besides, we'll see a good movie.'

"Well, I made him promise we'd come home right after the movie. Before the evening was over, I was saying, 'I'm going to marry that girl' and a few months later, I did and she resigned her position and went on tour with me."

During the conversation, it had become obvious to Bulla that the Senator was a good friend of President Quirino. She had been asked by the President to help run his recent campaign for re-election because of her broad knowledge of the Philippines as a nurse and her experience in political circles. She had worked hard for his support, so much so that she was romantically linked with him. The press and radio in Hawaii and on the Mainland had always found Senator Akana good copy wherever she went. When she was invited to join President Quirino for his election celebration, the media ran wild on her attachment to him. Some columnists insisted, over her protests, that she was flying to Manila to join the President in marriage.

She told Bulla, "We're good friends and that's all. I have a great aloha for the Filipino nurses and for all Filipinos in Hawaii and have worked with their heads of civic affairs. I am keenly interested in the progress of the Philippine Republic because their success affects the whole Pacific, including Hawaii. But I expect the rumor of the romance to keep bobbing up as it has before."

The pilot announced that terrific winds were buffeting Guam and the other islands, and because of the typhoon, they would make an unscheduled refueling stop in Tokyo, outside the typhoon zone. The pilot announced that they would remain at the airport in Tokyo until the weather cleared for the flight to Manila. Passengers were free to disembark for several hours, but the pilot asked that they keep in touch with the plane's representative at the gate.

Lotus Blossoms

This was the first trip to Japan for Dutch and many of the pro golfers, and they were eager to see Tokyo. World traveler Johnny Bulla volunteered to lead the group on a grand tour of the Imperial Palace and other tourist attractions.

Toward the close of the second hour the signal was given at the airport for return of the passengers to the plane and all gradually reboarded except the golfers. Senator Akana became more and more impatient as hour after hour passed. Finally, her impatience rose to a boil and she approached the pilot.

"My Philippine hosts are expecting us. Affairs of state are involved and a Presidential reception party is awaiting us. Leave the golfers in Tokyo! They knew when the plane was supposed to depart."

The pilot was told in no uncertain terms to prepare for take-off and found it difficult to postpone it much longer. The golfers finally appeared, laden with bundles of souvenirs and buoyed by Japanese libation. Johnny Bulla, acting as tour guide, looked a bit sheepish and apologized for losing track of time.

The pilot approached Bulla and Harrison to forewarn them of Senator Akana's distress, "The Senator lady in the back of the plane is about to have a hemorrhage. I don't mind the delay you caused, but that lady back by the window is really fuming. She's a friend of the President of the Philippines and the Philippine government owns the biggest hunk of this airline."

Dutch spoke up, "Don't worry, Captain. I'll smooth her ruffled feathers," and in his inimitable manner, he began.

This lovely woman immediately made him realize how lonely he'd been. His agonizing relationship with Emma had been tolerated only because of their separation; his romance with Jeannie had no future.

After apologizing, he gradually captured the Senator's attention, then her interest. There was immediate empathy between them as an electric conversation quickly warmed from polite chit-chat to cozy, more intimate dialogue, and easy laughter. So engrossed were they in each other that neither recalled another brief stopover before arriving in Manila.

"She was mad as a hen waitin' in the rain for a lost rooster. I thought I was goin' to get a Hawaiian war dance, but I got lotus blossoms instead," said Dutch.

Thelma recalled, "One moment I was resentful and about to have a conniption and the next moment I was enchanted by the charm of this person. It was on my way to Manila that I met the everlasting proof that I wasn't engaged to Quirino."

Dutch was fascinated by her family and background. He listened intently as she spoke, "I guess I represent the new Hawaii. My mixed blood is as diverse as the demographic profile of Hawaii. I'm about one-quarter Hawaiian, one-eighth Chinese and the rest equal parts of English, Irish and Norwegian. Like all the rest of Hawaiians today, though, I am American. My two younger sisters and I attended schools of high American standards. All our background is American and we think American. But I'd rather talk about my four children. I have three sons and a daughter."

The four children and their birthdates are: Raymond Kekuhaupio Moore Akana, 1928; David Yim Kawai Akana, 1935; Martha Ann Kaaihele Akana, 1940; James (Kimo) Palinakona Akana, 1942. The Hawaiian names were bestowed by family tradition from Grandmother Eulalie "Lalla" Liftee of Honolulu.

Dutch liked the soft melodious voice of his friendly flight partner as she described her life, her children and their heritage and personal interests. With her lovely fair complexion, hazel eyes and softly curled dark brown hair, she was a striking, very feminine woman who carried a full figure on her 5-foot, 7-inch frame.

When Dutch asked Thelma what her association with the President of the Philippines was, she replied, "As head of the Hawaiian Nurses Association, I had been supportive of Filipino nurses. Their hiring had been difficult in Hawaii, but I enthusiastically endorsed them because they made such excellent nurses with their characteristic warmth, timidity, and dedication. I realized that through President Quirino, nursing in the Philippines would be promoted and encouraged."

Sunsets and Gin Rummy

On arrival at Manila International Airport, the plane was met by a large group that included dignitaries, newsmen, photographers and a contingent of Filipino nurses carrying corsage bouquets. Thelma's many friends in the Philippine Islands were on hand to welcome her to the fiesta.

After a sumptuous banquet that evening, many of the golfers became ill with dysentery, including Dutch. They complained of severe stomach pains and were afraid that they would be unable to play exhibition matches the next morning. Remembering Thelma's nursing career, Dutch sought her help for their ailing stomachs. Thelma teased him about his "opu-ache" and concocted a homemade kaolin-rich medicine. By the next morning, Dutch and the other golfers were fully recovered.

The visiting guests were quartered at the Manila Hotel known as the "Queen of the Philippine Hotels," and the "Waldorf" of Manila society. It had been MacArthur's headquarters prior to World War II, and was nearly destroyed during the war. Now remarkably restored and divided into suites, it served as the official guest hotel for the Philippine government.

Thelma occupied the Presidential Suite portion of the General MacArthur Penthouse, which consisted of the entire upper floor of the hotel and contained five spacious, elegantly furnished rooms that offered breathtaking views of Manila Bay, including a spectacular view of one of Manila's famous formal gardens.

Thelma was the center of much attention in Manila. She attended a variety of social and political affairs, speaking at a number of them, including a special meeting of the General Federation of Women's Clubs, a packed Rotary luncheon, graduate law classes, a meeting of Filipino nurses and war victims, and miscellaneous gatherings of civic, industrial, and educational leaders. She received more press coverage than the visiting U.S. Congressmen or other dignitaries.

The Senator was also a special guest at luncheons, dinners and cocktail parties given by President Quirino at the Malacanang Palace, which included the visiting Congressional delegation, Senator William Knowland, U.S. Secretary of the Treasury, John Snyder, and Admiral Old.

"It's characteristic of Filipinos to find as many excuses for a party as they find for occasions to eat," said Thelma. "When you go to the Philippines, you are bound to gain weight...so many gala dinners and cocktail receptions. The magnificent buffets make your mouth water. Filipinos are famous for their *merienda*, an afternoon full-meal with its assortment of hot dishes and confections."

There was music and dancing every night in the Fiesta Pavilion, but Dutch and Thelma preferred the solitude of her suite or a stroll along the promenade surrounding the penthouse. Together they viewed the fabled sunsets across the graceful half-moon of Manila Harbor. She showed Dutch the places on the promenade where the twin flags of the United States and the Philippines had been replaced just seven years before by the red sun flag when the hotel became the Japanese military headquarters of the Islands.

Some of the golfers found the Champagne Room of the hotel an inviting bistro. Merrymaking for them generally began around 9 p.m., about the time that Dutch and Thelma were returning to her suite, where Dutch was said to have taught her gin rummy.

"Dutch began showing up at my door each evening with his playing cards. It was only when I discovered that he wasn't even bringing the cards with him anymore that I realized what was happening," Thelma remembered.

The Philippine World Open Championship was played at the exotic Wack-Wack Golf and Country Club, located five miles east of the hotel, so named from the cry of the crows nested there, not from a caddies' description of his golfer's inept efforts. The Club was completed in 1931 and is a championship course that has gained worldwide recognition.

Golf stars from Australia, Spain, Taiwan, and the Philippines competed with the U.S. contingent. Porky Oliver overtook Dutch in the last two rounds to win the tournament, but squandered most of his $10,000 winnings at the race track before leaving the Islands. His attempts to recoup his losses only led him further into debt until he had no money to get home. He borrowed a sizable sum from Dutch, who commented, "Ol' Pork Chops stayed in the Philippines too long. He was about to go home stone-broke."

This was Thelma's first experience on a golf course. "I liked to follow Dutch around the course, but had he asked me for a mashie, I'd have probably tried to supply him with a potato masher, instead of a 5-iron."

Hawaiian Christmas

Johnny Bulla remembers that during the entire trip, Dutch was seen only in the company of Thelma, either strolling on the golf course or dining together.

"From the time we arrived, to the time we boarded the plane nearly three weeks later, Dutch didn't mix with us golfers. It wasn't a case of his avoiding us, it was a case of courting Thelma."

Dutch's roommate at the hotel, Marty Furgol, remembers, "I didn't see hide nor hair of him outside the room, but Thelma sure did."

"Midway through our Philippine stay," Thelma recalled, "I thought how nice it would be if Dutch would return to Hawaii over Christmas, so I approached him, saying, 'Christmas will be magic in Hawaii. Please stay, Dutch, with me and my children at my beach home.'"

"I'll stay if Johnny stays," was the reply. But when Thelma asked Johnny, he said, "There's no way I could stay, Thelma. I have a wife and three kids expecting me back on the Mainland before Christmas."

Disappointed, but not about to give up, Thelma devised a plan. "Johnny, you have to do at least this for me. When we arrive together in Hawaii, please agree to have your bags taken off the plane with ours, as if you were remaining in Hawaii. You can drive home with us, enter the house, then slip out the back way to my car, which will be waiting. I'll have the Philippine Airlines hold the plane until you get back to the airport."

The golfers' plane landed in Hawaii at 1:15 a.m., December 5, 1949. Thelma's family and a few newsmen, eager to pursue the romance between President Quirino and Senator Akana, met the plane but the only quote Thelma issued was, "It was a most enlightening trip. I found the Filipinos eager to hear details of political ideas and practices in the United States. Great progress has been made in repairing the terrible ravages of World War II."

The big family Cadillac arrived at the Akana beach home about three that morning. Although Dutch and Johnny entered through one door, Johnny departed out another when Dutch retired to his guest room, just as planned.

Thelma recalled, "The children and I were so happy that we could share a Hawaiian Christmas with Dutch. Shazam! It was a magical time for us. And I believe Dutch was glad that he had made 'his' decision to stay."

Dutch confided that he had a wonderful time with the Akana family, "She sure made it a smooth trip for me."

Never once was it reported that he was unhappy with the ploy to keep him for Christmas. When Johnny was asked if Dutch ever scolded him about it, he replied, "If Dutch had, and he didn't, I'd have reminded Dutch that I returned his good deed of introducing me to Polly by introducing him to Thelma, courtesy of Philippine Airlines."

The Philippine experience opened up a new world to Dutch. Thelma remembered it as a "nostalgic, dreamy trip," with a moral to the story: Never, never come down with an opu-ache in the company of a nurse!

Playing Through

Please release me, let me go,
For I don't love you any more.
To waste our lives would be a sin,
Release me and let me love again.

From the song "Release Me"
by Eddie Miller, Dub Williams, and Robert Yount

Soon after the sojourn to Hawaii, Dutch began discussions in earnest with his attorney in Little Rock. His mind was clear: Emma's threats would not deter him any longer. The marriage had to end. Nevertheless, he continued to sweet-talk Emma into understanding that he would help her and would never forget her devotion to him.

When a friend told Dutch that he got new golf clubs for his wife, Dutch exclaimed, "Oh, that's wonderful, Mr. Jim! I wish I could make a trade like that."

Unresolved Issues

On February 15, 1950 Dutch filed for divorce, citing that he and Emma had been separated for more than a year. In his complaint it was stated that Emma had treated Dutch "with such indignities as to render his condition in life intolerable." These alleged indignities consisted of "studied contempt, neglect, abuse, unmerited reproach, and continuous fussing and nagging."

Privately, he had shared, "She could be hostile, like a tornado on the horizon. The vinegar she dished out never attracted any bees, I can tell ya. I had about as much chance winnin' an argument as a grasshopper in a hen house. She'd make a preacher kick in a stained-glass window."

In her cross-complaint Emma denied both the indignities and the separation, stating that she "assisted him in the development of his ability as a golfer and that his present station in life in the field of professional sports is due in considerable measure to the assistance rendered him."

She pleaded ill-health and maintained she was unable to work anymore. She sought $800 per month in alimony and called on her brother's wife to appear in court on her behalf.

Dutch flew to Little Rock for countless meetings and hearings between January and July. A preliminary hearing in April awarded Emma $200 per month, pending settlement of the case. At the hearing Emma agreed to return income tax records for the last several years and the winner's trophy for the Canadian Open in 1949 (valued at $1,500), which Dutch was required to bring back to Canada after keeping it for one year. After Emma failed to return the trophy and tax reports, a sheriff was ordered by the court to retrieve them. Emma said she could not find the tax reports, but finally did yield the trophy. Shortly thereafter, her attorneys resigned from the case and waived any right to receive their legal fees established by the court. Emma secured a new lawyer and persisted with her cross-complaint.

Meanwhile

During the same time Dutch was in Little Rock arranging to divorce Emma, Thelma and President

Quirino flew to San Francisco aboard his Philippine Airlines flagship and again were being queried about plans to marry.

Thelma responded, "It's not true. We are just good friends."

The President laughed and said the trip had "nothing to do with romance."

Actually, there was a romance between the two. It involved Thelma's son, Raymond and the President's older daughter, Vicky, who served her father as First Lady and played a leading role at social functions.

Vicky was Tournament Queen at the inauguration of the Philippine World Championship in 1949. When the President visited in Hawaii he was accompanied by young Vicky of "moonbeam beauty" and a legion of bodyguards. On these occasions, Raymond would date Vicky, somehow managing to ditch her bodyguards and make them furious.

The bodyguards pleaded, "Don't you realize that if something happened to Vicky, we'd be shot?"

Thelma had two suitors after her husband's death. According to her son David, "Raymond and I ran both of them off our property. One was a no-good charlatan who later escaped to Canada with Mother's investments. But when Dutch came on the scene, we liked him immediately. In fact, we kidded Mother that after running two of her suitors away, one with a gun, we might shoot *her* if she ever said no to a proposal from Dutch."

During early 1950, Thelma was on the Mainland pursuing a central objective of her political life: Statehood for Hawaii. She was able to see Dutch on tour while helping to lead Hawaii's fight to become the 49th state.

When legislation in Congress died in the U.S. Senate in 1947, Thelma did not give up. She spearheaded Congressional visits to Hawaii, appeared before U.S. Congress, and lobbied Congressmen. After her strong pleas for statehood, Estes Kefauver was among the many who promised their support.

Thelma also continued speaking before public

groups on the advantages of statehood. She pointed out that Hawaiians were second-class citizens without being able to elect a governor and vote for President in the United States. She urged high school and college student bodies to pursue their education and work for statehood, which "would be a true demonstration of democracy in action." Thelma's education had been broad. She attended St. Luke's School of Nursing in San Francisco, graduated from the University of California at Berkeley, completed an administration program at Columbia University and later a business program at the University of Hawaii.

She told them, "I want to give you students the same advice I give to my own children, who are a mixture of Caucasian, Chinese, and Hawaiian. And that is, racial understanding is a two-way proposition. We must prove ourselves worthy of other people's respect. We must put a high value on ourselves and show the world we have a great contribution to make."

Thelma had planned to run for Congress if the Statehood bill passed, but it didn't materialize until 1959, after Alaska had become the 49th state. By then she and the Farringtons were no longer in office to receive the credit due them.

Widow Emma

The final divorce from Emma was granted on July 14, 1950 in Chancery Court of Little Rock. Emma had the satisfaction of obtaining the decree of cross-complaint and a large property settlement, which proved to be a financial disaster for Dutch. She received all of Dutch's War Bonds, valued at over $50,000, a cash settlement and her Hillcrest home. Dutch was reportedly so short of money prior to the World Championship of Golf that he had to borrow car fare to Chicago.

Emotionally, the divorce was devastating for Emma, who never fully accepted the end of her marriage. She continued to list herself in the City Directory for a number of years as Emma Harrison (widow Ernest J.).

She had kept scrapbooks of Dutch in meticulous order through 1946, and continued to collect news stories of Dutch after that. She clung to a smorgasbord of Dutch's memorabilia such as his 1947 Ryder Cup golf bag. Even 30 years later she turned down a request for the scrapbooks. At no price was she giving up these keepsakes of the past.

Emma did not have to bear her grief alone. Jeannie had neither seen nor heard from Dutch since his Philippine trip. After Jeannie learned Dutch had married Thelma, she called Emma several times to commiserate on their mutual loss. For a time, Emma took great solace in these phone conversations with his former companion.

Emma's resentment and bitterness about the divorce were broadcast by her claim that the Lutheran minister who officiated at Dutch's marriage was destined for the devil. She also maintained that opposing counsel was a womanizer like Dutch, a topic that did not enter any of the official court records. Yet, she hung on tenaciously, refusing to accept the finality of their divorce.

On more than one occasion Emma managed to shock and embarrass him. On a bright October Sunday afternoon in 1952, a golf exhibition was held in Little Rock. This event was widely advertised, listing participants as Cary Middlecoff, U.S. Open Champion and Dutch Harrison, Canadian Open Champion. The pair held a clinic and played at the Riverside Golf Course with two local golf professionals. A large crowd, including Emma, turned out.

As she drove past the railroad tracks to enter the golf course, she shouted to the golf assistant taking tickets, "I'm Emma Harrison, Dutch's wife, and I'm not going to pay one cent. I'm going to shoot him," whereupon she brandished a pistol as she drove past the wide-eyed ticket-taker.

Emma caught up to Dutch and kept on his heels during play, snarling threats heard by his group. A sense of fear and embarrassment kept the crowd at bay, and though Dutch repeatedly apologized for "this woman's actions," he finally confronted her and matter-of-factly said, "Well, if you're going to shoot me, shoot me. Let's get it over with."

Only then did Emma retreat and leave. Dutch went on to score an amazing 67, five under par and the lowest score of the day.

Chilling Frost

Emma's evaluation of her marriage to Dutch contrasted sharply with his. Although he generally refused to discuss the situation with anyone, his friends were not as reticent.

One golf professional spoke about feeling the chilling frost of Emma's disfavor whenever he won more money in a tournament than Dutch, "She would put my wife and me down and try to get her comeuppance."

Another famous professional spoke about the distance that Emma built between the Harrisons and his own family. "She'd say, 'Good morning' to us and that was all. They'd not invite us to dinner and we never invited them. It was not Dutch we were avoiding, it was Emma. Socially, I don't believe she helped him."

One of the best known professionals asked rhetorically, "I wonder how many tournaments Dutch would have won if it wasn't for his wife badgering him? I know I stopped riding with Dutch when Emma was traveling with him. How could you relax with her along?"

Emma maintained a self-righteous posture to the end. To summarize her comments: "We were happily married until the war and then the devil got into Dutch and he developed a wild streak. That other woman in Hawaii was out to get Dutch and the devil played his role. Dutch had a mental lapse. I was told he didn't love her, but she had lots of gambling money to finance him. I made my Dutch what he became. I wish now that I had traveled more with him before he got out of hand."

Wedding in Little Rock

Rumors of the romance between Dutch and Thelma persisted through July 12, 1950, when Walter Winchell reported during his Sunday night broadcast: "Mr. and Mrs. America and all the ships at sea — Hawaiian Senator Thelma Akana will marry E.J. "Dutch" Harrison, Arkansas golf professional."

This was two days before the divorce from Emma became final. Thelma, en route from New York City to Chicago to meet Dutch, feared that adverse publicity might damage out-of-court settlement negotiations. She immediately responded to Associated Press with a firm denial of the rumors.

Days later at the World Championship of Golf, held at Tam O'Shanter Country Club near Chicago, Dutch finished fifth on August 13th, despite a tumultuous week with the press, friends, and admirers. Associated Press asked Dutch about the marriage rumor.

"I didn't get married. It might be one of these days, but it wasn't yesterday. If the good Lord willin' an' the creek don't rise, I just might," Dutch responded.

Some close friends received word in early August of a tentative late August wedding, but were sworn to secrecy. The *Honolulu Star-Bulletin* announced on August 18 that Dutch and Senator Akana were to be married August 23 at the Chicago home of Mr. and Mrs. Joseph L. Block, "close friends of Senator Akana," and that Dutch would be participating in the Eastern Open in Baltimore. The news was picked up by all the wire services and published coast to coast.

On August 16, Thelma and Dutch quietly checked out of their Lake Shore hotel in Chicago, leaving no forwarding address. The strategy did not appear clear to close friends until it was discovered that Dutch had not registered for the Eastern Open that week. The announcement of the Chicago wedding had been simply a decoy. Publicity had to be avoided at any cost lest their plans to be married in Little Rock be disclosed to Emma. Dutch and Thelma needed to move the wedding date forward so they could journey to Montreal, where Dutch was to defend his Canadian Open title at the end of August.

"Besides," Dutch quipped, "I always get married in Little Rock."

The following evening, August 18th, Dutch, age 40, and Thelma, age 45, were married in the small Lutheran church in Little Rock, with Henry Levy as Dutch's best man and Irene Lewis as Thelma's matron of honor. Although only immediate members of the family, including Dutch's parents, attended the ceremony, a large party was held the following night.

Dutch publicly proclaimed, "The preacher really teed off on us." The marriage was such a well-kept secret that Thelma's two youngest children, Martha and Kimo, staying with her mother's secretary in Waikiki, first heard the news on a radio broadcast. Walter Winchell broadcast, August 20, 1950: "Dutch Harrison, well-known professional golfer, just married Thelma Akana, territorial Senator from Hawaii, in a little brown church around the corner in Little Rock, Arkansas."

Son Raymond was serving in the Pacific, but son David arrived from New York the next evening and joined Thelma and Dutch in Little Rock.

Local newspaper accounts did not appear until Monday, August 21st, but speculation flourished on the effect of the marriage on Thelma's political career.

The Republican Party Chairman opined, "If Thelma remains in Hawaii, she'll be just as strong as she has always been. In fact she'll have an even wider circle of friends."

Happy Trails

After spending two days at the Little Rock home that Dutch had built for his father and mother, the newlyweds set out for St. Louis with 15-year-old son David. As they approached the crest of a hill in southern Missouri, David, who was sitting in the middle of the black Cadillac's large front seat, noted with glee the speedometer reading of practically 100 miles per hour. At the crest they were startled to see a state policeman monitoring an accident less than a quarter of a mile ahead. Dutch slammed on the brakes. The stately sedan screeched to a stop opposite the trooper, leaving an incriminating trail of burned rubber behind them.

The policeman strode over, ticket book in hand, but before any words were exchanged, Thelma exclaimed, "Any state policeman with any sense would have left his patrol car with lights blinking at the top of the hill or else set flares."

She continued to make point after point on how derelict the policeman had been in his duty. Dutch winked at David and feigned putting his hand across her mouth.

Finally, the policeman said to Dutch, "Well, I'm not going to give you a ticket because you have more problems than you need."

A bit shaken, the three continued on their first family trip at a much slower pace. A close family bond had already developed. Thelma's beautiful voice broke into song with some of her Hawaiian favorites. Dutch and the children loved her voice and would encourage her to sing.

"Sing, Mom, sing," Dutch would say. "I ruined my voice a-hollerin' for cornbread when I was a young-un."

The family treasured the songfests for years to come. All began on the first trip to St. Louis.

David remembers how Dutch would like to tease Thelma and the children on trips:

"Big Mom, did you know that short skirts are the new style?"

"They are?"

"Yep, the stores are advertisin' 'em: 'All summer skirts - 20 percent off.'"

"Dutch had us children convinced that one leg of his was shorter than the other because he was the original Arkansas Ridgerunner," David reflected. "The only way he could run along the ridge crest straight was to have one leg longer on the lower side."

David laughs about sharing most of their honeymoon with the newlyweds before they returned to Hawaii. "We didn't make Montreal, and I don't think anyone gave it a second thought. In St. Louis we stayed at the home of Fred Bowen, attended the St. Louis Cardinals games, and the race track at night. I was thrilled to be able to go to the Cardinal dressing room and be introduced by Dutch to my favorite players, Stan Musial and Enos Slaughter."

Thelma's children latched onto Dutch with gusto and looked forward to becoming a family again. Dutch had to catch his breath. "One day I had no kids. All of a sudden I had to take roll call. I found I had four of 'em," Dutch remarked.

Dutch and Thelma had planned to be in Hawaii the middle of September through October, but they stayed on the Mainland so Dutch could play in three tournaments — all close to St. Louis. The big attraction: Fairmount Park Race Track, located ten miles east of St. Louis. There were just no race tracks in Hawaii.

A Fond Aloha

Thelma returned to Hawaii in October to preside at Hawaii's 60-day biennial session as Vice President of the Legislature. She was the first woman to receive this honor.

Often she had spoken to the women of Hawaii on how they must make their voice heard, "Politics is hard for women, but it is good for them too. Women, I find, don't give up as easily as men."

Privately she shared with Dutch, "If you only knew the finagling that goes on among politicians. I came into this with St. Andrew's Priory ideals. Sister Olivia Mary Matthews, the principal and a registered nurse, was my role model. I thought all senators were men of integrity who cared about common people, who really cared about Hawaii. If you only realized, Dutch, how much bargaining and nonsense goes on."

She found time to entertain and give parties on behalf of Dutch, aloha shirts required. In Hawaii, she was known as the "busiest woman in town" and the "Hawaiian hostess with the mostest." She had also been named the "outstanding woman in Hawaii." She thrived on combining a political, civic, social, and home life as Dutch had discovered the previous Christmas, but she always had ample household help. A Japanese maid, Fujino, was a second mother to the children.

Dutch accepted her admitted ineptitude as a cook: "I can boil water, but as a cook, I'm a superb horticulturist. You never tasted such cooking. My children would rather have me stick to my flowers, especially my anthuriums, which I love."

After the legislative session, Thelma rejoined Dutch late in November at Pinehurst, North Carolina, both returning to the Islands in the spring for her last legislative session. Dutch assumed a new role — in the Hawaiian Senate! The caption of a picture taken of Dutch and Thelma at the podium read: "When Senator Thelma Akana Harrison's husband, Dutch Harrison, visited the Legislature Monday, Senate President Wilfred C. Tsukiyama yielded the chair and gavel to Mrs. Harrison, who is Vice President. Then with her golfer husband sitting behind her, Mrs. Harrison presided over the afternoon's business."

Dutch told friends afterwards, "Thelma is the fair-haired angel in Hawaii, I'm convinced."

At the end of the 60-day session, Thelma, attractive

in a red dress with a huge vanda orchid lei, announced while presiding that she was retiring from politics.

Tearful but ever smiling, she told her colleagues in the closing minutes that she would not be a candidate for re-election after her three terms in office, "I am retiring from elective politics. My duties as wife of one of America's leading golf professionals must now supersede my duties as a public official. This is my seventh and last year in the Upper Chamber. I have a moral obligation to my children and my husband. It's hard to find a good husband and I'm going to keep him...

"I hope I can someday persuade Dutch to make Hawaii his home, but as long as he tours the lonely circuit of professional golfing competition, I will be with him. . . I shall retain my official residence and my voting registration in Honolulu, of course. This is my home."

Thelma's aloha speech was greeted with thunderous applause by her Republican colleagues and by the Democratic senators alike. When the session adjourned, many senators gave her a fond personal farewell with a hug and a kiss. Thus ended the political career of a brilliant and vivacious woman, one of Hawaii's most colorful political figures.

She served by the Hawaiian motto: *Mau Ke Ea Ka Aina Ka Pono*: The life of the land is preserved in righteousness.

Friends sometimes remarked, "Thelma can raise you, build you and put you away. And whichever stage you're in, you enjoy it."

For Thelma this was a traumatic time, but she was overjoyed to be able to rejoin Dutch. For Dutch it was a happy solution to a bitter dissolution.

At a later date when Doug Sanders asked Dutch if he should get married, Dutch threw up his hands and replied, "Whew! Get the right one when you do. If you get the wrong one — oooh — look out!"

Ardmore

Many waters cannot quench love,
neither can floods drown it.
If a man offered for love
all the wealth of his house,
it would be utterly scorned.

from "The Song of Solomon"

Fellow golfers took a shine to Thelma almost immediately. Sam Snead was one of the first to climb on her bandwagon when Dutch and Thelma traveled with Sam and his wife, Audrey, during the summer of 1950.

A Real Asset

On their way from a tournament in Toledo to play an exhibition at Sharon, Ohio, Thelma casually asked, "Sam, when are you coming out to Hawaii?"

"Oh, whenever you ask me," he replied.

"I'm asking you now," offered Thelma.

Sam told her that he didn't expect it would be so sudden and that he'd have to discuss it with Audrey. Dutch knew that Sam didn't like flying, particularly overseas. It took a little time, but the pressure from Thelma combined with Audrey's desire to see Hawaii was enough that Sam finally gave in.

"Thelma is one smart woman, a real nice gal," he praised her later.

Arrangements were made for Dutch and Sam to hold a series of clinics and exhibitions in Hawaii and California the following year, a series that was eminently successful for them and for charity. It all began with the invitation from Thelma.

Paul Runyan got to know Thelma much better than he ever knew Emma. "Thelma was outgoing, intelligent, and did everything that would help Dutch do well. She was a real asset to him as a public relations person, as a front person. Everyone liked her and enjoyed her company a great deal. We all saw more of Dutch when Thelma came into the picture," he said.

A born athlete, Thelma's third name, Kalaokona, was after her great great-grandmother, direct descendant of Kekuhaupio, the famous warrior chief who taught the great Kamehameha I swimming, wrestling, spear throwing, and the art of Polynesian warfare. Thelma excelled in swimming and basketball. "Little wonder she was so well-received," said one close friend. "She succeeded in everything she did.

"Thelma was an outstanding solo vocalist, a straight A student and a true leader in school, politics and nursing. She epitomized the best of the three bloods that formed her background, Caucasian, Hawaiian and Chinese. She might have been a lousy poker player, but she was a leader in about everything else. However, when she wanted to become Dutch's wife, that was the time Thelma decided to play second fiddle. And she did just that. It was marvelous. She loved traveling with Dutch."

Thelma's daughter, Martha, would later say, "When Pops would get upset, Mother would play the shrinking violet. This would then bring Dutch to say, 'Oh, Mom, you're so good.' And Mother would say to me afterwards, 'How can you not love him?' She followed in his footsteps in addressing everyone at the golf and country clubs as

Miss or Mister, and she wanted to be known as Mrs. Dutch.

"I remember that Mother pretended to be naive about the previous women in Dutch's life. Some of them would still phone from time to time, and she would act as though she didn't know that the caller was a former girlfriend even when she met one or two. She played dumb. Later she told me this was the way to be, unless you wanted to drive your husband in the other direction."

The Richest Greenskeeper

Little did the Harrison clan realize what was in store for them on the mainland in 1952. It all began with Waco F. Turner, an Oklahoma oil tycoon and golf enthusiast, and his wife and business partner, Opie. The two had always wanted to bring a major golf tournament to the Sooner state, more specifically to the Dornick Hills Golf and Country Club in Ardmore.

Ardmore, Oklahoma, was named after the city of Ardmore in Pennsylvania. It lies near the Texas border, 100 miles north of Fort Worth and 100 miles south of Oklahoma City, in the foothills of the Arbuckle Mountains.

The golf and country club was owned by the Dornick Hills Corporation of which Waco became President. Ardmore was already known as the second wealthiest city per capita in the U.S. with 50 to 60 oil-rich millionaires among the 20,000 inhabitants. Waco set out to find the best golf professional possible to add prestige to his club. In late 1951 he contracted with one E. J. Harrison then playing out of St. Andrews Golf Club, West Chicago.

Between 1952 and 1954 Dutch worked at and represented Dornick Hills, a golf course he called, "One of the best in that part of the country. If you shot par, you'd played yourself some real golf — you really did. It was a wonderful layout, with a nice lake an' a doozy of a cliff hole — oooh, it was one tough golf course.

"Waco an' Opie followed the tournament trail coast to coast and lent a helpin' hand to Thelma an' me when we were in Florida the previous year. Our friendship bloomed with the opportunity to come to Ardmore. We arranged to arrive in February after the winter tour ended in Phoenix, with plans for the children to follow later. Waco an' Opie sure had the welcome mat out. They threw a big rip-hummin' shindig for us an' the 300 members — an' went whole hog doin' it.

"Waco an' his wife had been former schoolteachers in Texas until he hit a gusher. That started 'em in the oil business. He was the kinda man who might get turned down by a bank on loans for wildcat wells — an' if he did, he'd go someplace else an' get the loan, then invest it in his next drillin' deal. One time, he actually bought the bank that turned him down an' fired everbody.

"With those horn-rimmed glasses an' that cowboy outfit, he sure looked the part of one eccentric multi-millionaire. He wore that western-cut suit with bolo string tie an' a cowboy hat an' boots. It seemed that he was always doin' things his way an' tryin' to do everythin' himself. He'd load those oily drill bits in the backseat of one of his four or five Cadillacs — what a mess! He also owned six Chevrolets an' one Lincoln. He'd give me a new Chevrolet ever year since Thelma needed the family car. Waco would drive a different car every day. He'd drive out on the golf course, get on a bulldozer an' forget he had the car. Once a car sat there so long, weeds grew up around it an' almost hid it.

"Waco even served as our greenskeeper. He'd be toolin' down the fairways in a Cadillac. I called him the richest greenskeeper in the business.

"He even offered to build a home for me, an offer I was sorry I'd turned down. Waco an' Opie were real good to Thelma an' me. I didn't have a hard time pleasin' him, but it was hard to please all 300 club members. I sure tried."

The Grand Tournament

"Waco had always wanted to put on a golf tournament that would be Ardmore's first big-time golf classic. What Waco wants, Waco gets — we all found out. Money talks an' Waco had a bundle. I reckon he had a hundred oil wells spoutin' that black gold. First he sold the PGA a mighty sweet money package, then he remodeled the golf course an' clubhouse — built a new two-story pro-shop east of the clubhouse, all at his expense. He put Dornick Hills in top shape for the first Ardmore Open (June 5-8, 1952).

"Waco an' Opie hatched up a slick reward system for the tournament pros — in addition to the regular purse of $15,000. He got the idea of bonus money from his offerin' bonuses to strugglin' minor league ballplayers when they'd hit homeruns at Ardmore Park — awarded $15 for birdies, $500 for eagles an' $500 for best score of the day. He'd give $2,500 for a hole-in-one — an' I missed one by an inch the followin' year. Yes-siree — ol' Waco would sit at a table near the 18th green an' peel off the greenbacks to the bonus winner at the end of each round. I guarantee those pros were in Cracker Jack heaven. He even offered to double my regular first place money if I won the tournament. He musta shelled out $100,000 puttin' on that tournament an' makin' sure no pro went home without havin' his expenses paid. Reminded me of George May who started the real big purses at Tam O'Shanter in Chicago. Nothin' was too rich for their blood. Those two P.T. Barnums revolutionized tournaments an' lived their pipe dreams, I'll tell ya.

"The last round of the tournament was a real dog fight for the championship between me an' my playin' partners, Dave Douglas an' Roberto De Vicenzo. The turnin' point was on a par-3 hole. Mr. Dave's tee shot dropped in the water short of the green an' his provisional shot wound up in a deep bunker. Walkin' to the green, he notices his ball on a lily pad out in the water. So he rolls up his pants, wades in barefoot, an' plays that shot from the lily pad. As I live n' breathe, his ball went right in the hole for a deuce! The gallery was goggle-eyed. He had expected six or seven strokes on that hole with the pickle he was in. What a recovery shot! Well, he beat me by two strokes an' I was runner-up. That tournament was a lot of fun. Everyone had a good time.

"Waco helped to pioneer women's golf that year. He had one of the first tournaments with all of the best women golfers includin' Babe Didrikson Zaharias. Now there was a real golfer, a champion in every sport. She reached the long par-5 green on the cliff hole in two — an' this was when we all knew she had cancer. At a news reporter gatherin', Wilbur Johnson told me that he asked her what she foresaw for the future of women's tournament golf an' what it would take to keep it goin'.

"She had a ready answer. 'Simple,' she said, 'All it takes is to keep those gals from getting pregnant.'"

Teamwork

The work at the club proved challenging for Dutch who hired his own work force.

"Thelma was a natural for the golf shop," Dutch remarked. "She had no experience at merchandising so she had to learn the trade. Golly, what she took on when she took over a household with a strugglin' golf pro. I left the finances up to her an' alotta correspondence was handled by her personal secretary, Eva Hart."

T. D. Morris, a future eminent PGA pro, was a chubby caddie who became caddie master before Dutch brought him into the pro shop to assist Thelma. He was one of ten children and came from a poor Ardmore family.

Morris said of his own start in golf, "I must have been picking pecans on the right side of the house at the right time in 1946, because that autumn afternoon a wealthy judge pulled his shiny sedan to the curb in

Ardmore and asked me if I wanted to make a buck as a caddie. I jumped at the opportunity, and I've been in golf ever since."

Morris continued, "Dutch was well-liked at the club. Even though he was a famous pro, he insisted on carrying members' bags from their cars. He remembered names so well and made everyone feel special. Thelma ran the shop, but Dutch was around when he was needed. He'd not hustle members and never played them for more than a two-dollar nassau. Always, he'd give the opponent a chance to get even. He was good at purposefully missing putts by rimming the ball around the hole on the short ones. He always paid the caddies well and they appreciated that."

Harrison Household

Soon after the Harrisons arrived, Frank Anderton, Vice President of Dornick Hills Corporation, let them occupy, without charge, his ranch home 12 miles northwest of the Club. There, a cyclone fence was built and Dutch kept two of his race horses in the field behind the home.

"I pulled Bo-Co in a trailer behind that Cadillac for a ton o' miles. Ol' Calico-Sis broke down in her first race an' I had to give her to a farm outside Ardmore," Dutch recalled.

Thelma's 16-year-old son, David, arrived from Hawaii in March and enrolled at Ardmore High School as David Harrison.

He recalled, "I was afraid the Okies would have a hard time with Akana."

Daughter Martha, who was 12 at the time, and Kimo, the youngest at 10, also took the name Harrison.

Not all of the Ardmore days were blue-ribbon ones. After David and Kimo were given golf clubs and shoes, they would wear the shoes with spikes home and forget to take them off before entering the house. The beautiful soft wood floors soon became pitted and scarred. It took only a year before the Harrisons were "invited" to move, which they did, dutifully, to a rented home much closer to the Club. Later they decided to purchase their own home.

David was an ornery young man and easily rankled, but said, "I loved Dutch and never fought with him. I knew he was always trying to help me even though I made little progress with his golf instruction. One day as we left the practice tee, he turned to me and said, 'I know how you can make money at golf.'

"'How?' I asked him, incredulously.

"'Sell your clubs,' Dutch joked.

"I was a pretty wild kid at a time when Dutch had his hands full at the Club. One time my older brother, Raymond, gave me a good beating in a fight at the golf course. I was so upset, I ran to the car Waco had loaned to Dutch and drove it accidentally over a cliff and totally wrecked it. That was the only time I ever heard Dutch swear and he came pretty close to losing his temper that time. Later, I enrolled as an embalming apprentice at the funeral home in Ardmore and lived at the funeral home part time. Driving the ambulance was the part of my assignment that I loved most.

"When I turned 17 in August, Dutch and Mother decided it would be best for me to join the service and benefit by disciplined military training. Dutch contacted a captain in the Air Force who was a friend of his, then drove me to the recruiting station at Little Rock, 360 miles away. All the way there, we debated whether Dutch was actually drafting me or as Dutch maintained — he was volunteering me. I think there was genuine disappointment 80 days later when I was discharged because of my asthma. In 1953 I went to Albuquerque to live with Raymond and finish high school."

One person close to the family spoke of how Thelma must have been concerned while in Hawaii with her two oldest sons who made it impossible for her to continue seeing her two prior suitors. It was suggested that perhaps this was why, for the first year and a half of marriage, the children remained in Hawaii, the two younger ones with their grandmother.

The children never forgot their big collie, Ekolu, that was shipped from Hawaii to Ardmore after the family was settled. David remembered, "The dog had been given to Mother as a puppy by Buddy Cole, bandleader of the orchestra she had entertained. Ekolu means "three" in Hawaiian and was named from being a third generation removed from the original Lassie. The collie was about seven years old and when the weather grew hot and humid, Dutch felt so sorry for the dog that he had it sheared, leaving a big ball of hair on the tail. The dog was so embarrassed he stayed under the house and would come out only at night. Dutch always said he was such a big friendly dog that he would lead twenty burglars into the house. Ekolu disappeared the following year and we got a black cocker spaniel. Dutch kept bringing home stray dogs from the golf course — he had a real soft spot for animals — and that continued until Mother finally put her foot down."

Martha remembers coming to the Mainland with Kimo during the late fall season of 1951 and arriving in Chicago on a very cold day. "This was the first time that Kimo had worn shoes, because he and his brothers had gone barefoot in Hawaii up until seventh grade. Mother and Pops will never forget meeting us and seeing Kimo walking down the airport corridor carrying his shoes. Kimo and David went barefoot as much as they could at Dornick Hills and wore Hawaiian shirts which became popular at the Club.

"Skinny Kimo took delight in demonstrating how he could walk on broken glass without injury. Walking on the sharp coral reefs had made the boys' feet tough and leathery. Kimo learned to caddie under T. D. Morris and he would come home from the caddie shack and tell hilarious stories about the caddies and how naughty they were."

Kimo recalled, "Dutch had top-grade clubs cut to my size with my name on them. One time I failed to get the ball up the rocks of the cliff on the famous 16th hole and beat my club against the rocks, ruining it. Dutch helped me learn to control my temper."

Kimo reported, "After a stint at Dartmouth University, Raymond went into the service and was sent to the Marshall Islands. From there he returned to Kirtland Air Force base in Albuquerque. During summers he visited Mom and Dutch and worked at Ardmore. Raymond was a fine athlete, a 9.9 sprinter, an excellent football player, and a fine professional golfer. The family always maintained that if Dutch could play in the tournaments tee to green and Raymond could do the putting, Dutch would win all of the tournaments."

The cooking in the Harrison household always brought a few chuckles. David recalled how his mother had baked her first Thanksgiving turkey in 1952. Raymond, who had learned good Hawaiian-Oriental cooking from his father in Hawaii, had a question for his mother. "What's that concoction on the stove?" he asked.

"Oh, that's the dressing," Thelma replied. "But I'm not sure what to do with it."

Thelma's Philosophy

Thelma did not always accompany Dutch on his tour trips, but she did accompany him on his successful winter tour of 1952 when he tied for the Los Angeles Open championship, placed second in the Phoenix Open, and won the Thunderbird pro-am in Palm Springs. She was also with him when he won the Reno Open for the second time in October and the Havana pro-am in December.

David recalled what wonderful conversations he and Thelma would have when Dutch was away. "Mom wanted our attention to be on our new life, so Hawaii was seldom discussed. We held our sides laughing about some of the experiences at the club or funeral home, talking far into the night." It was at this time that Thelma expounded on her philosophy of life to David, namesake for his biological father, David Akana Sr. who was 42 years old when he suffered a fatal heart attack in 1943. A widely respected Senator, he was the son of a Cantonese businessman who came to Hawaii circa 1880 and married a native of Maui.

She told David Jr. that his father was a patriarch who gave a lot and usually bought and provided everything for her. Although she had been happy with him, she was happier with Dutch.

"Dutch has more wisdom than anyone I've known. Our marriage is based on mutual support. I used to lead an outgoing public life, but now Dutch and I don't like to socialize that much. We are content with our family and Dutch's professional life."

Thelma shared with David and Raymond how Dutch and she had entered the marriage believing that both had a lot of money.

"We laugh about this now," she would say. "Dutch lost his money through divorce and I lost mine through poor investments with people I trusted. That Tom Davis (former suitor) absconded with the contracts that I and my attorney-senator friends had approved and signed. He resold the contracts and then slipped off to Canada. I won the lawsuits but there was no money left after he reached Canada. In all, I had to sell four businesses, my mortuary, a construction firm, an asphalt company, and half interest in a restaurant. I had a debt of honor to repay, and I didn't want to leave an unpleasant stigma in Hawaii. I guess I trusted people too much. Never did I meet the kind of person I considered a four-flusher until I went into politics. This man, Davis, was an opportunist and he saw us as people who could raise money and get him help from the Philippines, China, and Japan — get whatever support he needed to enter the lucrative scrap metal field."

Tragedy and Expertise

Late in 1953 Dutch became afraid Waco was losing control of the Club. In addition, the suicide of a gin rummy addict deeply affected him. Dutch had been a whale of a gin rummy player, "the best I ever met," exclaimed Everett Watkins, former President of the Club. He was so skillful that legendary investor Joe Jemsek, "Chicago Joe," backed him at one dollar per point and was willing to bet Dutch against any player in the world. Others called on Dutch for lessons in gin rummy. Realizing that card players have a habit of putting their hands in a certain order, Dutch could tell when his opponent would draw a high or low card by where they placed it. He never held his cards in the same arrangement in order to keep his opponent guessing. This particular gin opponent kept losing to Dutch in friendly games and couldn't stop playing. He reportedly owed Dutch so much money that he committed suicide. Thereupon, Dutch swore he'd never play gin again. As a consequence of this decision, many of his new friends in later years never knew that he was once a gin rummy expert.

Dutch was better known in Ardmore as a shrewd betting expert on pro-am tournaments. He loved to team with top amateurs in Oklahoma like Charlie Coe and Wilbur Johnson.

That year Wilbur Johnson, who had become an Oklahoma City scribe, stayed with Dutch and Thelma at Ardmore while on vacation. "Early one morning, I was sleeping soundly and Dutch comes in and says, 'Wake up, Mr. Will, we got to get to Hobbs, New Mexico. There's a $5,000 tournament over there an' we're invited to play.'

"'What are you talking about, Dutch?' I asked.

"'Don't worry, Mr. Will, I've taken care of everything. I'm borrowin' one of Waco's cars,' he said.

"Well, we left at five a.m. and the car conked out in Texas. Dutch had to borrow another car from a pro friend there, and we finally made it to Hobbs.

"While Dutch went out to practice, I retired to the clubhouse lounge to enjoy the hospitality. The members were raising a large betting pool on the low pro score. Everyone tossed in $10, including me. The fellow who drew Dutch really wanted Raymond Gafford, the favorite pro. I threw in another $10 to get Dutch. Dutch and I not only won the team championship, but Dutch won low medal and set a competitive course record of 61! He walked away with it all—including the jackpot I turned over to him to help defray expenses. He was hard to keep up with in those days."

Chatterbox

During the PGA Championship of July 1954, Dutch advanced to a quarter-final match with Sam Snead in St. Paul, Minnesota. The two golfers were equally popular in the Midwest, and seemed to enjoy entertaining the crowd with conversation as they walked down the fairways. When a long-time friend greeted Dutch, he beamed and responded, "The things ya see when ya don't have your gun."

Dutch introduced Little Rock friend David Menkus and his wife to the fairway audience as they continued to stroll along. Menkus related, "Dutch had a sharp eye and an incredible memory for names, places, and faces. He could recognize an old friend in any crowd from a distance, and would wave and call out the friend's name. He had a way of making everyone feel important."

Jimmy Demaret told a writer, "We used to call Dutch 'Chatterbox,' because he was always talking to his opponent."

Former caddie, Otto Kohl, said, "The more Dutch chattered the better he played. He'd talk to everyone when he was swinging. If he had laryngitis he'd probably shoot 90."

On occasion, Dutch's well-intentioned enthusiasm could backfire. In the 1954 San Diego Open, free dinners were being awarded for an eagle on any hole.

Dutch was paired in the third round with Bill Ogden who hit a splendid second shot onto the 11th green, five feet from the hole. Dutch kept chirping, "C'mon, Mr. Bill, we got a free dinner in the fridge." This so unnerved Ogden that his putt didn't even come close.(Dutch won top money of $2,400 at that San Diego Open, the only San Diego Open to be held at the Rancho Santa Fe Golf Course in Rancho Santa Fe. However, *amateur* Gene Littler actually won the tournament.)

Golf galleries hadn't known anyone like Dutch. His style was a projection of himself. Having a good time on the golf course came naturally and he played as if life had birdies in store for him. In the U.S. Open in Chicago, Dutch was playing with Bobby Locke when Locke's critical approach shot of 140 yards rolled to the front edge of the cup, almost poised to drop.

As Locke stepped up to knock it in, Dutch quipped, "Watch that blade of grass there."

Dutch was clearly a favorite of the crowds. Marv Dahl, an avid fan, recalled, "Dutch was comfortable as an old shoe and simply a joy to be around."

Spectators won't forget the thrilling Los Angeles Open in 1952 when Dutch rallied with a spectacular birdie-3 on the difficult 18th hole at Riviera Country Club to tie Tommy Bolt and Jack Burke, Jr., for first place. It was at the Los Angeles Open that Marv Dahl introduced Shirley, his bride-to-be, to her first professional tournament. They picked up Dutch's foursome at a tee on the second nine holes.

Marv told Shirley to watch for Dutch. "He will greet the crowd with, 'Hi y'all,' and then he'll hit the ball out of sight."

Shirley had been accustomed to viewing golfer's frowns, scowls, and pensive countenances without a word spoken and was doubtful. But as Marv predicted, Dutch proceeded to give a friendly "Hi y'all," and calmly sent the ball out of sight, leaving the bride-to-be duly impressed with her fiance's clairvoyance.

Old Warson

Enjoy a lark? Make golf a ball?
Hit the links, watch "Hi y'all!"
Don your shoes and walkin' shorts,
Shed life's worries, all its warts.
Pay attention, listen up
Laugh a lot, you'll fill the cup.

"I've been on the go ever since I got out of the Army. And now I'm goin' to try to enjoy life a little more," Dutch said after clinching the Vardon Trophy for the lowest average score in 1954.

Thelma echoed the hope of his slowing down while she was visiting political friends in Washington, D.C. She predicted that 1955 would be a less strenuous year and then she broke the news: "Dutch has been appointed Professional Director of Golf at Old Warson Country Club in St. Louis. The new golf layout is scheduled for opening next April — we've already purchased a home in Brentwood near St. Louis."

Talking Money

Prestigious Old Warson had its formal opening in April 1955. A championship course founded by W. Alfred Hayes, Sr., and designed by Robert Trent Jones, it has been the host to major tournament events. It is similar to Augusta National of Masters fame with its oversized greens and bunkers.

Jack Berkley, a banker, had been in charge of the committee to find a name pro for Old Warson. "We had our eyes on Dutch and wanted to lure him to St. Louis," he recounted. "I found out his contract at Ardmore expired in June 1954, so I went to ask him what kind of money it would take to interest him in the job. He scratched his head a little, then said, 'I'll tell ya, Mr. Jack. Give me $400 per month and everythin' else that goes with it, the concessions, the drivin' range, golf lessons, together with the understandin' that I can go on the tour.' I couldn't believe it. We practically had to talk money into his hands. I told him, 'Whatever you want, Dutch, it's yours.' It was an eight-month deal because we were closed during the winter. He was free to go elsewhere during the winter and play in a few summer tournaments of his choice."

Dutch was happy with his appointment. "Old Warson is a good track, and I'm proud of it. I know one thing. When they move the tee markers back and hide the pins, it will be one tough course."

William "Bill" McDonnell who Dutch had caddied for in Little Rock, had moved to St. Louis, and recalled meeting Dutch in St. Louis. "When Dutch came to Old Warson he needed some money to buy the inventory for the pro shop. I was President of the First National Bank. Dutch didn't have any collateral, and he was about to be turned down by an official of the bank when he asked to see me. The official brought Dutch up to my office and said, 'Mr. Harrison wants $2,500 to stock his pro shop at Old Warson Country Club. He says he doesn't have any collateral and he can't suggest anybody who would endorse a note for him.'

"I replied, 'He doesn't need any collateral with me, and he doesn't need an endorser. I know Dutch is a hard worker and a good pro, and I know he'll pay back the money. And if he doesn't, I will.'

"Well, Dutch got his $2,500, which he quickly paid

back. Afterwards, he'd always be trying to give me gifts and lessons free of charge. I explained to him that in my position as a bank loan officer I couldn't accept the gifts, but he tried his best to shower me with them anyway. No matter how I tried, he wouldn't let me pay for lessons. He always said, 'You befriended me when I needed it an' I'll always be grateful to you.'"

After moving to St. Louis in 1944, McDonnell became a civic leader and held the chairmanship of the finance committee of the St. Louis McDonnell Douglas Corporation that designed and built the space capsule that carried the first men into space in the 1960s.

With Dutch as celebrated pro, the membership at Old Warson swelled to 325 members before opening day in April, 1955. Thelma managed the books and a smooth running day-to-day operation at the pro shop, which was small but attractive. Thelma was popular and there was little doubt that she was in charge. Occasionally she would have to admonish Dutch for selling merchandise at practically cost.

"But Dutch was such a cagey guy that he usually got his way," said one member. "He'd refer to Thelma as 'the best match of my life.'"

"I'll Write Ya a Check"

Thelma's son, Raymond, had met and married Helen Dillon in Albuquerque when he was a supply sergeant at Kirtland Air Force Base in 1952. He left the service in 1954 and joined Dutch as Assistant Professional along with T.D. Morris. By 1957 the Raymond Akana family had grown to five children — three girls and two boys, one named Dutch Harrison Akana.

While attached to Old Warson, Dutch was permitted to hold a winter job as Tournament Professional at the El Rio Country Club in Tucson, Arizona. This enabled him to stay in Tucson for a month or so before and after the Tucson Open and at intervals between tournaments in California and Arizona. Through Dutch's efforts,

Raymond Akana became the resident pro and a new clubhouse and pro shop were built. Dutch made the down payment for Raymond on a handsome and spacious four-bedroom home three miles from the Club. The whole family looked upon El Rio as an appealing rendezvous spot during the winter months.

Jack Berkley recalled, "Dutch was liked by all the members. He'd kid them and exchange small talk, always calling them 'Mister' or 'Miss.' He'd even carry their golf bags to their carts. We all loved to play with Dutch because he was such a fantastic shot-maker and a nice gentleman. Dutch also attracted a lot of celebrities to the club, like Bob Hope, Forrest Tucker and Randolph Scott.

"Once Dizzy Dean came to play with Dutch in a foursome with other celebrities. Ol' Diz just loved to bet. They came to number 13, a par-3 of 190 yards with a lake at the front of the green. The stakes were high.

"Dutch said, 'I'm hittin' a 4-iron here,' and then hit it right on the green.

"All the others hit into the lake. Dutch had been setting them up by hitting soft iron shots on preceding holes.

"One time a golfer who consistently lost to Dutch won twenty dollars from him. 'I'm going to frame this!' whooped the man who accepted the $20 bill. 'Will you autograph it for me?'

"Dutch eagerly took the bill and said, 'I'll do ya one better. I'll write ya a check.'"

Running Room

Thelma loved to discuss politics with the hired help at Old Warson. She closed the door of the little pro shop when business was slow and would start debating politics, usually on the Eisenhower side of the Administration. Spud Carter was her chief adversary in these sometimes heated debates. He recalled, "She was real intense and we'd get an earful. She loved to argue."

Dutch grew up in a primarily Democrat environment in Arkansas, and generally avoided discussing politics. According to son David, "If he ever voted Democrat, he wouldn't tell Mother because she was such a rabid Republican."

Senators Symington and Kefauver were Thelma's favorite Democrats. One morning in the 1940s, David had been awakened to find a man sleeping in the twin bed next to his. He ran to his mother's room and told her, "An old man is sleeping in my bedroom!" Thelma calmly explained the man was a house guest, and when that guest awakened, David was introduced to Senator Estes Kefauver, key Democrat who paved the way for statehood in Hawaii.

Martha recalls her mother would occasionally bend her ear for hours regarding men and the handling of men. "She had the habit of tweaking my nose when she was scolding me in her nice, friendly way. Only when my brother or I upset Mother would Pops intervene. When Mother went with Pops on tour she would generally remain in the clubhouse. She always had a nice ear for the young pros and spent considerable time with their wives, offering cheer and solace. Her therapy helped a number of devoted wives who were experiencing rocky marriages."

Thelma was a very giving person. Kimo remembers when they flew to Chicago once and landed at Midway Airport with only a three-mile trip by cab to Sportsman's Park Race Track. "The cab driver complained the entire route about such a short fare. When Mother tipped the cab driver $10, I was really annoyed. Mother countered with, 'Maybe he'll be a nicer person for it.'

"Every Christmas Mother would mail boxes of clothing to the grandchildren, commonly five or six dresses for each girl and pants for the boys. Then on birthdays, each of the grandchildren would receive money. Once she sent a wool vest and pant outfit to Molly, a friend of Martha's, just because she liked her. Molly later became my wife," said Kimo.

The Harrison family enjoyed their large colonial two-story residence while Martha and Kimo attended school in Brentwood. Martha recalled how the spaciousness of the home and yard reflected the "running room" Dutch and Thelma gave one another.

"Mother wanted to paint and redecorate the front of the house," Kim recalled. "She waited until Pops was on a golf trip. When he returned, he drove past the house without recognizing it and had the taxi go around the block again.

"After he finally found the house, he kidded Mother, 'Big Momma, I'm afraid to leave next time not knowin' what's gonna be done when I'm gone.'

"Pops never got upset about it even though he probably would have said no if she had asked him in the beginning. They gave each other a lot of room and were trusting and generous in nature."

A Car Full

Dutch was real handy around the home. He could skillfully extricate the newspaper from the mailbox and cheerfully give up its principal parts to his wife, retaining only the sports page. He could operate the TV but was not quite as adept at screwing in a light bulb or replacing the batteries in the flashlight. He would gladly undertake this handiwork when his wife, one of the children or another helper wasn't available.

Dutch and Thelma's beloved grandchild Nalani Akana, was the oldest of Raymond Akana's growing family. While a senior in high school she became Junior Miss of Hawaii and was sent to the national championships in Mobile, Alabama, where she was unanimously selected "Miss Personality."

Nalani remembers staying with Grandpa and Grandma at the Brentwood home as a five-year-old, "Grandma Thelma had my favorite dish of hot rice porridge, and I loved her french toast."

Dutch gave away stepdaughter Martha Harrison in

a St. Louis Church wedding on December 23, 1958. Nalani remembered, "When my parents moved from St. Louis to Tucson, I stayed with my grandparents so I could be the flower girl for Martha at her wedding. It was an exciting time for me.

"Before the ceremony I cut my hair and practically ruined it. Martha spanked me, and I felt so bad about the spanking that Grandpa came upstairs and consoled me," said Nalani.

"I remember what a loving, comforting, and humble man he was. Grandpa and Grandma needed only to raise their voices and I obeyed. The housekeeper took care of me, but I looked forward to evenings with Grandpa and Grandma.

"Typically, Grandpa and Grandma were in their lounge chairs with their feet up, Grandma doing her needlepoint and Grandpa either reading or watching TV. They never hassled or argued. It was such a fantastic relationship and such a good model for me. I can remember them giggling throughout the night in their bedroom. One night I shouted, 'Shut up!' and learned the next day from Grandma in no uncertain terms, that was a phrase never to be used."

Kimo recalled the trip that Dutch took with Nalani from St. Louis to Tucson in 1958, "Dutch adored Nalani. He called her Nanni when she was small, and Miss Nan when she became a teenager. During this long trip, Dutch would stop at gas stations and restaurants and always buy Nanni something. By the time he reached Arizona, the car was full of presents."

Hide an' Go Seek

It was while at Old Warson that Dutch took Doug Sanders under his wing as a protegé in 1955. Dutch had already become legendary for selecting talented golfers who at first blush were not impressive. Doug filled this bill.

Dutch recalled, "I brought Doug to Old Warson and

looked him over to see if I could help him. Even with that goofy swing he would blister our course. He was such a handsome dude, I'd lock up my daughter, Martha, when he was around. When I roomed with Mr. Doug on outin's I'd be hard put to keep him corralled. I'd even try to block the door at night with a big sofa or somethin' before I went to sleep. Late one night before a tournament match, he disappears an' I didn't see him 'til I got to the third tee the next mornin'. Finally, he comes puffin' up, grinnin' like a tomcat, an' says, 'I knew you'd hold 'em for me, Pops.' Mr. Doug would have been one of the greatest players of all time had he concentrated on golf."

Doug Sanders turned pro in 1956, the year he won the Canadian Open as an amateur at age 22. He proceeded to win 21 PGA tournaments before joining the PGA Senior Tour in 1983. When he teamed with Dutch in the 1950s, they won nearly all of their four-ball matches.

Once while staying overnight with the Harrisons, Doug Sanders recalled, "Dutch and Thelma were all smiles about her hitting the Daily Double for $1200 that afternoon at the track.

"Dutch exclaimed, 'Lookee at that big purse she's got. Betcha she won't let me close to her.'

"The next morning when Dutch came downstairs I said, 'Dutch you look a little tired.'

"He said, 'Oh Lordy, Big Mama wouldn't let me sleep last night. Ever' time I moved over a little bit she says, 'get away from me! You're tryin' to get my $1200!' I kept snoozin' a bit, then tried to find that purse an' all that money. We kept playin' hide an' go seek all night.'"

Super Mex Slacks

Harold Wiesenthal, owner of Harold's Mens Wear in Houston, helped sponsor some pro-am tournaments and became attached to Dutch, "Dutch had very little in his pockets in the 1950s when I met him. He came to me and said, 'I have a sure bet in a golf game in San Antonio.

If you could loan me $500 I'll bring back your $500 and more.'

"After the tournament Dutch returned and said, 'Mr. Harold, here's your $500 an' $500 more. If I hadn't three-putted the final hole, you would have had $800 more.'

"That's how I found out what a good man Dutch was. He could have pocketed the cash, you know, but that wasn't his way. And we were close friends from then on.

"Dutch and Thelma stayed at my brother's apartment while in Houston and Dutch stopped by my shop to buy slacks and coats. He then referred a lot of young players to me. He'd encourage them to dress well by telling them if they wanted to become professional golfers, they should dress sharp.

"Once he phoned me from Dallas and asked me, 'Mr. Harold, would you kindly send two pairs of slacks to a poor Mexican golfer in Dallas an' send the bill to me?'

"I can still remember mailing those slacks to Lee Trevino.

"Dutch always bought good quality clothes, and I helped coordinate them. Even if the size-44, extra-long coats didn't fit too well, when I asked how he liked them, Dutch would reply, 'Oh, Mr. Harold, this charcoal mohair coat is beautiful.'"

The Ponies Call

Joe Switzer, "licorice king," was an Old Warson member who had sought Dutch's appointment. "I became a good friend and played with Dutch in pro-ams, including Crosby rain-drenched clambakes and the Greenbriar Invitational in 1957 when Dutch won the whole jackpot. Dutch put all his money in a sack, woke up the next morning, and said, 'I got to get this to Mom.'" Dutch had fired a 29 on his last round for a record 62 to slip by Sam Snead, the perennial favorite, and Ben Hogan. In 1959 the tournament became known as the

Sam Snead Golf Festival.

"I accompanied Dutch to the race track a time or two before Chicago tournaments. One time Dutch called me at home and said, 'I'll pick you up, Mr. Joe, at 3 p.m. to drive to Chicago.' Then about 3 p.m. he called and said, 'Sorry, Mr. Joe, it'll be about 5 p.m.' At 5 p.m. he called and said, 'I'll be right over.' Then at 6 p.m. the phone rings and he says, 'I'm on my way.' Turns out, the timing was perfect for us to attend the events at the Fairmount Park Race Track in Collinsville, Illinois on our way to Chicago."

David Akana accompanied Dutch to the Carlings Open near Detroit in June 1957. His description of the trip was revealing, "I chose to drive my car since it was the only air-conditioned car in the family at the hottest time of the year. We left on a Tuesday about 6 p.m. and about midnight Dutch climbed into the back seat, saying he was going to rest his eyes. About Hammond, Indiana I stopped to ask directions and I asked Dutch to drive because I was tiring.

"Dutch cooed, 'Son, you're doin' a good job. Keep drivin'.'

"So we continued, and about daylight I woke him up again and said, 'Whether you're hungry or not, I'm going to stop and get something to eat.' After stopping, I asked him to take the wheel again and started to head for the passenger side of the car.

"Dutch said, 'No, no, no, you're doin' a whale of a job.'

"I couldn't believe it — I'd heard his sweet-talk for years and there I was again, still behind the wheel. Just north of Toledo, I woke Dutch again and told him flatly, 'You have to drive. I'm going to wreck this car and we're both going to get killed.'

"He refused again, conning me with, 'Son, you're doin' a fine job.' And so I ended up driving clear to Detroit.

"As we drove into the city, Dutch started giving me directions. I thought he was intent on getting out to the golf course so he could get his entry squared away. Suddenly he said, 'Turn right on Nine Mile Road,' and I wondered what we were doing in that section of Detroit until all of a sudden the Hazel Park Race Track came into view. I reminded Dutch that I had only a quarter in my pocket. 'Don't worry about it,' he kept saying.

"As we walked up to the entrance, Dutch says to his friend the ticket-taker, 'My son is dead broke today.'

"And the guy says, 'Oh, okay. Come on in — it's our turn to pay your way.'

"Inside Dutch loaned me $50. We lost the first race but won the second one and then the Daily Double. I paid Dutch back and had about $700 left. I figured Dutch had about $2,000, because he usually bet between two and three times what I did.

"In the tournament for the first two days, Dutch was paired with Tommy Bolt. Tommy had been playing well and had not displayed his famous temper. I walked with Dutch that second day and noticed at the 14th hole Dutch drove the ball without really establishing his normal stance. The ball went out of bounds.

"Before that first ball got over the fence, he was teeing up the second ball. He took the same unprepared stroke and hit it out of bounds the same way.

"Tommy Bolt started laughing after those two shots and yelled out in front of the 30 to 40 spectators, 'Dutch has got a horse at the race track, and he's gotta get there fast. He's not gonna qualify because he's got a favorite running tomorrow.'

"Dutch was a little embarrassed at that, but didn't say much the rest of the way. At the 17th hole Tommy got mad and broke a club. The rule had just gone into effect that if you broke a club you were automatically disqualified. Dutch had some choice words for Tommy. That tickled me so much I laid down on the fairway and split my sides laughing. Tommy took out a golf club and was going to come after me because he was so mad. I grabbed a club from Dutch's caddie and told him to come on. Dutch became quite upset with me, but after the round he went up to Tommy and suggested that he turn himself in because Dutch didn't want to have to do it. Tommy did report his violation and received a large fine. Unlike Dutch, he survived the cut.

"Next day we headed for the race track and wound up $15,000 ahead. Then came Black Saturday. We checked out of the hotel, and left for the race track intending to win another pot. Our sure winners became losers. The race track got back all except $2,000. We did go home with money in our pockets, but more importantly with the feeling that we had a good time. I guess it was a typical week at the race track for Dutch."

Little Check, Little Speech

Dutch's self-effacing charm was not lost on himself, and it was not uncommon for him to go out on a limb and predict himself the tournament winner. Confidants kept track of these victories and were amazed at his record of winning the tournaments he expected to win. Dutch correctly declared himself a winner before the Richmond, Reno, Hawaiian, and Wilmington Titles. He'd deny this with a grin to those outside his inner circle, but inwardly he was a real crystal-gazer.

Dutch confided, "I'd never talk about it, because you can play well in some tournaments only to have someone shoot the lights out an' edge you the last day."

Few edged Dutch when he secured the lead after three days. He could withstand the pressure to win that fourth day. Thelma recalled that Dutch promised her the winning trophy in the Texas Open of 1951. He fulfilled his promise, coming from behind with a spectacular 64 in the last round to tie Doug Ford for the championship, then beating Doug in the play-offs by one stroke. His total score set a tournament record.

After his victory in a distant city, Dutch commonly delivered this message to the crowd at the awards ceremony: "You folks have been mighty good to me. This golf course was built for me. I should move to this city sometime."

At one awards ceremony (St. Louis Open Gold Golf Tournament) Dutch was presented as the third-place winner. "I had a big speech all ready," he said, "because I thought I was goin' to win an' take home a big check. But little check, little speech. Thank you."

Jonesboro, Arkansas was one city that fell in love with Dutch. Barney Osment and Earl Toler, both of Jonesboro, attested to this. "Dutch donated his time for worthy causes in Jonesboro by being the main attraction in our annual tournament. People grew to realize how big-hearted he was. Our good young amateurs had a tough time keeping up with him.

"Dutch told us, 'I'll tell ya one thing, Mr. Barney an' Mr. Earl. The young dogs may be snappin' at my heels, but they'll have a tough time passin' the ol' Dutchman.'

"Dutch was like a fresh breeze to cool the summer air."

Troubled Times

Dutch suffered a heavy blow when his close child-hood friend, Eugene (Gene) Granville Smith, Chief of Police of Little Rock, committed suicide. Little Rock had become an explosive world-wide symbol of desegregation resistance in 1957.

"Daisy Bates related, in *The Long Shadow of Little Rock,* how Smith was literally hounded to death by segregationists along with other public officials being run out of town. A long succession of threats on the Smith family as well as his son's run-ins with the law shattered Smith's spirit. A short time after the historic confrontation between Governor Faubus and federal authorities the humid afternoon of September 24 on the doorsteps of Little Rock Central High School, Smith ended his life.

Dutch was shaken by the news and found the suicide difficult to accept and understand. He remembered Gene Smith as Daisy Bates had: "... a courageous, dedicated police officer who did his duty as he saw it, standing for law and order even when the Governor of the State did not."

Although Dutch had inherited many of the traditions of the plantation south, he was never racially prejudiced, a gift he attributed to his evolution as an athlete. He had become a good friend of boxer Joe Louis, "the Brown Bomber," and was deeply disappointed when Louis and other black golfers were banned from playing the tour and most private courses.

He became part of the movement for nondiscrimination led by Walter Winchell in 1953, "If Joe Louis could carry a gun in the U.S. Army, he should be able to carry golf clubs in tournaments."

Shortly thereafter, the PGA amended its constitution to permit black entries and finally in 1961 dropped its "Caucasian-Only" membership clause. This blended well with Dutch's philosophy of everyone enjoying life to the fullest.

Assorted ailments stalked the Arkansas Traveler in 1958 after a brilliant tournament start. Dutch won the Tijuana Open and placed second in the Los Angeles Open. Sciatic nerve trouble had almost put him out of commission in 1952 and the rainy, cold weather at Old Warson still bothered him. Dutch went on the shelf with the flu, was diagnosed as having diabetes, and had a double hernia operation in the fall.

On October 8, 1958, Dutch's father, David Walter, died of congestive heart failure at age 80. He had retired as a night watchman following a lengthy career on the Little Rock police force. Dutch's mother lived until 1963. Both parents were buried near Conway, Arkansas in the little Baptist church cemetery known as Oak Bowery.

To cap the calamitous year, Dutch suffered an arm and rib injury when he slipped on an icy road. Little wonder he became good friends with Dr. Dean Sauer that year.

Dr. Sauer warmly recalled his friendship with Dutch, "We operated on him for double hernia. While he was under the general anesthesia, we were able to closely inspect the marvelous hands of the master, without embarrassment to him. Not a callous or blemish could we find — mute evidence of his capacity to caress a golf club in the execution of his utterly amazing shots. Tough, uncomplaining man that he was, within two weeks he was raking balls from Old Warson's east lake.

"He knew everything about every member but gossiped about no one," continued Dr. Sauer. "Secrets were always safe with him. He made it a practice never to socialize with members, declining even to attend the wedding of my daughter. Always a great and gracious gentleman he was — and Thelma was just as lovable.

"Dutch loved to teach and enjoyed most of all those talented and elite golfers like Jack Berkley and Joe Switzer. With the high handicappers like me, he was the essence of patience. Never did I receive a bill from him. When one was requested, he'd invariably say, 'We'll get around to that later.'

"When I was privileged to operate on him, I felt that in some small measure I was able to even the score. That's what I thought. But later in his career, he called my son Fred and me to come to his house and presented each of us with a set of matched Wilson clubs. Then he turned to Thelma and said, "Mother, I think they need some bags, too. I want to do this because Dr. Sauer has done so much for me."

Greener Grass

One Sunday morning in September 1959, Dick Shaiper, St. Louis pro, was leading Dutch by one stroke at the start of the last round of the St. Clair Invitational at Belleville, Illinois. Shaiper met Dutch in the locker room. "Dutch was complaining about his leg and the need to drop out of the tournament. I pleaded with him to play. 'You're only one shot behind me, and it's only right that you try to play,' I told him. Dutch pulled up his pant leg and showed me his varicose veins, the source of his pain. I found a doctor who wrapped his leg well enough for him to walk the final 18 holes. Do you know that old son-of-a-gun went out and beat me by one shot for first place?

"After the round, I remember Dutch smiling real big, and saying, 'Mr. Dick, you oughta know better than to help a cripple. They'll jus' beat ya every time.'"

After Thelma left Hawaii in October 1951 she did not return until November, 1959. She flew to Hawaii with her good friend "Teddie" Hager, who was known as the Auntie Mame of the Club, with her bubbly personality and flare. Teddie remembers how Hawaiians welcomed Thelma back with open arms and how royally entertained they were by Doris Duke, Mrs. Joseph Farrington, the Frank McKinleys and the Lyle Guslanders.

"President Eisenhower had just signed the proclamation declaring Hawaii a state, and we celebrated the statehood Thelma had helped pioneer. We had sumptuous Hawaiian-style dinners eaten with your fingers without tableware—to the melodious music of Hawaiian groups. The volcano, Kilauea, was erupting on the Big Island, so Thelma arranged a picnic party at a safe viewing distance. We sat on beach blankets and watched the magnificent eruption."

In July 1959 Dutch was offered the Head Professional position at Waialae Country Club near Thelma's former residence in Hawaii. It was a tempting offer in many respects, but Dutch turned it down and recommended Tony Anthony of Louisville, Kentucky, who filled the position. Hawaii was just too far from family, friends, and race tracks.

How much had Thelma missed her native land? Her sister, Anne, sensed that Thelma had tired of the stress and strain of life as Territorial Senator. "Thelma not only wanted to be with Dutch, but she enjoyed getting away from the rat race in Hawaii. Someone was always at her doorstep with a problem. It was, 'Will you help me with the police?', or, 'I have a problem with my job at Queens Hospital,' or, 'We need some financial help desperately.' I remember Thelma told me this story, 'One night a wife phoned about her husband beating her and she wanted him put in jail. I told her to call the police. Then about 3 a.m. she remorsefully called again and not only asked me for money, but wanted me to go down to the police station and bail him out!'

"Thelma wanted her children to have a little more than Hawaii could offer them at that time academically, and to be able to mingle with people on the mainland. In addition, little David had terrible asthma, and she wanted to get him away from the pollen-laden atmosphere. We used to ask her, 'Thelma, don't you want to come back to Hawaii for a visit?' 'No, ' she'd reply, "It's not the right time.' Never in the years that she was away did she write that she missed the beach or any part of Hawaii. There was never any regret that she left. Her heart and mind were always focused on Dutch."

Dutch and Thelma were happy at Old Warson, but the Arkansas Traveler was getting restless to move on. His days as an underfed scrambler were long past, but there was always greener grass growing under his feet. One of the places that captured his eye was the beautiful Bay Area in California. An opportunity there would provide the catalyst for the next move in the Dutchman's adventurous career.

Olympic Club

I'm just breezin' along with the breeze,
Trailin' the rails, roamin' the seas,
Like the birdies that sing in the trees,
Pleasin' to live, livin' to please.

From "Breezin' Along with the Breeze"
by Haven Gillespie, Seymour Simons
and Richard A. Whiting

In November 1960, Dutch announced his appointment as Head Professional at the famous Olympic Club in San Francisco. Was the Arkansas Traveler really going to Nob Hill City? The golf world buzzed with surprise. His friends wondered how Dutch would react to this royal and elegant city with its Victorian tradition.

The Olympic Club of San Francisco was known as the premier social and athletic organization of the West, and as the *tour de force* of golf in the city. Members of the Club were addressed as fellow Olympians whose "Spirit of Olympia" created a large, enthusiastic society. Not the least of the area's attractions for Dutch were the nearby race tracks of Bay Meadows, Tanforan, and Golden Gate Fields.

The Welcome Mat is Out

The Olympic Club's golf courses consisted of the championship Lake Course and the adjoining Ocean Course. These two 18-hole courses, stretching from the Pacific Ocean to the shores of Lake Merced, represented one of the most picturesque and demanding layouts in the country. Bobby Jones called the Lake Course "the Best in the West." Dutch raved about it as "the longest short course in the world. It has small greens in a woodsy settin' of pines an' eucalyptus. There's a pretty view of Golden Gate Bridge from the third hole. Ya can't be sprayin' your tee shot on any hole. Sometimes it's like drivin' out of a chute an' playin' down a bowlin' alley. Those tough three finishin' holes — whooee!"

The Lake Course is famous for Jack Fleck's upset of Ben Hogan in the 1955 U.S. Open and Billy Casper's upset of Arnold Palmer in 1966. In 1964 the Club produced three national champions in one year: Ken Venturi in the U.S. Open, Bill Higgins in the U.S. Senior Amateur, and Johnny Miller in the USGA Junior Championship.

Jack Hickey was a member of the board of directors at the downtown Olympic Club, and said, "Dutch was chosen because of his tournament record, his personality, and the high esteem golfers had for him, as well as his off-the-cuff commentaries on World Championship Golf, which smacked of both spice and perception."

A news story noted, "The Dutchman comes to Olympic Club with a bag full of talents — Player Extraordinaire, Raconteur, Diplomat, Teacher, Manager, Television Announcer — all these are a part of the Harrison personality...his droll wit is as crisp as a 7-iron spanked stiff to the pin."

Dutch's best showing in the National Open had come that year, when he was 50 years old. Against the best field in the world, at Denver's Cherry Hills, he went down to the last few holes with a good shot at first place, and finished strong with a 69, three strokes behind

Arnold Palmer's smashing finish of 280.

The Olympic Club welcomed "another team member, Mrs. Thelma (Mama) Harrison...who has special capacities for record-keeping and ladies fashion-wear in the pro shop."

Thelma was one of nine on Dutch's payroll at the club. Two professionals accompanied Dutch from Old Warson, namely Derek Hardy and Vic Giron, and on the staff of assistant professionals were Art Armstrong from Hawaii and brusque, but loyal John Perelli. Kyle Burton also joined the staff and later became Head Professional.

In addition to a handsome salary, Dutch was awarded the concessions for pro-shop merchandise, the practice range and golf carts. Moreover, he could select the tour tournaments he wished to enter. The image of the club professional had markedly changed since Dutch became one. Not only could he walk through the clubhouse front door now, but he had an aura of glamour. Skill in merchandising golf equipment, and apparel had become an important function of the pro. His shop was a most profitable sideline until discount stores in the city began to shrink the profit margins.

Stepson Kimo helped with the record-keeping in the pro shop, caddied, and also attended San Francisco City College. He recalls, "Besides caddying a lot, I went to the races with Dutch and we became very close. I remember he caught me playing poker once with friends and warned me never to play again with friends. He also cautioned me to never bet with members."

Haircuts and Cookie Jars

Dutch and Thelma spent less time in Tucson with the Raymond Akanas during the winter, but enjoyed the opportunity to visit the grandchildren. In the 1960s a subject of some discussion in nearly every household with young boys was the proper length of the haircut. After all, this was the new age of Beatlemania, rock and roll bands, and jet aircraft. Dutch's generation had difficulty understanding the trend to long hair. He believed a well-groomed boy should have short hair. When Dutch wanted to show off his five-year-old grandson, Dutchy, during a celebrity tournament at El Rio Country Club, he received permission from Dutchy's mother to take him by the barbershop on their way to the tournament. Upon their return that evening in good spirits, Helen Akana was surprised to see Dutchy with a close-cropped crew cut.

Flashing his mischievous grin, Dutch teased, "Miss Helen, the barber had a real field day, didn't he?"

Nalani and Kahala, Raymond Akana's two oldest daughters, traveled from Tucson to San Francisco for a two-week vacation with Dutch and Thelma.

Kahala recalls, "We left crying because we had such a good time. Grandpa would always come in and kiss us in our beds every morning before he left for the golf course. He would take us to the club and want to introduce us to everybody."

She also remembers literally having her hand caught in the cookie jar once. "They had this big cookie jar in the San Francisco apartment. After I had received my quota of one cookie, I was caught taking another one. Grandma started to scold me severely and wanted to restrict me. Grandpa was sitting in the room and spoke up. 'I think Kahala has learned her lesson an' doesn't need to be restricted.'

"I remember getting up on his lap and his telling us stories. We would always have to ask him questions because he would never volunteer information on his victories and awards. He had such a fantastic memory of the golfers and golf events. We were both so proud of him."

One Club member recalled Dutch's prodigious memory for names. "It was amazing that he knew the names of the 600-plus regular-playing members within two weeks. I remember starting to introduce my daughter a second time to Dutch, and before I opened my mouth, Dutch said, "Hello, Miss Cecil — How are you?'"

Of his customers, Dutch remembered best the one who wasn't satisfied with his putter. "He bought a new one from me an' then brought it back. I allowed him $5 for the trade-in an' he bought another one. He brought that back an' I allowed him $5 again. That went on, $5 at a time, until he'd bought 17 different kinds of putters. An' do you know which one he settled on? The one he had in the beginning!"

Calcuttas and Trusted Lieutenants

In 1962 Dutch decided to turn the pro shop over to someone else in order to spend more time on the golf tour. Kyle Burton was chosen to handle the day-by-day affairs and serve as Teaching Pro. Burton was a good merchandiser whose advice was sought by Thelma. He described Thelma as "articulate and jolly with a lusty laugh. She was extremely popular with the touring pros and club members. She was the ideal golf pro's wife."

Burton observed, "In practice rounds Dutch liked to play with low handicap golfers. Even the high handicap players stood in awe of him and never said a derogatory word. Dutch could turn down an invitation to dinner or an invitation to play with a high handicap player and the inviter would wind up hugging him for the way he said no. He'd never bet large sums of money with the members, and treated them all fairly. He was an artist at bringing their handicaps down to what they should be."

Burton recalled, "Sometimes Dutch disappeared for two to three hours at a time, telling no one that he was out looking for golf balls. I'd catch glimpses of his white cap bobbing up and down in the tall brush and the woods."

Vic Giron was one of Dutch's trusted lieutenants in the pro shop. One day a friend phoned him, curious about Dutch's mysterious lunch time disappearances from the club. Ever the loyal employee, Vic was not about to reveal the whereabouts of his mentor, but over the phone came the telltale sound of fingers drumming on the table to hoofbeats of the William Tell Overture.

Dutch helped introduce George Archer to golf when he was 19 years old and gave him lessons. In 1962 Archer was one of Dutch's amateur "ringers" entered as a partner in the pro-am at Odessa, Texas.

Archer later related, "Dutch and I ate a hearty down-South breakfast early in the morning, practiced, and played 18 holes of golf, then returned for a big lunch. After a nap, we went to the race track. We placed third in the tournament, but faltered at the track.

"Dutch would always keep an eye on me after his experiences with that night owl, Doug Sanders, but he grew to trust me and selected me to deliver sizable golf bets in sealed envelopes to the Calcuttas at tournaments. Once I took an envelope to a Calcutta event in Las Vegas where I joined a couple of ringers and saw the odds rise dramatically. I'm sure I returned more money to Dutch in that envelope than I took to Las Vegas. Dutch was one shrewd bettor on golfers."

In a Calcutta, pro golfers were divided into teams and each team was auctioned to the highest bidder. The pool from the auction was divided between the owners of win, place and show similar to a horse race. This form of golf gambling was popular through the mid 1950s and early 1960s, but was banned in the middle 1960s from the pro tour, because many of the teams auctioned included amateurs with inflated handicaps.

Assistant Arthur Armstrong was a Hawaiian golf champion who knew Thelma's family in Hawaii before she married Dutch. Francis Brown, illustrious Hawaiian golfer and tycoon, had sponsored Armstrong for 14 years as an amateur golfer. Dutch played in tournaments with Art as early as the 1940s and was a close friend.

Arthur remembered the magnetic attraction the race track held for Dutch, "On Mondays the Olympic Club was closed and Dutch usually had his mind on the racetrack. Early one rainy Monday, I swung by his Park Merced apartment to have breakfast and drive him to a pro-am tournament in Sacramento.

"'Dutch, are you ready?'

"'Mr. Art, how's the weather?'

"'It might be raining here, but it isn't raining in Sacramento.'

"After breakfast Dutch asked me to phone Sacramento and make sure it wasn't raining there. After phoning, I reported, 'They say it rained all night but the course is playable, Dutch.'

"I remember our trip across the bridge out of San Francisco. Dutch turned to me and asked, 'Are you sure it's not rainin' in Sacramento?'

"I was curious, 'Dutch, tell me something. Would you rather go to the races than go up to Sacramento?

"'Well, Mr. Art, we're gonna be passin' by the track.'

"'Well, if you want to go to the races just tell me.'

"'Maybe not,' Dutch chuckled."

Celebrities and Caddies

Arthur Armstrong continued, "It seemed all the pros coming through San Francisco would look up Dutch. He'd have them to lunch and invite them to play with him. He was always doing something for somebody. The celebrities loved him. Tennessee Ernie Ford and Randolph Scott would fly in just to play with him. And the pros loved staying with Dutch and Thelma in their wonderful apartment overlooking the ocean.

"At clubhouse parties, Dutch was a terrific emcee. His golfing jokes actually brought cheers from the membership. They loved him and all called him Mr. Dutch.

"Dutch always had a great feeling for caddies because he was a caddie once," said Art. "When the weather was so bad they couldn't caddie, he'd give them a couple of bucks just to clean the rubbish around the landscaped areas. If he had old shoes he'd give them away to the caddies, remembering how poor he had been as a young boy."

Dutch's favorite caddies at Old Warson had been two brothers from Roswell, New Mexico named Spud and Tobe Carter. Spud and another brother, Reese, accompanied Dutch to Olympic Club, where Spud handled the driving range, Reese the golf carts, and both caddied.

One day, two old friends from Little Rock, Frank Pace, former Secretary of the Army during World War II, and Jim Murphy visited Dutch and Thelma. They came to Olympic Club for a match with Dutch and John Swanson, an amateur from Olympic Club. The visiting golfers were furnished caddies, Reese and Spud Carter, who provided putting tips. At the end of the round, the Little Rock golfers were settling their debt when one of them asked Spud where he was from. Spud answered, "My brother and I came from St. Louis along with Mr. Dutch."

Turning to his partner, the golfer exclaimed, "Son of a gun, he's done it to us again! He did it to us when we were kids, and now he's done it again. We actually fell for these caddie's putting lines!"

"Make sure your caddies get their fair share of what you've earned today," the partner interjected.

Dutch replied, "Well, Mr. Jim, what was aworryin' me was that you an' Mr. Frank couldn't putt where those caddies were tellin' ya to."

Turning back to the young caddies, Mr. Jim laughingly warned, "Dutch has already beaten us out of our money — just make sure he doesn't beat you guys out of yours."

In August 1961, Olympic Club hosted young Jack Nicklaus in a friendly match.

Nicklaus had won the NCAA championship that summer, then his two matches of the Walker Cup in Seattle. He was on his way to Pebble Beach, where he would win the U.S. Amateur Championship. He then turned pro in November 1961.

Nicklaus arranged a round with Nelson Collinward of the *San Francisco Examiner* who called John Swanson as a third golfer and told John to find a fourth. John told

■ PGA Championship Semi-finalists in July 1939: Byron Nelson, Dutch, Henry Picard, and Dick Metz. Dutch advanced by beating Horton Smith, his boss, 4 and 3.

AP Wire Photo

■ Sergeant E. J. Harrison accepting War Bond after winning the Miami Open in December 1944 at Miami Springs Country Club.

■ Dutch and Sam Snead, soft drink fans, celebrate a hot tournament round, circa 1946. "Our drinks were as weak as well water."

■ Dutch while leading the qualifying round of the PGA Championship in Portland in 1946.

■ "The winnah, Dutch Harrison." Bobby Locke, runnerup, raises arm of Dutch, the winner of the Reading Open in 1947, at Berkshire Country Club.

■ Hustling Days— Dutch with arm around partner Bob Hamilton at the Inverness Round Robin Four-Ball Invitational, Inverness Country Club, Toledo, Ohio in June 1948.

■ **Dutch and Emma are among contingent of pros and their wives after arrival at Hawaiian International Airport for the 1948 Hawaiian Open.**

Defending Champion Dutch is seated second from left. Emma stands second from left. Seated left to right are Ed Furgol, Dutch, Skip Alexander, Lawson Little, Cary Middlecoff, Lloyd Mangrum. Johnny Bulla is standing at far left.

■ **Dutch and close friend Porky Oliver after a hot round, circa 1949.**

■ **The winning Ryder Cup Team of 1949.**

(left to right): Dutch, Johnny Palmer, Bob Hamilton, Sam Snead, Ben Hogan, Clayton Heafner, Jimmy Demaret, Lloyd Mangrum, Chick Harbert.

■ Second day of
Ryder Cup
Matches,
Ganton Golf
Club, England,
September
1949. Dutch,
calm and cool,
and his con-
cerned oppo-
nent, Max
Faulkner.

Courtesy of Ganton Golf Club

Courtesy of Ganton Golf Club

■ Before Ryder Cup practice round in September 1949 at
Ganton Golf Club, England. *Left to right: "Happy Boy" Dutch, Ken
Bousfield of Great Britain, Ben Hogan, Fred Daly of Ireland, and Johnny
Palmer.*

■ Everyone is smiling including Dutch as he cracks a joke while in tournament play with Chick Harbert (left) in 1949-50.

■ Dutch in one of his colorful Hawaiian golf shirts, circa 1950.

Courtesy of Anne Kauaihilo

■ Thelma Akana in the late '40s when she first met Dutch.

■ Top money winners
Dutch Harrison
and Byron Nelson
after Dutch cap-
tured the Bing
Crosby pro-am in
1950 at Pebble
Beach.

■ Dutch at the zenith
of his career (circa
1949). Publicity
photo for Wilson
Sporting Goods.

■ Dutch, Hoagy
Carmichael, Phil
Harris, and Jimmy
Thomson at Bing
Crosby Invitational
in January 1952,
the year after
Dutch and Phil
captured the pro-
am.

■ Dutch signaling Hole-in-One, on Hole 3, All-American Open, Tam O' Shanter Golf Club, Chicago area, August 1953.

■ Cary Middlecoff, Ed Crowley, Phil Harris, and Dutch Harrison at Cypress Point during first day of the second Bing Crosby tournament that Dutch won (1954).

■ Dutch and movie star Randolph Scott in Arizona, circa 1958.

■ Bob Crosby and Dutch Harrison on the televised World Series of Golf in 1959.

■ Dutch with celebrity group rooting for the Lucky International Golf Tournament held at Harding Park, San Francisco in January, 1961.

Seated from left to right: Jess Watson, John Raitt and wife, Ed Crowley and wife, Cecil Roarke, Vic Ghezzi. Standing: Tom Harmon, John Brodie, Dutch, Bob Rosburg, Crowley secretary, James Garner, Doug Sanders, Cary Middlecoff.

■ Dutch and Joe Garagiola
humorously come to grips
and vie for honors at the
Arkansas Hall of Fame,
January 1963.

■ Tennessee Ernie Ford and Dutch at
Olympic Club, circa 1963.

■ Dutch while representing Wilson Sporting Goods (1937-1972), circa 1965.

■ Dutch with Walter Hagen trophy emblematic of his fifth victory in six years in the U.S. Seniors Open, Las Vegas (1966), chatting with Monica Lind of Tropicana Hotel Folies Bergere.

■ Dutch with close friend Tommy Bolt at U.S. National Seniors Tournament in Las Vegas, October, 1968.

■ Dutch and Shirley
on their wedding
day, February 16,
1973 in Hot
Springs, Arkansas.

■ Pals Doug Sanders and Dutch Harrison at
Bob Hope pro-am in 1977, St. Louis.

■ Dutch and Bob Hope playing in the Bob Hope pro-am in 1977, St. Louis. Dutch was 67 and Bob 74 years young.

■ Bob Hope singing a special version of *Thanks for the Memories* to Dutch Harrison (standing) at the Bob Hope Testimonial Dinner October 22, 1977.

Dutch that they had some "easy meat... a 21-year-old kid from Ohio."

Dutch asked, "Mightin' that young kid be Jack Nicklaus?"

When told it was, Dutch said, "I'm sorry, but I'm headin' to the races an' won't be available." He recognized the Nicklaus destiny for greatness even at that early stage.

John Raitt, the celebrity baritone, was one of the low handicap golfers that played often with Dutch. An all-time heartthrob of Broadway theater, John Raitt performed in *Oklahoma, Carousel, Pajama Game* and other musical productions.

Since meeting in the early sixties while Dutch was on tour, they played many benefits together, a couple of times at the Bing Crosby Tournament. One year after the Los Angeles Open, Raitt noticed that Dutch was limping and was complaining of a bad back, with one leg a bit shorter than the other.

"Dutch said, 'Mr. John, I don't believe I'm going to be able to play in the Crosby with you. My back's out.'

"I said, 'Mr. Dutch, I've got a great chiropractor, the best. Wait here in the locker room.'

"A few days after his treatment, he was feeling well enough to play in the Crosby with me.

"We didn't make the cut as a team that year in the Crosby tournament. Dutch says, 'Mr. John, let's go to the Little Crosby Tournament where there's $3,000 prize money for non-qualifiers. I'll tell some stories over there tonight an' you can sing. We'll have some fun.'

"And sure enough, we did."

John always called Dutch his best public relations agent, "Dutch would tell everyone I was the best singer ever, and could really call the hogs. He was such a proud guy. He might let me pay for dinner or for shows, but when it came to golf, he paid the way. He'd give away a lot of golf clubs and tell me each time, 'Mr. John, this is the greatest iron I've ever had. Now you take good care of it an' don't let anyone else have it. It's a special club.'

"Dutch probably had six or seven more like it in the clubhouse."

During one golf round at Olympic Club in San Francisco, John became upset with one of his shots and threw a club high in a cypress tree where it stuck. It was his favorite wedge, a gift from Dutch.

The next day John entered the pro shop and said, "Mr. Dutch, I have a confession to make. I threw a club and it's up in a cypress tree."

"Oh, Mr. John, you didn't do that, did you? What do you need?"

"I need a golf cart, a ladder, and a caddie."

"Well, you don't need a ladder, but I'll give you a cart an' a caddie."

John went out on the golf course with cart and caddie, but couldn't find his wedge. Returning to the golf shop, Dutch grinned and said, "Mr. John, you're lucky. While you were gone someone brought that club into the golf shop."

Dutch had planned to teach him a little lesson.

"He was so good for my golf," John remarked. He'd say, 'You really buggy-whip that ball, Mr. John. Nobody abuses a ball that way. Each of your drives looks like an aspirin up there.'

"He'd give me lessons out at the practice tee and he'd say, 'Mr. John, I have 1,000 new range balls I've gotta break in.'

"So he'd tee up about ten at a time for me. Now, I'm very fast in my actions and Dutch is characteristically slow southern. He'd tee up about ten at a time for me and I think I hit about 700 that day. Mr. Dutch would say, 'Mr. John you're really dilapidatin' that ball. The only thing is that by the time I get ten teed up for you, you've got four in the air — you're runnin' scared!'"

Tennessee Ernie Ford first met Dutch at Olympic Club on an extremely cold morning. In that melodious bass voice, Ernie told Dutch, "But I don't want to play today, Pro. It's too cold. This is hog-killin' weather."

"Mr. Ernie, you sure speak the Mother tongue — that's why I think we'll always get along."

The late Mark Twain is remembered for his now-famous observation, "The coldest winter I ever spent was the summer I spent in San Francisco." When Dutch decided to leave the Olympic Club in 1964 he commented, "My old bones can't stand the foggy, chilly weather."

Bob Goalby asked, "Dutch, I thought you had the greatest job possible at Olympic Club. What made you leave?"

"Oh, Mr. Bob, those people are wonderful out there. The courses are just beautiful an' I love the town. But I couldn't take the cooooold weather. I'd get out on that lesson tee an' freeze up like a cold pipe."

When Dutch and Thelma left San Francisco that year, their sentiments were identical to those of Rudyard Kipling: "San Francisco has only one drawback —it's hard to leave." And it was always that way with Dutch. He enjoyed everyone and everyplace. Little wonder the Arkansas Traveler found each port in life "the greatest place in the world."

International Championships

That far away prize, a world of success,
It's waitin' for me if I heed the call —
I won't settle down or settle for less,
As long as there's half a chance I can have it all.

from "I've Gotta Be Me"
by Walter Marks

"You play in tournaments for your living; you play in the Ryder Cup for your country," Dutch said.

Participation in this premier international event, the Olympics of professional golf, is considered the greatest honor a professional golfer can attain.

First Ryder Cup

"I was as tickled as a boy goin' to the circus when I received my first Ryder Cup invitation. That was in 1947 when only British an' Irish pros came over to play at the Portland Golf Club in Oregon. What a picture layout with all those beautiful fir trees. An' I'm tellin' you it was the biggest international sports event they'd ever had in the Pacific Northwest, an' it was the first Ryder Cup since 1937. Without Bob Hudson, a grocer with the Piggly-Wiggly chain, it wouldn'a been held at all. He paid for everythin', flyin' from Great Britain to New York, winin' an' dinin' the team at the Waldorf Astoria, railroadin' from Chicago to Portland, an' livin' expenses for us all.

"He was buyin' gifts an' spendin' money like it was goin' out of style. What a patron saint he was. Why, he even asked the British team what sorta gifts they'd like to carry back home. You know what they selected? Sacks of seed. Food was so scarce over there they wanted to plant the seed in their gardens!

"I remember he bought wrist watches for the two teams an' he gave the British team pitchin' wedges, a golf club they hadn't seen before. They had trouble usin' those wedges an' noticed our wedges had the grooves much deeper so we could stop the ball on a dime when we landed on the green. Captain Henry Cotton of their team protested an' made us shave our grooves down. He was a tough cookie an' kept sayin' to everybody, 'We didn't come all the way over here to lose.'

"In practice, I managed a little ol' 66 (lowest score), so I knew I had a chance to help our team. Porky Oliver an' Jimmy Demaret scored low too, but Jimmy scored the best with his Beau Brummel outfits. The crowd got a kick out of those eye-catchers. I remember he dressed once in a green shirt, pink pants an' checkered cap. Whoeee!

"We practiced in the rain an' I think it rained every day...so heavy I can still hear it beatin' on our umbrellas — a real frog drowner. The sloppy fairways eliminated any roll on the balls an' many of our shots buried where they landed. Sand traps turned into lakes. Some of the players took their shoes off to play out of those traps. Knickers were passed out an' nearly all the golfers wore 'em. It was either that or stuff your pants inside your socks. At times, I thought they'd be callin' out the lifeboats.

"I played against Fred Daly, a tough Irishman who had the lowest practice round of their team. It was amazin' that 7,000 people came out to watch us on a rainy day. I was fortunate to win my match with Mr.

Daly, 5 an' 4 (five holes ahead with four to play). The American team won, 11 matches to one, but most were real close ones."

Visitation from God

One of the most exciting Ryder Cups for both nations was the September 1949 contest at Ganton Golf Club near Scarborough, England. This was Dutch's first trip to Europe, and both he and his peers learned that British and Irish performances rise to unparalleled heights under the gripping patriotic fever of playing on home soil.

"Our team arrived at Southhampton on the Queen Elizabeth. We were met by a fleet of Rolls Royces that were at our disposal throughout our stay," Dutch said, picking up on the story. "The British hustled us to a cocktail party at London's Savoy Hotel, an' we watched the drawin' made for an American/British tournament to follow the Ryder Cup. The reporters kept telling us what strong favorites we were. I told 'em we hadn't played golf in 15 days. Our trainin' consisted of hittin' balls into the net on the boat an' workin' out in the gym.

"The next day we motored some 250 miles north of London to the resort town of Scarborough, where we stayed at the Grand Hotel durin' Ryder Cup week. It took us all day to reach Scarborough because we stopped at Oxford, Stratford-on-Avon, an' York to see the sights. Though we were four hours late when our Rolls Royces pulled into the square in front of the hotel, thousands of people met an' cheered us. It was unbelievable. Bobbies had to escort each of us into the hotel. The next mornin' I told our team, 'Now don't go gettin' big heads — that crowd came to see the Rolls Royces, not us.'

"Ben Hogan was our leader an' non-playin' captain of the American team. It was hard to realize that in February he nearly died after his Cadillac collided head-on with a big bus. Herman Keiser an' I visited Mr. Ben at the El Paso Hospital two days after the accident. He was barely able to recognize us, but he asked, 'Where are my clubs?' We went down an' found 'em an' assured him they were safe. As we left, I turned to Herman an' told him, 'It doesn't look like he'll ever play again.' The doctors thought he was in a dream world when he announced he was goin' to play golf.

"I remember he would be sittin' in the locker room with bandages an' braces on his legs. We had to turn our heads as he was wrappin' an' unwrappin' those black an' swollen legs that were so badly mangled. Mr. Ben may have been broken in the body, but he sure wasn't in spirit. An' he couldn't turn down the challenge of this Ryder Cup. He knew it'd take a all-out effort for us to win again.

"The British were anxious to win the Cup an' dedicate it to the memory of Harry Vardon an' Ted Ray, two famous British professionals who had played outta Ganton an' had won the British an' American Open Championships.

"I'll tell ya, Mr. Ben's key to success was grit an' gumption. An' that meant practice an' more practice. So it was no surprise when he set up a stiff schedule for the team. We practiced harder than usual, even Jimmy Demaret, who would saunter in from the Picadilly Circus later in the day. I practiced more, but I sure-'nough ate less!

"I couldn't get used to havin' fish an' tomatoes with my cereal at breakfast. At our first dinner in London, we were served whole fish with the heads still on. That was too much for me. I couldn't eat my main course. At another dinner we were served stuffed grouse — I was told afterward. When I stuck my fork into the bird, it spurted blood. It was a rare bird, indeed. I suggested that they leave the feathers on one leg so we would know what kind of bird we were gettin'. I sure developed a bird-like appetite real quick. I like 'em cooked.

"Great Britain was still on war-time rationin', so it didn't set well with the British when they learned that the team was bringin' a ton of steaks, ham, an' bacon across the ocean with them, through the generosity of Bob Hudson. In fact, the press was full of food shortage messages an' cartoons showin' the American golfers carryin' a cow or pig off the boat. The meat was really intended to be shared with the British at the team dinners.

"Mr. Ben told us, 'We'll never have a piece of that meat while we're in England unless the British team sits with us.'

"But some people thought the Americans were tootin' their own horn. Captain Ben asked that the subject of the meat be dropped, 'cause we came over here to play golf, not talk about eatin'.

"I became good friends with my Rolls Royce chauffeur, who, like many chauffeurs an' cabbies, was a golf addict. He drove me every day to the Ganton Golf Club — a real scenic route to the famous Club located ten miles southwest of Scarborough. One night after we got back to the Grand Hotel, I told the driver to wait outside. I came back with a thick slab of Virginia ham between two slices of bread.

"The chauffeur said, 'That's more meat than I've seen in five years.'

"I told him, 'Well, don't just stand there an' look at it. Let's see what you can do with it.'

"He was grinnin' like he'd just won the Daily Double."

The British press reported that a "sensational eve-of-the-match club inspection gave an edge to the international clash," after a heated controversy erupted over the status of the clubs used by a British golfer. Taking a page from the 1947 Ryder Cup when Captain Henry Cotton insisted the entire American team file their clubs, Hogan charged that opponent Dick Burton's clubs were illegal and should be filed because they were scored too deeply. The British press made light of the "rough" club surfaces, which "enabled greater stop applied to the ball." They were "treated," submitted to Hogan, then sent back for more "treatment," because they did not conform to his requirements.

The night before the matches, Hogan called the nine-man team together. Bob Hamilton related that Ben stood up front and with real emotion told them how much he wanted to win, but he didn't want to hurt anyone's feelings.

"Eight of you play tomorrow in the foursomes, then eight of you play in the singles the next day," he said. All knew that one player would have to be left out each day.

Dutch spoke up, "Mr. Ben, leave me out of the foursomes tomorrow. I'll beat the devil out of somebody in the singles for you, but I don't believe ol' Dutch can go 36 holes two days in a row."

And he looked around the room at this array of the greatest players of his time (Skip Alexander, Jimmy Demaret, Bob Hamilton, Chick Harbert, Clayton Heafner, Lloyd Mangrum, Johnny Palmer, Sam Snead).

Ben looked Dutch straight in the eye, "Dutch, you are the last man in this room that I would leave off the team. You are my number one man."

Dutch always felt that was the greatest honor he could be paid. He wasn't a glory player, just a team player and these were team matches. He wanted to do what was best for the team.

The crowd of 7,000 watched the first day of the foursome matches and had much to cheer about even though it rained. One newspaper reported, "Great Britain beat America 3-1 today in the Ryder Cup foursomes. And you can keep saying that, because it makes the most beautiful piece of golf writing in years. No British Ryder team has had such a lead. If we win half of tomorrow's eight single matches, the Cup is ours. Oh, what a wonderful change from explaining away no-alibi teams and playing coroner at the inquests into British failures... that burst of cheering and the waves of clapping that rejoiced over the winning putt by Dick Burton in the last foursome was music... Burton had gone out coldly angry after the clubs incident... but he found the clubs just right today... at every hotel in Scarborough there are celebration parties."

Another newspaper responded, "Britain was in the ascendancy (today) and as the rain came pouring down in the afternoon, American hopes were washed away."

Clearly, the British were hungry for their first Ryder Cup victory since 1933 and the odds were now overwhelmingly in favor of the hosts.

"I was pretty down after that first round," recalled Dutch. "An' I sure was sick of seeing so much heather — especially that prickly gorse. You could lose your caddie in that stuff— ya need a sledge hammer to get out of it. I told my chauffeur that Mr. Hogan would probably replace our Rolls Royces with lorries an' that we'd dadgum better turn things around tomorrow.'

"He patted me on the shoulder an' says, 'You bloody well will, mate. I'll knock you up in the morning.'

"Well, I did a double-take on that. Over in England that means he'll pick me up in the mornin'. He was such a nice gentleman."

On the second day, spectators turned out in force. National passions soared and the applause swelled as each British-Irish golfer was introduced. Max Faulkner was the British 'Number One' golfer and was to play Dutch in the first singles match. His many successes in representing Great Britain were extolled, and his accolades seemed interminable.

Then it came time for Dutch. The announcer proclaimed, "And now on the first tee representing the United States of America, former Ryder Cup player, E.J. 'Dutch' Harrison." Dutch smiled and tipped his cap. He wasn't overawed. He was ready.

On the first holes, Dutch chatted and visited with the crowd. He was his amiable, loose self. And his buttering up of his opponent exceeded the customary spirit of open friendship and good neighbor policy between the United States and Great Britain. He had complimented Max Faulkner off the tee and then also with his long irons, "Nobody hits irons better than you, Mr. Faulkner."

Then on his putting, "That's the greatest putt

anyone could possibly make, Mr. Faulkner."

Finally, Faulkner stopped and said in his clipped British accent, "Mr. Harrison, you've been telling me how well I drive, how well I hit my irons, and how well I putt. How is it that I'm three down to you?"

News that Dutch had scored five 3's on the first six holes spread like wildfire and ignited the Americans. By the time Dutch reeled off six birdies on the first nine holes, American hopes had been revived. Dutch turned his match into a rout and won 8 and 7. "I got outta the box pretty good," he admitted.

Dutch returned to the course after his victory to become part of the large gallery and cheer on his teammates. The adrenalin was running high for all of the team as they forged from far behind and captured five of the first seven 36-hole matches. Lloyd Mangrum added the capper in squeezing out a tight victory over Fred Daly and the Americans won the matches 7 and 5.

"Thanks to Mr. Ben, we really cleaned their Big Ben clocks that last day!" Dutch ventured.

The British press was kind to the winners, particularly Dutch. They had already dubbed him "Happy Boy," and he was chosen the most popular member of the American team.

Before the final day's play began, Dutch was quoted as saying, "I've seen sicker dogs than this get well."

The *Sunday Chronicle* added, "This sick American dog (Dutch) not only got well, but jumped over the moon and ran away with the dish and spoon." Another newspaper reported, "That wasn't a match — it was a visitation from God." Dutch's day at Ganton had taken on a mythical, almost divine note, and the press had been awestruck.

Henry Longhurst, revered columnist with the *Sunday Times* of London, and prominent amateur golfer, commented: "Harrison's iron play was a joy to watch and so was his demeanor and attitude towards the game and his unsuccessful opponent."

It was in the London Match-Play championship the following week that the British sporting world was truly bedazzled by a heart-rending display of sportsmanship by Dutch.

Desmond Hackett memorialized it in the *London Daily Express* of September 21, 1949: "The picture of 'Happy Boy' Dutch smiling over his grand, honest face with a massive hand outstretched to congratulate Fred Daly on his 19th hole win...was a sporting print to remember. No wonder the crowd cheered big Dutch all the way back down the fairway and to the clubhouse."

This came after what the British press termed ". . . the worst display of golf manners ever shown by a crowd. Three times Dutch's shots hit spectators who strayed onto the fairway... At the sixth hole play was held up after Dutch politely requested the crowd to move back and they refused. At the 14th hole he had to play a blind shot to the green because the crowd wouldn't move."

This shot went into a bunker and cost him the hole. On the 17th hole, "the big-hearted Harrison gallantly picked up Daly's ball instead of asking him to hole out a 4-foot putt."

A band struck up "When Irish Eyes Are Smiling," on the 18th hole for benefit of Irishman Daly. He later conceded the emotional rendition supplied the inspiration he needed to tie Dutch on that 18th hole. Some members of the British press may have been almost as partisan as the crowd, but their admiration of Dutch was unrestrained.

Before the American team left England, the British government decreed a 30% cut in the value of the pound sterling. Bob Harlow, writing in *Golf World*, observed that this act of financial legerdemain had "wounded the American team squarely in the pocketbook, a notably cruel place to cut a pro golfer." The rush for steamship tickets was immediate.

While hastily stuffing his colorful wardrobe into suitcases, Jimmy Demaret was quoted as saying, "What we want from this country right now is out. I feel like a rat deserting a sinking ship, but I want to get back to where I can play for those good old American dollars."

"It was a weak an' tired crew of golfers that returned to New York following a rough voyage on the Queen Mary," recalled Dutch. "Skip Alexander an' I were supposed to play an exhibition in London, an' return a little 'track green' to my pocket, but both of us were so anxious to return home that we bowed out an' flew home at our own expense. I loved the British an' Irish people, but ya know, I came back home awful appreciative of how good we Americans have it. You sure learn quick what good ol' fashioned patriotism is all about."

The year 1949 was an Olympic year for Dutch when he brought home gold medals from international competition and achieved prominence from the Ryder Cup matches. Dutch was on the Ryder Cup team in 1951 at Pinehurst, North Carolina, and although he was present for the team photograph, he didn't play because of a virus. He was selected again to play in the Ryder Cup matches at Wentworth, England in 1953, but declined with thanks "because of club duties."

His moments for sharing in the national pride of the Ryder Cup event were past history, but he, like other Americans, would never forget the crowning glory of victory...the raising of the British and American flags...playing of the national anthems, the team camaraderie, the pageantry, and the atmosphere charged with emotion.

The Canadian Open

Previously, the newspapers had treated Dutch as a steady contender, but not a champion. Now, as more than one journalist recognized, . . . "Dutch made practically no noise in the newspapers, but if you look closely, you saw that approximately every ten minutes Old Dutch was taking in another $600 or $800. When you realize that in 1948 Harrison won twice as much money as such highly publicized and excellent golfers as Sam Snead, Porky Oliver, and Lawson Little, the whole thing becomes slightly amazing."

In June of 1949, Dutch entered the Canadian Open, which he rated next in importance to the U.S. Open, PGA, and Masters. He made a big hit in Toronto where he led after all four rounds, winning the tournament by four strokes and clipping seventeen strokes off par "with the ease of an expert pruning trees."

Dutch proved as popular in Canada as in the United States and elsewhere. A crowd of 3,000 was drawn by Canada's equivalent of the U.S. Open. Nick Weslock, member of Canada's Golf Hall of Fame, could not recall a larger, more enthusiastic Open crowd than attended the presentation ceremony for Dutch: "His deportment and kindness to the gallery was a pleasure to experience — a 'Southern Gentleman,' indeed. He was the 'Flying Dutchman' in this show."

The newspapers were intrigued with his nonchalant manner on the golf course: "There was none of that hush, hush business for the gallery. He joked with them, ladled out advice to young Fred Hawkins and praise for Jim Turnesa. The gallery did everything but walk in Harrison's shoes. At times, they hardly gave the players enough room to breathe, let alone make a difficult shot. Instead of dressing them down, Dutch remarked that they were 'a mighty fine collection of golfin' fans.' He played the final round in the same casual fashion he drawled words, kibitzing most of the way, and acting as if he were out for a practice round and not gunning for top money."

They quoted Dutch as saying, "Ya know, I had a hunch I'd win this one — I was at the peak of my game an' kept my edge right through this tournament. I just rolled 'em up an' played 'em safe on those last three holes. Iffen I'd had to, I could have shaved another two strokes on that final 18 an' possibly three." That would have tied the Canadian Open record.

The Western Open

At age 43, Dutch earned his first major American golf championship. Winning the Western Open in 1953 on the demanding Bellerive course in St. Louis was a significant milestone in his career.

This Open was considered a major golf championship in the '40s and '50s. Dutch posted rounds of 70-69-70-69—278 to finish four strokes ahead of Lloyd Mangrum, Ed Furgol and Freddie Haas, Jr., and won the $2,400 first prize before a final day crowd of 5,000.

"This victory soothes all wounds," cracked the Dutchman, who was recovering from an infected heel. "My heart is light even if my feet are heavy."

He credited a putting tip given by Johnny Palmer before the tournament with helping him win, "Johnny pointed out how I had fallen in the habit of laggin' my putts instead of goin' for the hole."

Australian "Dinkum Dazzler"

Dutch's visit to Australia in 1954 was a championship international golf tour that he fondly remembered, "It was almost 30 days of tournaments an' matches in October an' November. The Ampol Tournament at the Lakes in Sydney was the first big one that had Australia's best golfers playin' some of our best. U.S. Open Champion, Ed Furgol, was to captain our team but he tore a muscle in his arm shortly after arrival an' Dave Douglas had to fly in to take his place.

"We were playin' for high stakes that last round, but I tried to play like we were havin' a Sunday social round. I was playin' in a threesome with Ossie Pickworth, Australian Open Champion. We were tied comin' to the last hole an' some gentleman told me I needed a birdie to win on this par-5. Brother, it wasn't rain that was runnin' down my neck. I hit my second shot over the green, but chipped four feet from the hole. I had a breathless moment on that last putt — somethin' like seein' a motorcycle cop behind you when you're pushin' 60. Fellah, I can tell you the cheers of the crowd on that birdie putt made the sweetest music I ever heard. Musta been 10,000 spectators that Sunday. You woulda thought an Australian won the tournament. I just got to the wire ahead of Mr. Ossie. Ol' Lady Luck was on my side.

"The fans were simply too marvelous for words. What do they feed 'em —besides vitamin pills? They almost ran me over pattin' me on the back an' shoutin', 'Good on ya, Dutch.' When I sank that winnin' putt, a half dozen guys started shakin' my hand like it was a car jack. Lordy, what's a dislocated collar bone when you're among friends!

"I had trouble handlin' the smaller Australian ball in those howlin' gales — they weren't just ordinary winds. But when we went to Perth it was perfect weather — just like Florida at its best. We played a four-day series of 36-hole double an' single matches.

"During the matches I had a hard time keepin' peace between Norman von Nida of Australia an' Tommy Bolt. After Tommy was beaten in their match, von Nida said to me, 'You told me this guy was a nice man.'

"I said, 'He is a nice man, but with his temper you don't have to get him mad. Startin' an argument with him is the worst thing you can do.'

"Von Nida said, 'I'm gonna give him a whippin'.' Now he weighs 130 an' Tommy is a big guy. You should have seen Tommy's eyes bulge. Von Nida persisted, 'Close those locker room doors. Once I give him a good whippin' that will straighten him out.'

"I told 'em they were behavin' like Brahma bulls. I don't know how I managed to keep them apart, but I did.

"Tommy had about four clubs when he left Australia because he had broken so many. He wanted to borrow some of mine to use in Hawaii, but I told him that I just couldn't afford to lose any of my favorites.

"Tommy reminded me a bit of that myna bird in Australia. He would fly over ya an' take a whack at ya.

Ya just didn't mess with him. When ol' 'Thunder an' Lightning' played with Porky Oliver it was a real show. Porky was golf's good humor man — I never saw him get mad at anyone. I recall playin' with Porky an' Tommy in the Colonial Invitational in Fort Worth. It was in the days when Tommy's temper was like TNT. He kept wantin' to break his putter, but Porky kept talkin' him out of it.

"When Tommy finished puttin' on the 18th green, Porky said, 'Tommy, let me see that putter.'

"Tommy handed it to him an' Porky reared back an' threw it into the lake. Ya shoulda heard the spectators howl.

"The Australians organized good tournaments. We were guaranteed $5,000 to appear an' on top of that we had the winnin's from the tour, so I came back with a mint an' six boxes of those big, long Australian cigars. I loved the land and its people — they were beautiful."

The Australians felt likewise about Dutch whose army of followers down under resembled Arnie Palmer's in the 1960s. Dutch won many friends for American golf and even had to take the phone off the hook several times because of calls from female admirers. The *Sydney Morning Herald* called him "a beautifully balanced player with a perfect temperament." As the Australians might say, the trip was "a dinkum-dazzler" for Dutch.

U.S. National Senior Opens

Another tournament with international competition in which Dutch excelled was the U.S. National Senior Open. Dutch won five Senior Opens in the '60s after reaching age 50. Following the 4th win in a row, scribes began calling the tournament "The Dutch Harrison Benefit" and "The Dutch Treat."

When Dutch entered the tournament for the first time in 1961 he won by 11 strokes, an awe-inspiring 15 strokes under par on four different golf courses in the Palm Springs area. The next year he repeated and again spread-eagled the field on the same courses.

The media descended on Dutch and photographed him riding a camel. Dutch quipped, "These critters are mighty friendly, but they remind me of some of those horses I've lost money on — painfully slow an' inconsistent."

In 1963 Dutch again waltzed through a competitive field, this time in Phoenix. He won the Senior Open by 10 strokes and tied the tournament record.

The gambling center of Reno was the backdrop for Dutch's fourth straight Open victory in 1964. After coming from behind to win by one stroke with a birdie on the last hole, Dutch pocketed the first prize of $5,000 and headed for the casinos. He celebrated at Charlie Mape's Hotel with Jimmy Demaret who sang with the band and entertained all night. At the crap tables, the crowd swelled when Dutch began talking to the dice.

He'd shout, "Here's seven for the caddie." To Charlie Mapes he confided, "I still love to play craps."

In 1965, Dutch arrived in Las Vegas seeking his 5th tournament victory in a row. Dutch and Marty Furgol went to a private club for a practice round. Marty related what happened when the guards wouldn't let them enter without more identification. "Dutch suggested to me that we withdraw from the tournament and have some fun in Las Vegas. I tried to talk Dutch out of withdrawing, but he was more persuasive. So we took it easy for the next four days."

By the time Dutch took the Open title in 1966, Thelma had run out of shelf space to display his winning trophies. After placing second to Tommy Bolt in the 1968 Open, Dutch said, "I've been a roamer all my life. I've played in more golf tournaments than any man, livin' or dead (no exaggeration in 1968). How times have changed. When I started to play tournament golf, Hoover was President, the country was dry, an' Arnold Palmer wasn't even born. I won $100 in my first tournament in 1937 an' $1,000 when I won the Bing Crosby in 1939. Today, the purses have skyrocketed, Arnold Palmer is a millionaire, an' golfers like Arnie fly their own jet plane. But maybe I wasn't meant to be rich."

Special Awards

Dutch received a series of coveted awards for his International Championship Days. He accepted them with characteristic humility. In November 1954, Dutch won the PGA Vardon Trophy for the annual lowest average score of any tour pro.   Consistency was his strong suit and he was known as one of the steadiest in golf. After winning the trophy, Dutch thanked everyone for treating him so well and told the throng, "Now I'm goin' to travel less an' try to enjoy family life more!"

On November 27, 1962, Dutch was inducted into the PGA Hall of Fame in Palm Beach, Florida, the only golfer elected by initial vote that year.   This honor is accorded to relatively few in the golf profession.

At the awards ceremony, PGA President Lou Strong said, "Dutch was selected by the PGA for this honor not only for his fine golf over a span of years, but also for his friendliness, understanding of golfers, whether experts or duffers, and his humorous speeches."

Dutch responded, "Bein' named to the Hall of Fame is the greatest thing that ever happened to me. It's quite a thing for an ol' cotton-picker."

Afterwards, Dutch said, "It's been a wonderful life. I started out as a caddie in Arkansas, an' that's a tough state to dig out a quarter. Ben Hogan an' Sam Snead were the finest I ever saw. Ben worked harder an' was more determined than any player, but my old buddy, Jimmy Demaret, could have been the greatest if he had worked harder. He was somethin' like me — he enjoyed himself out there. Arnold Palmer is the best right now, but Jack Nicklaus could be the man in two more years — if he would learn to play a little faster. This boy Nicklaus, he's a real gunner — even with those little hands..."

In January 1963 Dutch flew to Little Rock to be inducted into the Arkansas Hall of Fame. He stayed with Harry Lasker, a good friend from his caddying days. The first morning when Harry awakened Dutch, Dutch opened his eyes and said, "Thank you, Mr. Harry. I'll get up right away, Mr. Harry."

Harry told him, "For goodness sakes, Dutch, stop calling me mister."

True to form Dutch responded, "Sure, Mr. Harry. I sure will, Mr. Harry."

The first night of the festivities Dutch charmed the crowd of 50 guests with his stories and impromptu comments. He had become "golf's greatest storyteller." He pointed to Ray Winder in the audience as he exclaimed, "There is the man who turned me pro! That was in 1930 when Ray Winder put on a tournament (Arkansas Open) for all the pros. He handed me the first prize money of $100 an' that made me a pro. But you know, I never did get to spend that check. I put the check on my dresser at home that night, an' either my mother or a robber got it."

Dutch then pointed to broadcaster Joe Garagiola, master of ceremonies, and kidded Garagiola about being too young to caddie when Dutch was pro at Old Warson. Turning to Jack Pickens, President of the Hall of Fame, he said, "I used to caddie for Mr. Pickens. He wore tennis shoes an' I went barefoot. He helped me buy my first suit. I bought it at a place where you paid a dollar now an' a dollar when they caught up with you. I also bought a pair of English walking shoes with buttons on them an' a straw hat."

At the following evening's banquet Dutch was made a member of the Arkansas Hall of Fame with Clyde "Smackover" Scott, football and Olympic champion. In attendance at the dinner that evening were Governor Faubus, numerous dignitaries and sport celebrities such as Stan Musial, Joe Garagiola and former inductees, Bill Dickey and Lon Warneke. Dutch was presented with a plaque by Ted Darragh and toasted as "having more natural ability and more knowledge of golf than anyone in the game."

Dutch responded, "I know if it wasn't for certain people in this room I wouldn't have made it. Curran Conway — stand up, Mr. Conway — gave me encouragement to play, or I'd been pickin' cotton. This other man, Herman Hackbarth, taught me golf, an' I pestered him until he did. One of my most wonderful friends is Henry Levy, who pulled me out of many jams. There are many others who have been wonderful to me."

Nine years later Dutch was commissioned by the State of Arkansas as Arkansas Traveler, an "Embassador of Goodwill from Arkansas to the people of other states, the people of nations beyond the borders of the United States or wherever this Embassador of Arkansas may hereafter travel or reside."

It was an honor befitting the man who distinguished himself as a world traveler and whose motto, "have golf shoes, will travel," so aptly reflected his talents and charm. Dutch was the first American golfer whose popularity was based as much on charisma as on golf prowess itself.

Showtime

I've got the world on a string
Sittin' on a rainbow,
Got the string 'round my finger,
What a world, what a life...

from "I've Got the World on a String"
by Ted Koehler

Dutch's flair for showmanship began in 1932 when he put on exhibitions between games at the Little Rock baseball park hitting 9-iron shots over the center field fence and striking targets to the pleasure of the crowd.

Vaudeville

In January, 1941 Billy Sixty of the *Milwaukee Journal* wrote, "Dutch gave me one of the finest extemporaneous chats on the radio I've had the delight to hear on the air," and suggested, "If Dutch decides to give up golf, he might hit the circuit as an entertainer."

Dutch joined Rocky Marciano on the vaudeville circuit, while Rocky was reigning as World Champion Heavyweight.

"I'd storytell an' talk to the folks, then hit cotton balls into the audience," Dutch recalled.

On the stage Dutch was known for his superb timing with impromptu remarks. His lines were five parts humorous and five parts down-home humble.

"I worked some shows in Seattle, then in Canada. Gayle Sayers of the Chicago Bears appeared with us. I also MC'd some stag shows, but I'd never work a show where they used bad language or told dirty jokes — those I'd hear an' try to forget 'cause there were so many good clean stories. We'd have about ten people on the shows an' I was generally back there waitin' my time to talk."

While speaking at luncheons and dinners, Dutch would bring down the house and be given standing ovations.

"His charm always left us smiling and refreshed," recounted Jack Berkley.

Forrest Tucker, a true Irishman who loved drinking, golf, and acting, recalled Dutch's soft-spoken nature and slow drawl, "He would call me, 'Mr. Fo-est.' His easy manner appealed to me and I asked him to 'lay more on me.' We became good friends. Dutch moved about as fast as a turtle and I could always relax with him and enjoy his camaraderie — unlike Mickey Rooney whom I dearly loved, but could only take for about four hours at a time because he was so hyperactive."

In the late 1940s, Dutch received a letter thanking him for his stunt of driving his golf ball from a grapefruit in tournament play at the Harlingen Open in the Rio Grande Valley, citrus capital of Texas. The favorable publicity generated was welcomed by sponsors and gallery alike.

"I was kidded," said Dutch, "as bein' the only grapefruit driver in the game."

Three-Ring Circuses

Golf tournaments gradually became three-ring circuses, combining a professional-amateur contest with the regular tournament plus clinics. Audiences became enchanted with the televised Bing Crosby National Pro-

Am tournament that illuminated public celebrities: Phil Harris and Jack Lemmon appeared on screen while encountering the average golfer's dilemmas of hitting out of the brush or failing to get out of a bunker. Indeed, the pro-am, generally a one-day tournament before the regular tournament, was a legacy of the first Bing Crosby tournament and more than likely paid the expenses of most tournaments. Dutch attributed the rise of golf in the 1950s not only to television, but to President Eisenhower's enjoyment of the sport, the thrill of Arnold Palmer's style, and the many contributions of entertainers like Bob Hope and Bing Crosby.

"The ol' game has come a long way," drawled Dutch, "since Henry Flagler, Mr. Florida, insisted golf was just a fad an' would soon pass. Lordy, I'd say its elevator is still risin', an' will keep on risin'."

Dutch's Patter

The advent of television brought the personality of Mr. Dutch to a much wider audience. David Akana remembers when he and Raymond watched Dutch's first TV performance.

"It was after the Bing Crosby Pro-Am about 1954 and Dutch was on the Colgate Comedy Hour. At the end of Dutch's lines, he started to walk off stage. Phil Harris had to run after him and literally pull him back. From the expression on Dutch's face, we could tell he was nervous, but he did well in public appearances to follow."

Golf emerged as a gold mine, and NBC's "World Championship Golf" in 1959 proved just that. Billed as a World Series of Golf with leading pro golfers as contestants, emcee Bob Crosby proved as entertaining a host as his singing brother, Bing. Matched with Dutch's magnetic personality as color commentator, the Saturday show lit up screens all across the country.

In one televised match, Dutch dramatically described the final difficult putt that Cary Middlecoff needed to win the match. "This is sure a pressure-cooker for $10,000.

If he plays it jus' right, he'll have 'nough gold to last a dentist like Dr. Cary a lifetime. But ya know, Mr. Bob, ever'body has his chokin' price."

"And what is your choking price, Dutch?" asked Bob Crosby.

"Ooooh, a dollah!"

As one pro observed, "If Dutch was as good with his putter as he was with his patter, he'd have won all of the tournaments. He brought out the best in Bob Crosby and Bob brought out the best in Dutch. If Dutch had been announcing a croquet match, people would tune in."

Dutch carried the message of golf around the globe with some choice interpretations of the English language.

About his English, Dutch commented, "I guess I was sometimes like Dizzy Dean when a schoolteacher told him that he didn't know the King's English. He answered, 'Heck, I don't care if he is.'"

Dutch became the prince of showmanship with his characteristic unsmoked cigar waggling in front of his nose.

He might comment, "When you're a winna', you can afford a dinna'." Or he'd say, "Ohhhh, that's a mean putt, Mr. Bob, a m-m-m-mean putt."

Once when a pro fell far behind, Dutch commented, "I think he's got about as much chance as a one-legged man in a butt-kickin' contest."

Peter Thomson recalled how Dutch influenced the Japanese language in the early 1960s as television commentator. "When a golfer reached a green with his shot, Dutch's phrase, 'Nice on'— became a part of the Japanese culture."

Dutch greatly simplified the art of golf to listeners: "There's not much more to golf than ya can shake a stick at. It's jus' like sweepin' the floor. Ya take it back an' ya bring it through — an' ya jus' keep hittin' the little ball 'til it goes in the hole."

Dutch would explain how difficult a shot was and what was in the mind of each competitor. When it became possible to create the instant play-back, his analyses of the shot techniques in slow motion were of equal interest to the audience. One pro described him as a cross between Dizzy Dean, Will Rogers, and Bob Burns.

Dutch could be the subject of television scripts like this one:

Comedian: How does Dutch finance all his race track bets?

Straight Man: Pigeons! Amateurs who think they can beat Dutch.

Comedian (to audience): Why is he staring at me?

Straight Man: Did you ever play Dutch?

Comedian: Sure, and I almost beat him. I was even until the last hole when we doubled the bet. Hey, wait a minute! You don't think...he...

Straight Man: Welcome to the flock!

College of Golf

Pro-am tournaments were great fun for the amateur, especially those receiving tips from Dutch who often became more concerned with their game than his own. "Being around him was like going to the College of Golf," one amateur said. Dutch's enjoyment of the pro-ams is indicated by his record of winning so many.

Dutch often appeared at exhibitions and clinics held in connection with the pro-ams or would go on exhibition tours where he demonstrated his repertoire of shots to the delight of the crowd. The announcer would say, "Dutch, show our guests how you can drive the ball to Hot Springs" (or whatever the next town was) and Dutch would respond by hitting the ball out of sight as the crowds oohed and aahed. After his demonstration he'd take the microphone and explain with his typical finesse and humor how simple is the game of golf — that is if your name was "Dutch" Harrison.

A crack amateur told of Dutch's remarkable demonstration of approach shots at these exhibitions, "He'd take his wedge and hit balls to the green from about 100 yards. "He'd tell the crowd, 'Now this ball will land beyond the hole, then spin back to the hole.' Applause. 'My next shot will land to the right of the hole an' end up on the left of the hole.' Louder applause. 'Next, the ball will strike to the left of the hole and wind up just to the right of the hole.' Thunderous applause. It was uncanny. He could take that wedge of his and make it do whatever he wanted."

The Duke of Windsor

One of Dutch's favorite partners in eastern pro-am events was the Duke of Windsor. Dutch met the Duke in 1940 at the exclusive Seminole Golf Club in North Palm Beach, where the annual Latham R. Reed Pro-Am was played between 1937 and 1961 with the exception of the war years. It was a fancy affair with a lot of wealthy amateurs playing with the golf professionals. Of the elite, Dutch said, "Some of those fellers were so high-collared they couldn't see the sun exceptin' at high noon. On the first tee when Mr. Duke pulled out one of those flat English wood clubs, teed the ball real high, an' then dug a divot on his practice swing, I knew right then my winnin's was in jeopardy.

"After my first meetin' with Mr. Duke, a couple of the sponsors took me aside an' talked to me about not speakin' too much to the Duke until I was spoken to. They told me he was the man who gave up his crown for the woman he loved, Ms. Wallis Simpson, an' left England to marry in France — then became Governor of the Bahamas durin' World War II. They explained to me that Mr. Duke was an honorary member of the Seminole Golf Club an' they wanted me to treat him respectfully as His Royal Highness. They talked about the Duchess as 'Your Grace.' I was tempted to call her Mrs. Grace, but wound up callin' her Mrs. Duchess. Your Grace an' Your Royal Highness were too high-falutin' for me. But I was always polite an' respectful to her. She was quite a dresser, an'

174

I guess she should be, 'cause they carried 'bout 100 pieces of baggage — mostly hers. She favored the arts, which he found borin' an' he loved golf, which she found borin'.

"Mr. Duke had been playin' golf since he was fourteen. When he was Prince of Wales, he was captain of a royal golf club. In the Bahamas an' Florida he'd love to play golf every day. He would phone me an' say, 'Oh, it's the Duke. Would you be able to join my greensome?'

"He was pleasant to play with — never made excuses 'bout his poor shots. When he hit one, he'd say, 'Dreadful, dreadful.' After he'd miss a short putt, he'd say, 'By jove, I missed it.' Once I told him to hit his drive toward the right side of the fairway. He swings an' hooks the ball far to the left.

"I said, 'Oh Mr. Dukie! You done knocked it out there on the beach. You're out there with the sharks!'

"He says, 'Tch, tch, tch — what a pity.'

"Everyone recognized him in those baggy knickers an' old pullover sweater. He'd bring his dogs onto the golf course — I remember once he stopped playin' an' rushed one of his dogs to the hospital, 'cause the dog was limpin' behind a bit. But he was sort of a miser when it came to tippin' the caddies.

"I had some fun times with Mr. Duke. In the Bahamas we were playin' in a pro-am an' the Duke had played over his head on holes 15 and 16. "I said to him, 'Mr. Dukie, you can let up now. I'll carry it the rest of the way.'

"At the Greenbrier Pro-Am I had Mr. Duke as a partner an' I was on the green in two an' he was in the trap in six. He called me over and asked, 'How should I play it, explode or chip it?' I didn't have the heart to tell him to pick up.

"One year at the Seminole, Mr. Duke placed his approach shot about three feet from the hole. He had a downhill putt, the toughest kind. I coached him a long time before he hit it. He slid it about four feet past the hole, missed it coming back, then missed it again an' I don't think he's holed out yet. When the scorekeeper asked me what he had, he answered, 'Four'.

"Well, that shook the scorekeeper an' it shook me, so she asked me what to do an' I told her, 'Lady, if Mr. Duke of Windsor says he had a four, he had a four.'

"At those celebrity turnouts there were people like Connie Mack, Babe Ruth, Dizzy Dean an' a bunch of princes, princesses, an' other royalty. The Duke an' Duchess would invite us to dinner — that's where those fingerbowls really threw me."

Bob Hamilton recalled one of the first rounds Dutch played with the Duke of Windsor. "On the first hole Dutch put his arm around the back of the Duke of Windsor and said, 'Come on Dukie, we've got to getum.'

"When Dutch did that, about three secret servicemen started to grab him, but to Dutch it didn't make any difference. After one of those rounds, the Duke, who liked Dutch so much, slipped him a couple of $100 bills. Mr. (R.R.) Young, head of New York Central — we called him Railroad Young — motioned as if to remove the money from Dutch's pocket and said, 'Dutch, you know the Duke is a guest of mine in this country and we don't do things like this.'

"Dutch replies, 'I know that, but I'll tell you what, Mr. Young. You run that railroad, an' me an' the Duke will get along just fine.'

"And he pushed that $200 deep into his pocket and grinned at Mr. Young. The Duke loved it — he wouldn't play without Dutch. He'd always say, 'I want Dutch for my partner.'"

Phil Harris

Dutch and Phil Harris formed a popular showtime team on the course and on the stage. Phil, orchestra leader, comedian, actor and singer, was a throwback to the romantic legend that the 18-hole golf course is related to the 18-jigger bottle of Scotch that was to be drained by a golfer at the rate of one jigger per hole.

As Phil would kid, "I truly can't remember when I had a pure glass of water. You've gotta put something in it. Dutch never put a little something in his, but I sure did."

Dutch and Phil always put on a show, especially on the golf course. "Ol' Mr. Phil liked to play the course sideways an' be in the brush an' trees where he could take a nip unobserved. I think he had more Jack Daniel labels in his golf bag than club labels," Dutch said.

The most memorable moment for Dutch and Phil came during the week of the Bing Crosby Tournament in 1951. Phil tells the story.

"This was my first year with Bing and Dutch. I was the amateur and Dutch was my pro. I bought ourselves into the Calcutta pot and we sold for practically nothing, you know, because at that time I was a 12 handicap and I probably played higher than that. But Dutch and I just seemed to ham-'n'-egg it and we played well together. We had a best ball of 59 in one round and that was some sort of record. Well, in that last round we were playing Pebble Beach. Byron Nelson and Ed Lowery were the other twosome with us. It was a storybook finish.

"We were on the 17th hole and it was cold and blustery. All of us had to use drivers into the wind on this par-3, but Dutch used a 3-wood and drove his ball over the green and into the ocean.

"I managed to slice the ball onto the right corner of this kidney-shaped green that had a big hump right through the middle of it and the pin was on the other side of the hump about 65 feet away from my ball. My caddie, Scorpy, comes over to me and says, 'You're gonna have to hit the ball off the green to get over the hump and down to the hole. You see that brown spot up there? Well, just aim for the left corner of that circle.'

"So I start to putt and he says, 'Hold it'. Now there is a tremendous crowd around the green because we're leading the tournament by one stroke and Scorpy had never done this before. He comes over and says, 'Aim for the center of that little brown patch.' Well, that's a difference of about one inch. So I hit the ball and it goes way up off of the green, makes a left-hand turn, then goes downhill—right into the cup. You know, I've putted on that green for over 30 years since that time and every time I tried that same putt I couldn't get within 15 feet of that hole.

"Well, after I made that putt I said, 'This is a terrible blow to clean living.'

"When the newsboys asked Scorpy, 'How long was that putt that Mr. Harris sank on 17?', he said, 'Well, I don't know how long it was, but I'd like to have that much frontage on Wilshire Boulevard.'

"And then they asked, 'Well, was it 40 or 50 feet?' Scorpy said, 'The putt broke that much.'"

Dutch told the rest of the story, "When Mr. Phil sank that putt, everybody went bananas. It put us three shots ahead with one hole to play. Mr. Phil's legs almost buckled an' tears were streaming down his face. He was shakin' all over. He told me he didn't know if he could play that last hole so I told him, 'You just put your clubs away an' head for the clubhouse. I'll take it from here.'

"So I played that last hole myself. Even with the wind blowin', No. 18 was the purtiest hole I ever played. Thanks to Mr. Phil's wonderful putt we won that pro-am with a near-record score. You know, the greatest thing Mr. Phil did was to offer Scorpy, a heavy drinker, his own share of the pro-am prize an' Calcutta money if Scorpy would promise never to take another drink. He arranged to get Scorpy a job at Tamarisk Country Club in Palm Springs an' old Scorpy probably owes his life to the pledge he made to Mr. Phil."

Dutch and Thelma stayed with Phil and Alice Faye while in Palm Springs, beginning in 1953 with the first Thunderbird Invitational. They enjoyed the comfortable ambiance of the Harris home and the beautiful oasis of golf course that rose from their patio door.

"You could walk right out on the sporty Thunderbird course from their home," Dutch recalled. "Miss Alice could really dole out a barrelful of good southern cookin' — fried chicken, black-eyed peas, cornbread an' all the trimmin's.

"An' Mr. Phil an' Miss Alice put on some rip-snortin' parties. I can remember Peter Lorre rearin' up from behind the bar an' those big rollin' eyes scarin' everybody to death."

Phil Harris may have been an unpredictable shotmaker, but he was as popular in pro-am tournaments as he had been on Jack Benny shows. The kinship of Mr. Phil and Mr. Dutch was treasured by both throughout their careers.

Dutch would joke about Phil adopting as his signature song, "That's What I Like to Hear about the South."

"I always thought you were from the South, Mr. Phil, but you're just a carpetbagger from Linton, Indiana," Dutch quipped.

The typical response in that molasses baritone was, "Dutch, I was eating more ham hocks and black-eyed peas in that Nashville area than you ever eyeballed."

John Raitt

John Raitt was another "singing cousin" of Dutch's. They were close on the golf course, at dinner shows and other social functions. Together they'd go to sports events. Kyle Burton, assistant pro to Dutch at Olympic Club, told this story about John and Dutch.

"Dutch was toying with going to the racetrack rather than playing in the Almaden Open in 1963. He recognized that I preferred to go to the tournament, so we drove to northern California in his big Lincoln. At each of the toll bridges out of San Francisco, I happened to be snoozing and Dutch paid the toll. I remember awakening at the second toll station to see Dutch looking over to see if I was awake and when he saw I was, he said, 'Mr. Kyle, would you be interested in eatin' an' drinkin' on the house at this tournament?' I told him that would be fine and he said, 'Mr. Kyle, just do as I say an' I'll work things out.'

"When we arrived at the golf club, Dutch met the manager and asked, 'How would you like to have John Raitt sing at the awards party after the tournament is over?'

"He said, 'That would be wonderful, Dutch. How can you arrange that?' (John Raitt had just become famous after appearing with Doris Day in the *Pajama Game*.)

"Dutch replied, 'I think I can arrange it but it will probably take quite a bit of expense to handle this if I get him to do it, 'cause he'll expect to be freeloaded.'

"The manager jumped at the opportunity. Dutch phoned John Raitt to be a spectator for a day and benefit from watching the pros. We waited after the tournament to see if he would appear. When John came in the door, there was a three piece combo with young students playing. Dutch knew that he would have to talk turkey to pull this one out.

"'Mr. John, the people here would love to hear you sing. I think it would be real nice if you could entertain the people a bit.'

"John questioned how he could sing with that combo. 'Oh, Mr. John, you'll be able to show them how great you are.'

"So John went over and made arrangements with the combo and entertained all of us. The people really loved it. That Sunday was a day I'll never forget. Not only did Dutch place second in the tournament, but he negotiated the coup of the tournament. To this day I don't believe John Raitt realized that his performance paid the expenses of Dutch and myself.

"Returning home, I remember that we got to the first toll gate and I was asleep again so Dutch paid for it. At the last toll gate, I had one eye open and Dutch looked over and winked at me and said, 'Mr. Kyle, three out of four is all you get!'"

Music City U.S.A.

Dutch joined the other pros and celebrities at the annual Music City U.S.A. Pro-Celebrity in Nashville, Tennessee, an event that could be as much entertainment as golf. Dutch's instructional show fit the music theme. He demonstrated — to music — how it's possible to swing imperfectly, but still hit the ball well if the swing is rhythmic.

"The average golfer," Dutch maintained, "shouldn't beat his head against the wall tryin' to create the perfect swing. He should be concentratin' on buildin' rhythm an' blendin' the swing into one smooth, continuous motion."

He was dubbed on the spot, "The Rhythm Man."

Music brought great joy to Dutch. He said, "I'm a country music man from way back, especially a fan of the 'King of the Country,' Roy Acuff. He mails me some of my favorite recordin's. An' I love Tennessee Ernie Ford, too."

Dutch's tastes in music were as varied as his one-liners and included jazz, polkas, Hawaiian melodies and Mexican music, particularly "Vaya Con Dios," the enchanting Spanish love theme.

"Thelma an' I would polka until all that whirlin' would make me dizzy. I guess I dance like I was plowin' the North 40."

Leading the Lawrence Welk band in *Moon River* was a special thrill for Dutch. Thelma had taught him to hula and with almost no hips and an atrophied behind he'd dance so that his pants would gradually fall down, much to the delight of his audience.

"Dutch would say, "I can sit on a dime an' have five cents showin'!"

Five-Star General

Many stories are told about Dutch and five-star General Hilario Moncado, a visionary guerrilla leader in

World War II, who later came to the U.S. to negotiate the Labor Organization for the Filipinos. He became so wealthy importing labor for agriculture and such an avid golfer that he sponsored a tournament every year at his nine-hole course in Stockton, California. Most pros thought of him as a charismatic, friendly Filipino. A very generous man, he would pay everyone to come to the tournament.

One pro said, "If a guy needed money, General Moncado would whip it out. Dutch and Porky Oliver were two of his favorites."

Dutch often spoke of his friendship with General Moncado, "He'd call me in Philadelphia an' say, 'Dutchy, we've got a pro-am on Monday. Can you be there?'

"An' I would usually say, 'General, I'll be there.'

"He sorta took a likin' to me an' ya know, he was almost as tall as me — unusual for a Filipino. He treated me like a member of royalty wherever I was with him — Hawaii, California, Mexico."

The General was also remembered for treating his caddies at the Stockton golf course like chickens. He'd come out with several rolls of dimes, and as he peeled off the rolls, he'd throw the dimes in the air and call, "Caddies, Caddies, Caddies."

His caddies would see to it that no one outdrove the General, except the professionals. If the General's drive from the tee was shorter than his competitors, the caddies would see that the ball was advanced the necessary distance by picking it up under their bare toes. The General was known to claim a hole-in-one on a green located over a hill from the tee, and was known to distort his score and hold a much higher handicap than deserved.

In one pro-am contest, General Moncado was playing with Dutch and Porky Oliver. After the game he drew them aside in the locker room.

"I'll give each of you $100 if you'll testify that I shot 78," the General earnestly requested.

"Oh, we couldn't do that," Porky answered.

"Now hold on a minute," Dutch cautioned Porky. "Personally, I thought he shot a 77."

Reportedly it was General Moncado who lodged his tee shot in the high crux of a tree during a pro-am. He surveyed the ball's precarious position, turned to Dutch, his playing partner, and asked, "How would you play that?"

Without hesitation, Dutch replied, "Under an assumed name."

Dutch handled the media as he handled golf, smooth and free-flowing. He liked all of the writers, interviewers and announcers and treated them with respect. They returned the compliment. "Dutch intoxicated us with that southern friendliness and knack for storytelling," said one writer. "He was always good copy."

Of greatest fascination to the tour pros was Dutch's delightful wit and humor as he entertained the golfers after a round.

Bob Goalby recalls, "Everybody loved it when Dutch held court. I'd heard some of the stories a hundred times, but I'd laugh every time 'cause he was so funny telling them. The tourney grind was lightened immeasurably when Dutch joined the entourage. He really enriched the game."

Bob Hamilton recalls when he and Dutch were principal speakers at a large Chamber of Commerce luncheon, "We were seated at a conspicuous head table breaking bread with an illustrious throng. I happened to look down the table a couple of seats and there is Dutch breaking his cornbread into a glass of milk. He smiles big at me and says, 'Boy, this is good eatin', Mr. Bob.'

"That was Dutch, bless his heart."

Touring and Forest Hills

"Meet me in St. Louie-Louie
meet me at the Fair...
Don't tell me the lights are shinin'
any place but there..."

from"Meet Me in St. Louis"
by Andrew B. Sterling

Dutch and Thelma accepted Judy Garland's tuneful invitation to St. Louis and returned in August 1964 to the riverland Dutch loved.

"I came back to hear the St. Louis Blues on my river," chortled Dutch.

Bless Mr. Barnes

Dutch was brought back by Donald L. Barnes Jr., son of the former President of the St. Louis Browns, to the Forest Hills Golf and Country Club on the old Barnes farm in the suburb of Clarkson Valley. Landing Dutch was tagged a "coup" by the local press.

"The Dutchman was sought not only for his personality and golf skills, but because his name and prestige will sell memberships, even before he arrives," recorded one paper.

Dutch called the plans for Forest Hills, a subdivision and 27-hole golf course under construction, "mighty interesting. Bless Mr. Barnes. He's creatin' some beautiful green areas to build homes around. Golf courses are good for everbody."

The Eastern Missouri Professional Golfers' Association held a welcoming dinner for Dutch to celebrate his return to St. Louis after his absence of four years. As principal speaker, Dutch kept his fellow pros in stitches with anecdotes. He also encouraged the younger pros to practice and hit at least 300 balls a day.

T.D. Morris, Old Warson's Assistant Professional from Ardmore, remembered Dutch's arrival, "The first thing Dutch did when he got into town was to phone me and see if everything was going all right. I thought Dutch might be a little miffed at me for not offering to assist him at Forest Hills, but he was gracious as always. He was more concerned that I was doing well at Old Warson than about my availability."

Forest Hills was officially opened early in 1965. Prior to the official opening, Dutch regarded the golf course as playable but somewhat primitive.

"The first members had to play through the deer, foxes and Canadian geese. I'll tell ya, if I ever got the concession of golf balls lost here, I would have it made," he said.

Dutch and Thelma purchased a spacious ranch-style residence in the nearby suburb of Chesterfield. It was located in the Four Seasons Development with a patio that faced the first fairway of the Four Seasons golf course. Dutch had a hedge of low, thick bushes placed along the backyard boundary with the fairway.

A friend asked, "What's that hedge for, Dutch?"

"Oh, Mr. Tim, that's for the li'l dividend I get ever' day. I poke through the bushes with my 9-iron an' find five to ten golf balls a day."

Tim Crowley, youthful crack amateur at Forest Hills recalled, "One day I took Dutch home and we were out picking balls out of the hedge when a little lady comes down the fairway with her golf cart. She hits this awful shot from in front of the hedge. Dutch says, 'Missus, let me help you. If you grip the club like this an' swing easily like this...'

"And he just seems to tap the ball with that lazy swing. The ball soars in a high arc and stops within three feet of the hole a hundred yards away. The lady exclaims, 'Oh my! Mister, you should be a pro!'

"Dutch replies, 'Oh, not me, Missus, not me — too many hazards for me.'

"Dutch's language was sprinkled with his own golf-isms. In describing how to get some place, he might say, 'That place is two 5-pars down the road.'

"In judging girls on the sidewalk while driving with male friends in Fort Lauderdale, I remember he'd point and say, 'That one will qualify, that one won't qualify — there's an unplayable lie.'"

Dutch dug in at the newly opened Forest Hills Country Club. He said of that opportunity, "The job freed me for the winter tour an' a few summer events if I felt like playin'. A good club pro can find at the end of the year he's made just as much profit as a tournament player, if he's done his job properly. I don't have the itch for tournament play like I did — a sign I'm no longer young. The game's a bunch of errors an' I can't seem to eliminate them like I used to.

"It can be lonely out there, especially for a wife. She's got to be able to live out of a suitcase. In my younger days we didn't have jet planes an' good roads. Travel was difficult. But today, the pro's wife still has to be able to take the travel, bein' away from home an' in new surroundin's. Some can't do it."

Thelma eventually became hooked on the horses just like Dutch. She'd go up to Dick Kohlmann, leading St. Louis golf pro and owner of West Par Golf Course, and ask, "Hey, Dick, I need a little money — can you help me out?"

Dick would never turn her down and on occasion would loan her $500 to $1,000.

"She'd always pay me back," Dick reflected. "She was honest as the day was long. She breathed sincerity and had that effervescent Dinah Shore-type personality."

Kimo became a good golfer and an assistant to Dutch. Another assistant pro was Skip Toler, son of Earl Toler, a good friend of Dutch's from Jonesboro, Arkansas. Dutch had suggested Skip go to college before fulfilling his ambition to be a pro golfer.

Pressed by Skip and with the encouragement of his father, Dutch agreed to train him at Forest Hills and offered him this piece of advice, "Son, you'll reap what ya sow — prezactly. You're goin' to have to give it more than a lick an' a promise if ya expect to be choppin' tall cotton."

About a year after Skip entered his apprenticeship, Dutch phoned his father. "Your son has gotten in with a bad crowd, Mr. Earl. If he were my son I'd come an' take him out of this environment."

Earl Toler did, and later reported, "Skip went to college and got back on track, thanks to the great humanitarian that Dutch was."

"Bessie"

Many new friendships were struck and old friendships renewed by Dutch while on tour. One of the most interesting characters whom Dutch called a close friend was Al Besselink. Described as a 6'3", 220-pound New Jersey accent, Besselink was a standout on the University of Miami golf team in the late 1940s when he met Dutch. He joined the professional tour in 1950. Although Dutch generally avoided tipplers and carousers, "Bessie" was the exception. His coolness under match pressure and his propensity for gambling attracted Dutch's attention immediately. Conversely, Dutch's laid-back manner and philosophy of "Gentlemen, light down, an' put your legs up," suited Besselink to a "T". Bessie entered the 1953 Tournament of Champions in Las Vegas as a 50 to

1 shot. Without hesitation he bet $1,000 on himself in the Calcutta pool. Sam Snead sold high for $16,500 in the pool, ahead of Dutch, Jimmy Demaret, and the 16 other pros who had won tournaments in the previous year. To the surprise of most everyone, the first prize of $10,000 was captured by Bessie. Moreover, his winning ticket returned him $50,000 from the bookies. With his bundles of green in his car trunk, he set out for the race track and card tables. Alas! By the end of the week no trace of the money was left.

One Sunday Dutch was sitting in the clubhouse with Thelma, Kimo, and Tim Crowley watching the conclusion of a tournament on television. They cheered for Bessie as he emerged another winner.

Dutch turned to Kimo and suggested, "Let's get Bessie on the phone." The conversation went something like this:

"Congratulations, Mr. Bessie. We saw you on TV. You won some good money."

"Yeah, Pops. I had a pretty good day." After exchanging pleasantries Dutch finally got to the subject of his call, namely the money Besselink still owed him.

"Mr. Bessie, are you goin' to bring back some of that money?"

"Don't worry about the money I won, Pops."

After the ensuing conversation, Thelma asked. "Well, what about the money? When are we going to get it back?"

Dutch replied, "Don't worry, Mom. He says he's goin' to limit his spendin' to $1,000 a day."

Bessie entered the pro shop at Forest Hills one afternoon with a wad of century notes clutched in one hand. "Hi, Mr. Bessie. Glad to see you have something for me," said Dutch.

"Oh, Mr. Dutch, if I paid you, then I'd be broke and then I'd have to come around and borrow more from you," Bessie replied.

"Well, all right, Mr. Bessie, you just keep it then." Dutch's spirit of generosity provided wonderful reinforcement for Bessie.

Tim Crowley followed behind Dutch and Bessie like a little mouse.

He reported, "Bessie would borrow $50 from Dutch even though he had a tab of $800 at the clubhouse. I asked, 'Bessie, are you doing all right?' He answered, 'Don't worry about anything. See these clothes? They have fooled many a dude!'

"Bessie always dressed right out of Esquire Magazine. One day when he was visiting Forest Hills and unloading his clubs from his Cadillac limousine, I complimented him on his sartorial splendor. Bessie said, 'These alligator shoes, Varela slacks and this checkbook have fooled a lot of people!'

"The Varela slacks were an expensive brand that cost $65 when most golf slacks were costing $25. One day Dutch asked Kimo to track Bessie down by phone on behalf of a golf salesman in the Clubhouse. Kimo finally located Bessie somewhere in Florida.

"Kimo asked, 'Do you want any Varela pants and if so, what color?'

"Bessie replied, 'Kimo, you know better than that. Don't call me and ask those kinds of questions. One of each color, of course!'"

Tim Crowley recalled a typical conversation when Al Besselink and Dutch would meet.

"Hey, Pops, how're you doing?"

"Pretty good, Mr. Bess. How are you doin'?"

"Oh, wonderful, Dutch. What's going on?"

"Not much, Mr. Bess. What's new?"

"Not much, Dutch. What's new with you?"

"Same ol' country store, Mr. Bess. Everythin' okay?"

"You bet, Pops. How's with you?"

"Okay, Mr. Bess. You got things under control?"

"Yeah, Pops, how about you?"

This brather-palaver would continue for four or five minutes without seeming to go anywhere. Their ability to varnish nonsense with the charms of sound was unsurpassed. In reality their camaraderie negated complicated dialogue.

The Jemseks

Joe Jemsek, entrepreneur elite in golf circles, met Dutch in Orlando in the winter of 1948, and became a lifetime supporter of the Arkansas Traveler. A husky ex-caddie of Russian ancestry, Jemsek acquired a fortune by owning and operating golf courses, such as St. Andrews, Cog Hill, Fresh Meadow and Glenwoodie near Chicago. He was affectionately known as "Chicago Joe" and "Mr. Public Golf" for being the leading promoter of golf on public courses and originator of golf on television in 1949. Dutch had represented Jemsek's St. Andrews course while on tour in 1949.

"Chicago Joe" invited Dutch, Thelma and family to stay at his house at St. Andrews many times. Dutch looked upon Joe as a close friend, father-figure, and a Daddy Warbucks, particularly when it came to the race track. Dutch would often drive the 300 miles to the Sportsman's Park race track in Cicero, near Chicago to meet Joe.

He'd say to Kimo, "We know where we can get a good meal," and they'd stop at St. Andrews for some of the club's thick pork chops.

Joe returned the favor. "I felt sorry for Dutch's financial condition and wanted to help him more, but he never wanted anything for himself. Dutch never had his hand out or took advantage of anyone. He would have received ten times more than I ever gave him, because I liked Dutch and wanted to help him. He wouldn't hurt a fly."

Dutch adopted Joe's son, Frank, as a golfing protegé at Forest Hills and introduced him to the professional tour.

"I had trouble keepin' him under my wing, 'cause he stood 6 foot, 8 inches barefooted... a nice young man an' a good golfer."

Frank was accustomed to hitting about 75 balls per hour in practice. "Dutch showed me how to hit 750 balls in a couple of hours in rapid-fire fashion. He would set the balls down in rows of 75 and hit one after another with that easy swing of his. I went on tour with Dutch and roomed with him. When cooking for himself, Dutch's favorite meal was putting three pans of water on the stove with potatoes in one pan, hot dogs in another, and corn-on-the-cob in the third. I remember we both liked ice cream. He told me he'd show me the best place to buy it. Turned out the place was across from the race track! Dutch always raided my ice cream in the refrigerator until I learned that he was allergic to strawberries. Then I started to buy strawberry ice cream.

"Dutch was unexcelled when it came to betting on golfers. He had that uncanny ability to measure golfers by selecting those with the most promise, and nursing them along to get the most of their playing talents. I remember playing in the Alvin Dark Invitational in Lake Charles, Louisiana in 1965. Dutch explained how I should play the course to take advantage of my abilities. I scored five to seven strokes better than in my college days at Loyola of New Orleans, but I really wasn't a better golfer. Dutch won the tournament in 1967 with two shots to spare even though he waited until the November 23 deadline to file his entry."

Lee Trevino

Lee Trevino, who has given many golf lessons on and off TV, received his first golf lesson from Dutch. He tells the story: "I was playing with Dutch Harrison in the Alvin Dark Invitational in 1964. We came to a par-3 on the first nine and I saw Dutch pull out a 3-iron on this 178-yard hole. He takes that big swing and hits the 3-iron about 15 feet short of the hole, walks over to his caddie, rolls that cigar in his mouth, and says, 'Man, I hit that thing hard!' I'm just standing there watching him put that 3-iron back into his bag.

"I knew that hole was 178 yards, so I said, 'Well, I'm going to hit it with my 4-iron.'

"I took that 4-iron, crushed that ball and hit a house in back of the green and the ball went out of bounds. So I put another ball down and hit a 6-iron right on the green. I'll never forget Dutch looking at me and saying, 'Son, that's your first lesson. Never look in anyone else's bag.'

I'll never forget that as long as I live.

"Actually, my first and only real golf lesson came from Dutch Harrison a year or two before," Trevino continued. "I didn't know much about Dutch Harrison, but I remember when he came to Dallas for the PGA Championship in 1963. He stayed with Hardy Greenwood, for whom I worked on the driving range.

"Hardy told Dutch, 'I've got a little munchkin kid out at the driving range that can really play. I'd like you to help him out a little bit.'

"Well, Dutch came out, got out of the car, and watched me hit some balls. He's rolling that cigar in his mouth and he says after a bit, 'All right, boy. You're all right, boy, but you gotta get that left hand over to the left a little more.'

"I did and hit about five or six more balls, and Dutch jumped in the car and left. As soon as he left, I put my left hand right back where I had it in the beginning because I didn't feel comfortable. But I cherished that moment, and when people say, 'Did you ever have a golf lesson?,' I'd say, 'Dutch Harrison taught me one time when I didn't know who Dutch Harrison was, but I didn't know who Ben Hogan was, or Jimmy Demaret, or Bobby Jones when I was a kid. In my opinion, Dutch was right up there with them, a real stepping stone in golf. But I never forgot that first and only lesson from Dutch."

San Antonio, Texas

Lee Trevino's sentiments were expressed by the 500 fans and golfers who jammed the Oak Hills Country Club ballroom to honor Dutch at the Texas Open of April 1965. The tournament was officially dedicated to him by the San Antonio Golf Association.

"I've always considered San Antonio my second home," Dutch said in grateful response during the evening's program.

"Your local pro, Harold Blaylock, an' I barnstormed around here durin' the Depression years before Harold became a golf instructor at Duncan Field. The first championship I ever won was the Texas Open in 1939. It was ace golfer John Reynolds who predicted on the radio here that I would win. In those days he was huntin' raccoons where this Country Club is now. Ever since my win I've had alotta friends here — friends who have helped me keep the ball outta the woods. Ya know, golf tournaments are lost, not won. I jus' keep playin' — waitin' for my competition to stub their toes. So far they've been real nice about stubbin' their toes."

Comments after the banquet were flattering.

"The big guy couldn't have been happier had he won the Masters. His talk was pure Dutch Harrison," said one golfer.

Said another, "I'll never forget his modest little speech of appreciation when he first won in 1939. The San Antonio Golf Association spontaneously threw him a celebration dinner and Dutch said, 'I'll try my best to win it again sometime.' He not only did win again, but he won the hearts and admiration of San Antonio just like he did tonight..."

Echoed another fan, "The 1965 Texas Open belongs to Dutch — they couldn't dedicate it to a more deserving guy."

It had been 26 years since Dutch won the Texas Open with a record score, 271. He repeated as champion in 1951 and ten years later fired a 10-under-par 61 at Oak Hills. In 1964 he started the last 18 holes of the Texas Open with a one-stroke lead only to tire in the sultry heat and lose his lead on the last nine holes. Nevertheless, Texas would always hold many fond memories for Dutch.

New Orleans

A favorite respite that fit perfectly with Dutch's free-flowing manner and fluid golf swing was the city at the crescent bend of Old Man River, New Orleans. Dutch had a vast story collection about, "Do You Know What It Means to Miss New Orleans," a hit recording of the 1940s. When December rolled around, Dutch and Thelma would generally migrate to this Sportsman's Paradise to play the horses and the gambling tables. Wagering was second nature to New Orleanians and her riverboat crowd, and the two St. Louisians caught the fever. In 1966 Dutch fared better in a pro race than on a horse race when he captured the Yuletide pro-am, a two-day event.

"My winnin's helped support my favorite charities for Louisiana," Dutch said.

Dutch marvelled at the growth of the space program and the landing of humans on the moon. He was watching television when the Apollo group reached the lunar surface in 1971 and Alan Shepard hit his historic golf shot, a 6-iron at the "Fra Mauro Country Club."

Dutch kidded, "I thought I saw some awful big divots and pothole bunkers up there — shoulda known those holes in the big green cheese were really golf holes. The Orient and Australia were a fur piece to travel to play golf — never dreamed I'd see the day somebody played golf on the moon."

61-Year-Old Marvel

During the winters of 1967-1973 Dutch was engaged by a St. Louis pre-press production company for week-long golf outings to Georgia and Florida. These trips were intended to promote business with good clients of the company, who were invited to accompany Dutch and play golf with him. About 15-24 people took part. Dutch conducted a golf clinic in the morning and played 18 holes with the amateurs in the afternoon.

Leader Bob Nuelle recalls, "Dutch was so congenial he had the clients eating out of his hand. They would vie for who would room with Dutch so they could spend more time talking golf and hearing his fascinating stories. The first morning in Georgia, weather prevented getting out on the course. Dutch kept everyone spellbound with his stories. He had that way of making the clients feel comfortable and never offending them. I remember one client had a big curving slice, so bad that he would have to aim far to the left of his destination.

"Dutch told his caddie, 'Amos, don't you ever let him get cornered to the right. Keep him pointed to the left. If he ever points to the right we're going to lose him, because there's no way we can keep him on the golf course. Keep him pointed to the left an' we should be able to meet him on the green.'

"The company decided to transfer the outings to Doral Country Club in Miami, Florida in 1971. One afternoon after 18 holes of golf, Dutch put on an exhibition. The more Dutch demonstrated shots and talked to the group, the louder the applause and cheers became. Soon a huge crowd started to congregate. Here he was, 61 years old, doing all the tricks a golfer could possibly do.

"He took three balls and said, 'I'm gonna hit this 2-iron at that 200-yard marker. The first ball is goin' to fade into the wind to the right, the second ball is goin' to go straight, an' the third ball is goin' to hook to the left.' Well, the first ball went right over the marker and faded. When the second ball went straight and right through the middle zero in the 200-yard marker, there was spontaneous applause. As the noise level increased, more people were attracted.

"Next, he demonstrated the sand wedge. He took 20 golf balls, knocked three of them in the hole from 40 yards away, and the other 17 stopped not more than three feet from the pin. Imagine this at 61 years old! And he was smiling and talking all the time. We all enjoyed those trips immensely with Dutch as the drawcard."

Oscar Fraley, well-known sportswriter, was the namesake for a series of tournaments in Fort Lauderdale between 1969 and 1978 called the "Country Club Championships of America." It was generally a three or four-day event, involving the home pro and three members. The pros competed for $10,000 in individual money, and there was also $10,000 in team money for the event.

Dutch entered his team from Forest Hills Country Club consisting of Tim Crowley, Stan Grossman, and John Moore. Many states were represented in this tournament, most from the Midwest and the East. About 60 teams competed, and there were many betting pools. During the winter of 1971, Dutch was so worried about Thelma's health that he lost a five-stroke lead on the last day of the tournament. His team had been counting their chickens the night before, debating which one of them would drive home the new car that was the championship bonus.

Friends cheered for Dutch and Kimo Harrison to qualify for the U.S. Open in May, 1971 and make the trip together to the Merion Golf Course near Philadelphia. The local qualifying was a 36-hole grind in St. Louis in May. At the end of the first round, Thelma was well enough to meet Dutch with a tureen of soup, as was her custom. The scoreboard crew informed them that Kimo had a good start and was close behind Dutch.

"The King is dead, long live a new Harrison," kidded the crew.

"Listen," smiled Dutch, "Kimo better have his money out 'cause I'm gonna win it."

Sure enough, when the tournament was over, the 61-year-old marvel tottered to his car, allowing Kimo to pick up his first place medal by proxy. Dutch shot the lowest round of the day on the Normandie course, a 70, and possibly a world record for any senior citizen with varicose veins and a diabetic condition!

Two weeks later in the sectional qualifying, Dutch was the oldest player in a field of 132 to attempt to qualify. Before the tournament began, one would have thought Dutch wouldn't live until the next day.

"I'm so out of shape I can't make it to the first tee. Why, I couldn't hit a bull in the rump with a fiddle," he claimed. Then he walked away groaning and acting as though he were walking on razor blades. At the end of the tournament the winning check was made out to "Ernest Joe."

Dutch took one look at the check and with his usual outpouring of affection, exclaimed, "Well lookey here! Ernest Joe! Ernest Joe money is as good as any."

Thelma's Aloha

The sad part of that victory day was that Thelma was not at the 18th hole with her customary tureen of soup after the first round. She was far too ill. Dutch was worried and hurried home after receiving the winner's check.

Close friends Dick and Jane Kohlmann noted Thelma not feeling well toward the end of 1971.

"Dutch and Thelma would often stop by to see us at our golf course. One day, Dutch came in and said, 'Mr. Dick, Mama's feelin' mighty poorly. She's sittin' out in the car an' is not comin' in to say hello this time.'

"We knew she was supposed to diet because of her heart condition and high blood pressure, but we didn't connect those conditions to the way she felt."

In March 1972, Thelma suffered a mild heart attack. Although she had earlier carried 140 pounds on her 5'7" frame, her weight ballooned dangerously over 200 pounds. Apparently, only Thelma and her physician understood the seriousness of her progressive heart disease that was both coronary and rheumatic.

"I can't ever afford to get sick," Thelma said as she maintained her positive outlook and continued working at the same enthusiastic pace. If she harbored any fears or doubts during this time, she never shared them with Dutch.

Three months later, on June 28, Thelma suffered a

more serious attack, but this time she couldn't hide her fear. On the evening of the 29th, she called her children. David said he couldn't get her off the phone between 9:00 p.m. and midnight and finally suggested she cut it short because of the cost.

"I know, I know," she conceded, but continued talking.

On the 30th Martha flew in from Phoenix. David arrived from Reno on the first of July only to learn Thelma had passed away an hour earlier. A tearful Raymond flew from Hawaii the next day with two of his sons, Keku and "Dutchy." Although Martha had talked with her mother for a few minutes before she died in the St. Louis Hospital, Dutch sadly never had a chance that final morning. He'd spent a restless night and somehow, when the call came, half-expected the news.

Suddenly, their fabled romance had turned to grief. The loss was devastating for Dutch. Understanding his pain, the children did not bring up the possibility of taking Thelma's body back to Hawaii for burial. They knew it was her wish to be laid to rest beside Dutch. Services were held in St. Louis on July 3, followed by burial at Hiram Park.

Heartbroken and overwhelmed with grief, Dutch could not talk about Thelma without breaking down. It was only much later, when the healing process had begun, that he was finally able to speak about the woman he loved and the love she bestowed upon her family and friends, a love that bordered on worship, and a love that was returned by all the lives she touched, however brief.

Her Hawaiian aloha aina (love of the land) had been overshadowed by her devotion to Dutch. She had been content to be the wife of a golf pro, living serenely under the spell of Lord Byron's lines:

> Man's love is a man's life a thing apart,
> 'Tis woman's whole existence.

With Thelma's passing at age 67, Dutch was asked what he planned to do. "I'm just gonna chase that little white ball around. At 62, I'm too old to chase anythin' else."

A New Romance

Golf brought Dutch a good wage,
And lots of folks would say
"When I get to be your age,
I hope I still can play."

As Dutch boarded the plane enroute to the Las Vegas U.S. National Senior Open in September of 1972, it was with a renewed spirit. After three months agonizing over Thelma's death, it was time to start living again.

Mixed Baggage

Selecting a window seat next to his Texan traveling companion, Jack "Swifty" Swift, a golf-glove salesman, Dutch noticed an attractive woman in the aisle seat one row behind him. Before long, he asked where she was traveling, and in his usual smooth manner, politely changed seats with Swifty so he could turn and talk more easily. He was enjoying the conversation so much that he moved across the aisle from her after passengers deplaned in Denver.

Shirley Perlstein Rubin was a bright 46-year-old Jewish Pennsylvanian from a middle-class family. She had married shortly after graduating from Greensburg High School in 1943, and had one living son, Larry. An exceptionally gifted younger son, Michael, died of a diabetic coma when he was 11 years old. Shirley received her undergraduate degree from Duquesne University and graduate degree in social work from the University of Pittsburgh prior to the 1968 breakup of her 23-year marriage. At the time she met Dutch, Shirley was the Director of Special Projects for the Commission on Alcoholism and Drug Abuse in Edmonton, Alberta, Canada on her way to a much needed Las Vegas vacation.

When they arrived in Vegas, Dutch had Swifty handle Shirley's luggage and graciously offered her a ride to her hotel in their limousine. He had suggested earlier during the flight that Shirley should consider transferring to the Tropicana where he was staying, but she modestly declined, saying that due to heavy hotel bookings, it had been difficult to get her reservation.

"Well, if you decide you want to move over, I'll be sure to get you a room," said Dutch.

Upon arrival in his hotel room, Dutch received a call from Shirley inquiring whether he had taken one of her suitcases by mistake.

After checking with Swifty, he returned to the phone and said in mock surprise, "I'll be durned if your bag didn't get mixed with ours. I'll return it right now."

That he did, together with an invitation to dinner. At dinner Shirley learned Dutch would be playing golf in the pro-am the following morning with one of her favorite stars, Dean Martin. She joyfully accepted his invitation and took to the links the next day.

"What a thrill it was to see Dutch hit the ball. I remember one of his admirers saying, 'Dutch is older than I am and he still hits the ball so pure. It's like warm molasses.'

"So many people were rooting for Dutch, it was obvious how popular he was. Dean and Dutch not only made an entertaining team, they won the pro-am. Dutch went on to place fourth in the Senior Open, a tournament he had won five times and four in a row.

"After two nights at my hotel, I told Dutch that I'd move to the Tropicana if he could get me a room. He did and I moved. I stayed there three nights before returning to Edmonton."

Romance Revealed

"Dutch continued to keep in touch with me during that fall. He wanted me to come to St. Louis in October, then November. I must admit I was reluctant, because I was having a hard time understanding why he didn't come to Canada to see me. Little did I realize that a golfer wasn't about to travel to the cold weather of Alberta in October. I had finally decided to visit him since I had a meeting scheduled in Washington, D.C. in November, but the meeting was cancelled. Then I wasn't sure what I really wanted to do. My boss, who was also a very good friend and confidant, suggested I pack my suitcase and go to St. Louis in order to understand where I stood and what my next step would be. In St. Louis Dutch proposed to me, but he felt it was too soon after Thelma's death to get married right away so we agreed to wait."

Dutch would often be accompanied to pro-am tournaments during this period by his close friends, Stan Grossman and Tim Crowley, low handicap amateurs from Forest Hills. Both were successful businessmen, Stan in his mid-40s and Tim in his early-30s. Tim remembers an outing to Fort Lauderdale in early December of 1972 with Dutch, Stan and John Moore.

"When the phone rang in our hotel room, it was some girl calling from Canada and I told her, 'I think you have the wrong number, but wait a minute.'

"So I yell into the next room where we're playing cards, 'Stan, were you expecting a call from Canada?'

"Stan says, 'Nah, I don't know anybody in Canada,' and then all of a sudden I hear from one of the distant rooms of our suite, 'That call's for me.'

"Dutch comes paddling in clad only in his shorts, giving us high signs to make ourselves scarce and shut the door.

"I asked, 'Who's calling from Canada?'

"Dutch answered, 'Don't worry about it, Mr. Timmy.'

"That was the first we knew of any romance. It happened to be Shirley's birthday and Dutch had promised to phone her. I'm sure he had every intention to call, but he was so embarrassed about it, he didn't want to say anything."

"When he didn't call me, I decided to call him," said Shirley. "Dutch asked me to quit my job, sell my furniture and come down to St. Louis to live. He spoke about our driving to Florida, knowing that my mother and son lived there.

"He said, 'Drive down to Florida next time with me for my tournaments. You can spend some time with your family and when we get back, we'll get married.'"

The Merrymaker

Tim described their return flight from Florida to St. Louis, "The plane was crowded and Dutch had to sit some distance from us. We all had stereo headsets and I found a channel playing Dean Martin songs.

"Knowing Dutch liked Dean, I yelled to Dutch, "Hey, Pops, what channel do you have? Turn to Channel 2."

"After tuning in, Dutch beamed and exclaimed, 'Oh, Mr. Dean! How are you doin', Mr. Dean?'

"The people all around him broke out in laughter. No matter how many people were around him, Dutch would perform a monologue with a recording like that or with a TV program — we always had a good chuckle."

Both Tim and Stan fondly remembered the fun-loving conversations with Dutch, especially when they would stay together at the Bayshore Coast Yacht Club in Fort Lauderdale.

"What do you think of that golf pro, Dutch?," Stan would ask.

"You need a *Reader's Digest* when you play with him," replied Dutch.

"What do you mean by a *Reader's Digest*?"

"You need a *Reader's Digest* to catch up on your reading while he gets ready to hit the ball."

"What do you think of this professional golfer, Dutch?," Tim asked.

"Oh, he likes pitchers too much."

"What do you mean, pitchers?"

"Too many pitchers of martinis."

"Is this other pro fun to play with, Dutch?"

"He's hard on my stomach."

"What do you mean, he's hard on your stomach?"

"Give me a menu an' I would have time to select a full meal an' clear the table for dessert while he was sizin' up his shot."

The Big Step

It was difficult for Shirley to leave Edmonton and her work. "I made the big move to St. Louis in late December, and once in St. Louis with Dutch everything was good. We lived in the house which was previously occupied by Thelma and Dutch in the Four Seasons Development of Chesterfield. Kimo had just recently gone through a divorce and had moved in with Dutch, but soon after my arrival, he found his own apartment."

In February, Dutch said to Shirley, "We're goin' down to Arkansas an' get married." Shirley replied, "Why? We're in St. Louis." Dutch teased, "I meet all my new wives on airplanes an' always get married in Arkansas!"

"We drove to Hot Springs and were married by the Justice of the Peace on February 16, 1973, but before the 11:00 a.m. ceremony, we spent two hours trying to find suspenders for Dutch's trousers, which he had trouble keeping up. Dutch was happy when the ceremony ended just in time for us to make it to the first race at the Hot Springs track."

Shortly after the newlyweds returned from their honeymoon, Tim and Stan saw Dutch and asked if it was true that he'd been hitched.

"Well, ya know, Mr. Timmy an' Mr. Gross, it was just the right thing to do. We went down to Hot Springs an' we just had to let that preacher tee off on us," Dutch replied.

"It wasn't long before there was obvious tension between us over Dutch's wagering on the horses," lamented Shirley. "I enjoyed the race track, but not on a daily basis like Dutch. Every morning he'd take the sports section to read the race results and I got the rest of the newspaper. One time when I was extremely sick, Dutch had a speaking engagement in Kansas City and got home about midnight the next night. I said, 'Where have you been? It doesn't take that long to get back from Kansas City.'

"Dutch replied, 'Oh, I stopped at the Fairmount Park Race Track (in Collinsville, Illinois) on my way back.'

"I was upset. 'Since when did Illinois move between Kansas City and Missouri?'

"I didn't speak to him for several days. And we didn't go out to many social events. Sometimes Dutch would turn to me and say, 'Mom, I haven't taken you out for a long time.'

"Then he would take me to the race track. He never worried about a bank balance because he didn't believe in banks. His money was kept in shoes. When I asked him to take money to the bank, he'd refuse and ask me to get a Traveler's Check. He just didn't trust banks after his family's loss during the Depression.

"Not all of Dutch's savings went to the race track. He had built a new home for his mother and father and also provided them with a monthly cash reserve.

"He'd say to me, 'I enjoyed doin' that. Those kind of things mean a lot when a person gets older. It's nice when things are taken care of.'

"I wanted to move into our own place and not stay where Thelma had lived. There was friction over this, as well as the pictures of Thelma and the family that were still hanging. Dutch was very upset when the photographs were removed and put in storage."

Shirley received many compliments on her cooking.

Dick Kohlmann liked the ribs she fixed and remembered Dutch saying, "This is really livin' high on the hog."

Forrest Tucker spoke of what wonderful meals Shirley prepared during his visits with Dutch, "I needed to diet for three days after eating one of her feasts. She was a marvelous cook."

Shirley commented, "I quickly discovered that Dutch's fondness for simple cooking was a heritage of the southern farming community he came from. The first time when I served him hot dogs, sauerkraut, and cornbread, he turned to me and said, 'Mom, this is the best meal you ever cooked.'

"His other favorites were pork chops, fried chicken and ham hocks, but not lamb. I think his special combination was cornbread — all forms of cornbread — and milk. The spoonbread he loved was a far cry from the hushpuppies he used to have, little bits of cornbread that the southern cooks would break off and fry, then throw to the dogs with the admonition, 'Hush, Puppy.'

"Dutch had much the same attitude towards clothes as Will Rogers. He was cut from the same informal cloth. For evening he'd wear practically the same clothes he wore to the golf tournament. He almost always wore a golf shirt instead of a regular sport shirt, even though he was wearing a jacket and was supposed to be dressed up. And he wore golf slacks, usually ones he played golf in that day. When he wore knickers to golf in, he'd most likely keep them on to go to the race track that afternoon or night.

"The one and only time I didn't pack for him was when we drove to Florida, before we were married. The wardrobe he chose was unbelievable! He had golf slacks that were all patterns and colors, mostly blues and reds. The sport jackets were all casual, in browns, blacks and greens. He wore all these odd combinations and there was no way you could match anything. It was at that point I decided I'd never let him do his own packing.

"You rarely saw Dutch without a golf cap on, either a conventional type or the Ben Hogan/Dutch Harrison flat cap. He could be dressed up in formal wear and then reach in the cupboard for his golf cap. Dutch was often described as 'a cabbage in a rose garden,' compared to the peacocks of the links like Jimmy Demaret and Doug Sanders. He slowly became a presentable dresser — but not outstanding.

"One of his trademarks in the later years was the inevitable cigar stuck in his mouth. The longer and fatter it was, the better he liked it. He rarely lit the cigar and never inhaled it. He'd just chew on it without taking it out of his mouth as he talked and swung at the ball.

"In the beginning I asked Dutch if he were a church-going person. He turned to me and said, 'If I walked into a church, I think all four walls would collapse.'

"But in later years, he'd watch televised church programs.

"When Dutch would develop a paunch, he'd talk about walking the hills. One of his favorite pastimes, particularly on Mondays when the Club was closed, was to spend the whole day on the golf course looking for balls. He might go out for five or six hours with someone who would find 25 balls to his 125. It was a release for him and he enjoyed roaming the golf course and the woods."

Tim Crowley was amazed by Dutch's ball-finding ability.

"When I hit a ball into the rough or woods, Dutch could always walk directly to it, despite the bushes and terrain. When he was in the pro shop, he would often invite me to go to the back fairways, like the fifth hole at Forest Hills, and hunt for golf balls.

"He'd say, 'Now Mr. Tim, we're gonna go down in those weeds on the left an' I'm gonna find 20 balls an' you gotta find five.'

"It never failed; I'd come up with my five and shout, 'I have my find, Dutch.'

"I'd get over to him and he'd have more than 20 balls. Then he'd help me hit shots to the green with those balls and bet me a dime a shot for the closest to the hole. Needless to say, I would have run out of dimes real fast if he'd taken them."

Health Problems

Shirley recalled that for most of their marriage Dutch was not in good health, "When we drove to Florida that first time in 1972, he was sick most of the way with a bad croup and fever. I pleaded with him to see a doctor and he would say, 'My doctor is back in St. Louis.' I suggested he go back, but he'd say, 'No, I can't. My car is *here*.'

"He wouldn't fly either. Although he seemed to recover from that illness, he didn't feel well much of the following year. Finally, in December of 1973, he went to the hospital for a gallbladder operation. His blood pressure and sugar count were sky-high. The newspapers incorrectly reported that it was a heart condition.

"After his gallbladder surgery, he was in Intensive Care and was delirious for several days. Everyone knew what a gentle, kind person he was, but one night he became quite angry and refused to let the nurses come close to him. We couldn't get him to listen to reason. I called Dr. Koehler at 10:00 p.m. on Saturday and asked him if he could find the source of frustration for Dutch.

"Dr. Koehler came to the hospital through a raging blizzard and after five minutes with Dutch told me, 'I know what the problem is. He's worried about having his hands damaged by the nurses putting needles in them and drawing blood.' Even in that delirious state, Dutch was concerned with his hands.

"His hands were those of an artist, the most grace-ful and beautiful instruments I've ever seen. And he would take such good care of them. He'd keep his nails precisely trimmed and he disliked shaking hands with strong hand shakers. He'd just give them his fingertips so he could pull away. His hands meant so much to him in golf, and they were capable of such expressive nuance and humor."

Bob Hamilton described Dutch's hands as the most beautiful set he had ever seen. "He could have made a tremendous surgeon or piano player. He had those long, slim fingers. And what a sensitive touch. It was that of a safecracker. He's one golfer who could differentiate varieties of golf balls while hitting blindfolded."

Ten days after his surgery, while recovering in the hospital, Dutch had a stroke. He was kept in the hospital a total of 39 days.

"Meantime, my father was dying of cancer in Fort Lauderdale and passed away on Sunday, the day before Dutch was scheduled to come home," Shirley recalled. "Dr. Koehler told me, 'You go to Florida for your father and if the hospital can't keep Dutch, I'll take him home with me.' I buried my father on Tuesday, came back on Wednesday and took Dutch home from the hospital on Thursday.

"It was a difficult time for us. He was unable to care for himself, and I had to go back to work to make ends meet. A friend of Dutch's offered to come in every morning and stay with him until I got home from work. He came five days a week for two months and did this gratis, just to be with Dutch.

"Before his stroke, Dutch would be talking a mile-a-minute on the golf course to whoever was watching him play and would never stop talking while he hit the ball. After his stroke that became a problem. He lost his peripheral vision and couldn't concentrate enough on his swing while he talked. I said many times, 'Dutch, if you'd stop talking and concentrate, I know you could have hit that shot better.' But he was reluctant to change."

Dr. George Koehler was close to Dutch. He joined Forest Hills Country Club in 1969 at the age of 38, but didn't know Dutch until 1970 when he gave him an insurance physical.

"After I found that Dutch had diabetes and high blood pressure, I told him to forget about an insurance policy. The only one he had was an automatic $2,000 life insurance policy with the PGA.

"I got to know Dutch better as I took golf lessons from him. He'd call me Dr. George. I learned that Dutch grew up being afraid of doctors. When his back went out, he went to a chiropractor, a reflection of his upbringing. Prior to his gallbladder attack, I ordered a battery of tests to determine the cause of his fever. Dutch put them off until it was too late.

"After the stroke that followed his gallbladder attack, his vision was impaired. He could only see about 50 percent out of each eye because his optic nerves were affected. He couldn't see to his right and watch his backswing. After a car accident near his home, he realized the extent of his impairment. He swerved to dodge a dog and hit the back of his neighbor's car. He didn't drive after that."

Shirley was worried.

"In May of 1974 we needed a smaller place because of Dutch's health. Dutch was still reluctant to move, but I located a nice apartment on Kehr Mills Road about one mile from the Forest Hills Country Club. There were some good days when Dutch used to walk that mile to the club. He'd usually take a backwoods shortcut and on occasion friends would find him looking for golf balls. He could swing the golf club, but he didn't play much. Forrest Tucker was one of the few who were able to get Dutch out on the golf course. They were good for each other," Shirley recalled.

Pro-Emeritus

Forest Hills had become privately owned by its members after the original owner died. Following Dutch's illness, a few new directors on the Club Board explored replacing Dutch as Head Professional. They believed a more youthful professional would save the Club money.

One member almost single-handedly squelched this idea. He mailed postcards to the entire membership, reported the underhandedness of the action being initiated, and pointed out Dutch's devotion to the Club since its beginning. Sentiment immediately swelled in Dutch's favor. The membership stood solidly behind him and the movement failed.

Mindful of the Club's support, but still depressed with his slow recovery, Dutch was concerned with his future as Head Professional. In December 1974 he decided to step down after ten-and-a-half years at the post — but he already had a successor in mind.

Dutch first met Roger Williams in 1969 at a PGA fall business meeting. Roger, then 40, and the Head Pro at Spring Lake Country Club in Quincy, Illinois, introduced himself, "Mr. Harrison, I was in Quincy when you spoke on your 56th birthday at the tribute dinner for Scotty Glasgow. You inspired us with your message and your knowledge of the game. What would you charge to give an exhibition and clinic at my Spring Lake Club?"

Dutch responded, "Mr. Roger, I'll come to Quincy for $100."

Roger reflected, "I would never have believed he would drive from St. Louis to Quincy and be there all afternoon for $100, but he did. In fact the members enjoyed it so much we invited him back again several years later and he charged the same fee. Money was never a problem with Dutch — he loved golf and being with people. He'd always keep the crowd entertained through 18 holes of golf and a half-hour clinic. Every time he spoke to members he'd give the home pro a plug. All the pros appreciated that.

"Once while I was playing in the exhibition foursome with Dutch, he said, 'Mr. Rog, someday I'm going to get you a good job.'

"In December 1974 I sent my resume to him after being at Spring Lake Country Club for ten years. I had just resigned and was looking for a new position. Dutch stuck the resume in his dresser drawer but dug it out when he resigned, and recommended me for the Forest Hills position. I came down for an interview and was hired the day before Christmas. If Dutch hadn't recommended me, I wouldn't have had a chance, because the position wasn't advertised. I started as Head Professional on April 1, 1975.

"Our relationship at Forest Hills changed with the passing of time. It started out as Pro Emeritus/Head Pro, but it soon became Father/Son.

"My favorite story about Dutch goes back to 1970 when Jack Hull, City Champion of Quincy, wanted a top pro to look at his golf swing. I called Dutch and he agreed to help. It was raining like crazy when Jack and I left Quincy and it rained all the way to St. Louis. When we reached the club, Mrs. Harrison told us Dutch was at home with a cold and we might have to reschedule the lessons. She phoned Dutch, who insisted on getting dressed and coming over to the Club. Jack's wife and I stood under an umbrella while Dutch gave Jack an hour lesson in the heavy rain. Afterwards, Jack privately wondered how much the lesson would cost him, as he had only $15 in his billfold. To his surprise, not only did Dutch take us both to lunch, but told us, 'Anybody who would drive 125 miles to take a lesson in the rain can't be charged a dime.' I think Dutch convinced Jack, owner of a cleaning establishment, that there are people who do things out of the kindness of their hearts!"

As Pro-Emeritus, Dutch wasn't happy with his convalescence. He recalled, "I just can't seem to gain any strength. The worst part is I can't see out of my right eye. I just don't have any depth perception."

Paul Runyan was discouraged when he encountered Dutch, "He was in bad shape. I didn't think he would last another week. It was terrible to see a friend get that weak."

Dutch was at a crossroads. It was troubling him that he had no retirement income set aside and could expect little other than his Social Security check and what Shirley could earn. To make matters worse it was reported that the State Division of Alcohol and Drug Abuse was to be moved to Jefferson City, thus divesting Shirley of her employment.

Gradually, he started playing more, nine holes at a time. Shirley tried to pep him up and encouraged his playing.

"The more he played, the more he smiled. After golf he'd come home to dinner and josh with me. 'Mom, what are you doin' comin' over here an' puttin' those big dark eyes on me? Anytime you do that I just have to melt.'"

Together, a sense of hope was being restored. Spring was in the air and once again in his step. The twinkle in his eye symbolized victory in the struggle for recovery. New life breathed into his soul with the promise of enjoyment in his twilight years.

Golden Days

"If I never have a cent,
I'll be rich as Rockefeller,
Life can be so sweet,
On the Sunny Side of the Street."

From "On the Sunny Side of the Street"
by Dorothy Fields

Dutch was grinning ear to ear. His life-long love affair with golf was back in full swing.

"Watching him play again was like watching an eagle soar, a dolphin glide," marveled Forest Hills member Bob Nuelle, who had the pleasure of playing with Dutch at company-sponsored events in Georgia and Florida.

From frustration to fulfillment, Dutch had come full cycle. With better health he was "On the Sunny Side of the Street."

Cheerful as a Chipmunk

"Give me the health an' you can have the wealth," Dutch would say. "After my stroke the inactivity bothered me. All my life I'd been doin' somethin' — keepin' busy. At long last I'm feelin' cheerful as a chipmunk an' talkin' the leg off a mule. I won't feel like tearin' around the country forever, but now, I'm active again."

St. Louis was the crossroads and center of action for Dutch.

"St. Louis is my part of the country," Dutch then reflected. "I've lived here longer than any place an' this is goin' to be my home forever. I like to wander down to Arkansas whenever I can. You can take the boy outta the country, but you can't take the country outta the boy. Today, I'd rather see my varmints at the race track."

Stan Grossman observed, "Dutch never lost his country charm or his soft Arkansas accent. He made a wonderful ambassador of goodwill for St. Louis, singing praises of the area wherever he went and laying it on with a trowel. He'd talk about the exhilaration he felt just crossing the Mississippi and the joy of seeing the rainbow Gateway Arch that dominates the riverfront area. His reservoir of stories and reminiscences about St. Louis events was voluminous."

Roger Williams was so impressed with Dutch after he drove him to Canton and Springfield, Missouri, for golf banquets that he exclaimed, "Although the pro-emeritus hadn't spoken in public for years, he went over big. The way he worded things was perfect — the members of those clubs just loved him."

Dutch was asked by Bill Beck, popular St. Louis sportswriter, how many pigeons he planned to clip on his comeback campaign.

"Oh, Mr. Bill, I ain't sayin' I won't overlook a pigeon if I see one, but I'll sure look him over real good before I take him on. An' I'll bypass any Sam Sneads or Ben Hogans. Trouble is, I can't play a lick 'cause I haven't been practicin'," Dutch said. One of golf's elder statesmen seemed to be rehearsing his first-tee strategy.

Stan Grossman recalled being Dutch's amateur partner at the Bing Crosby Tournament, "The first night Dutch and I were having dinner at the lodge while many of the pros were there. The respect he was paid by them was an eye-opener to me. They came over to shake hands with Dutch, and I remember Bob Goalby and

Bruce Crampton saying to Dutch, 'Pops, will you please watch me hit a few shots on the range in the morning?' Dutch started helping many of these golfers when they first joined the tour."

Juniors

At Forest Hills, Dutch was well-known for the Junior Program of Golf. By 1974 there were about 140 juniors participating in the program.

Typically, Dutch gave credit to others, "That young feller, Roger Williams, put the program together. I helped where I could — always did like workin' with young folk. I had the feelin' I was puttin' somethin' back into the game. If a pro down in Arkansas hadn't taken the time with me when I was a kid, I wouldn't be here."

Roger Williams remembered how much Dutch meant to the juniors, "When our junior team announced they were dedicating their district championship to him, I was happy to help with the award. Every time Dutch gave an exhibition or clinic I saw the crowds brighten as he approached. The juniors were the same way. Dutch Harrison was the man who was raised on country sunshine and who let the sunshine filter through to everyone around him."

Steve Roussin was one of the teenagers at the Club who worshiped his instructor. "Dutch affected me more than anyone I ever met in golf. His inspiration was more than just teacher-pupil. He gave me lessons for four years and never charged a penny — not unusual for him, I understand. He was the kind that if you had the desire to play the game, money was not a consideration. He was always so nice to me and my mother as I grew up. We had a special friendship.

"Everyone at the Club put Dutch on a pedestal. I remember when he would see someone on the driving range display their temper or use bad language, he would say to me, 'You just can't do it that way.'

"He taught me to practice hard and long and with respect for the game. Soon after I met him he gave me a bunch of golf clubs. If anyone needed clubs and didn't have the money for them, he would give them a set. I know one summer he gave away at least four sets.

"He'd say to me, 'Here, hit some balls with this club.'

"After I did, he'd just stick the club in my bag and be almost insulted if I wouldn't take the club.

"You'd never know that he was famous. He always wanted to be just one of the guys and have fun with people. I think he recognized that some people were taking advantage of him, but he was always too nice to say anything or do anything about it.

"Once Dutch phoned and invited me to meet him at a barbecue with some of his cronies who got together every year and talked about old times. I reached the party before Dutch did and it wasn't long before one of the older golfers I was talking to said, 'You're going to have to go now — you know this is for the seniors.'

"I said, 'Okay,' and went outside to wait for Dutch.

"When we came walking into the room together, everyone stood and began applauding. I was in awe — here were all the pro golfers giving my friend, Dutch, a standing ovation. Being there meant so much to me. Sportswriters and pros flocked around him to have their picture taken.

"When the chips were down, there was no one who could play like Mr. Dutch. I remember when he was playing a one-dollar nassau at Forest Hills. His team was a shot behind going into the long 7th hole. He hit his second shot with a driver to reach the green and made an eagle. He could pull off some fantastic shots.

"Every time I saw him he seemed to have about ten cigars pushed into his shirt pocket. He kept handing them out. The cigar became his trademark. I don't think I ever saw him smoke one. He just kept one in his mouth. So many pictures were taken of him hitting a golf ball with a cigar in his mouth."

Wilma and Warren Van Norman had helped Dutch develop the Club's junior program and in the process became great friends and confidants of the Harrisons, particularly Dutch. When Dutch would drop by their home, their two dogs, Shadow and Rumples, would almost engulf him. Wilma remembers how much Dutch liked dogs and how he would treat them with respect.

"One day Rumples, who was spirited, tried to frolic and dashed in and jumped up on Dutch's lap. I can still remember Dutch with his arms flailing, saying, 'Where did you get this dog? Mr. Shadow is a real nice dog, but I don't know about Mr. Rumples.'"

In the Hunt

Bob Goalby recalled, "After Dutch returned to the tournament trail, he would slip off and try to win those itty-bitty tournaments like the Centralia Open and Peoria Open. I went up to the Winnebago Open in Iowa. It was a pro-am tournament and the winner got an air-conditioned 22-foot Winnebago motor home. I walked in the Clubhouse and there was Dutch. He grins and says, 'Mr. Bob, what are you doin' here? I slipped up here to win me a Winnebago, but man! I'm goin' to have to catch a train home with you here.'

"That was so funny. Dutch was in the hunt with me, but I did manage to drive out of there ahead of him with that brand new Winnebago."

Dutch also played with Stan Grossman and Tim Crowley in some Florida tournaments during winters. Stan reported, "Dutch loaned me some of his irons. When we got home to St. Louis I came out to play the following weekend and found the whole set of irons in my bag. They belonged to Dutch, so I asked him, 'What's the deal here, Dutch?' 'Mr. Gross, you're a young man an' I'm not goin' to play much anymore. I know you love these irons. They're for you.'"

Reluctant Endorser

When something went wrong, Dutch wouldn't show it outwardly. Rarely did a money matter upset Dutch, but a misunderstanding with a golf equipment company did. It happened in 1972. Since 1937 the Wilson Sporting Goods Company had paid Dutch an annual stipend that grew to over $4,000 with additional bonus clauses — all designed to market the Wilson name with the winning Harrison name on their products. It had been a long and friendly relationship and was a source of considerable personal satisfaction to have an illustrious company parade his name and have his own golf bag inscribed with *"E. J. 'Dutch' Harrison — Wilson Sporting Goods Co."* Those handsome bags were a far cry from the hand-me-down piece of shellacked cardboard with which he started in Arkansas. Even more important to him were the bonuses whenever he became a winner and the many free sets of clubs periodically issued to him.

In 1967 Dutch had dinner with Nat Rosasco, Jr. of the Northwestern Golf Company who enticed him to join their Advisory Staff. Stan Grossman, who was present, said, "Dutch accepted a ten-year contract which offered $5,000 per year and large bonuses to represent Northwestern and its aluminum-shafted clubs.

"By 1971-72, Dutch's public exposure was not as great as before and Northwestern wanted to cut him to $2,500. Impulsively, he terminated his relationship with the company. He was hurt that the company thought he was a lesser person, which wasn't the case at all. Dutch just walked away from that $2,500 check and I wish I had talked to him, because I'm sure I could have talked him out of it. He never signed with another company. Here was a legend of the game who in 1929 had won his first tournaments with hickory-shafted clubs before steel shafts were legalized, carrying on the fine tradition of the game with aluminum shafts and suddenly he no longer represented a golf equipment company. That was sad to me."

Nobody Asked Me

"One time in the mid-1970s he stewed a bit after playing in a golf tournament in Florida. Timmy and I had switched tee times with another golf group without talking to Dutch. As a result, it took our team much longer to finish the round. Dutch did not say a word during the entire round. The next day we were driving back to the golf course from our hotel. All of a sudden Dutch drawls from the back, 'I'm nothin' but a broken down ol' pro. I can't say anythin'. Nobody asked me.'

"What's that Dutch?" Tim and Stan were startled.

"What can I say? I'm just an ol' pro, I don't know anythin'. But you don't let people take your tee time — you can't do that. It took 5-1/2 hours for us yesterday. I should be in first place in the tournament. Now I'm in third place. I'm just taggin' along as an ol' broken down pro. Nobody asked me."

"Dutch continued this monologue the rest of the way into the parking lot. To this day, if anything goes wrong in our group, we'll say, 'Well, nobody asked me...'"

Bob Hope Salute

The Bob Hope Salute of 1977 that honored Dutch was one for the scrapbooks, one that evoked memories of golf's smorgasbord of Will Rogers, Casey Stengel and Mark Twain.

According to Hope, "Dutch has been a great and personal friend for more years than either of us likes to recall. He's not a perfect friend; he never lets me cheat on my golf score and worse yet, he's too funny."

Bob Hope fulfilled an invitation to salute Dutch on October 22, 1977, and the date was officially declared "Dutch Harrison Day" in the St. Louis metropolitan area and the whole County. Dutch was to be honored at a testimonial dinner that evening where Hope would preside. Earlier in the day, a celebrity pro-am tournament was planned in Dutch's honor at Old Warson Country

Club. Proceeds from the tournament and banquet were to be used to establish the "Dutch Harrison Retirement Trust Fund," a trust to provide for Dutch's necessary and emergency living expenses. The whole event was the brainchild of Forest Hills member, Wilma Van Norman. Together with her husband, Warren, they turned their rathskeller into a "Dutch Harrison Day" headquarters for the large group of volunteers needed to pull off a major event. Wilma coordinated the planning and preparation with the help of a Dutch Harrison committee. Jack Berkley, an old friend from Old Warson days, served as General Chairman.

It was an ideal fall day at Old Warson for more than 200 participants plus a large crowd of spectators and autograph-seekers. Dapper in matching blue cap, sweater and slacks, Dutch chewed on his perennial cigar and joined Bob Hope in his golf cart. Fittingly, Hope was the driver.

On their way to the first tee, Bob exclaimed, "Look how gorgeous the day is — just for you, Dutch."

The report on the golf was that "Dutch hit it straight as a string," and that "both Dutch and Bob Hope got off good shots and good quips."

The highlight of the day was the festive dinner, "Bob Hope Salute to Dutch." About 650 attended the banquet at the Chase-Park Plaza Hotel. Jim McKrell was the Master of Ceremonies and the program included speakers Doug Sanders, Tommy Bolt, Lew Worsham, Stan Musial, U.S. Senator Stuart Symington, Jack Berkley, William McDonnell, Deane Beman, and Alfred Hayes, Sr.

Many of Dutch's friends flew in from all parts of the United States and Canada to participate. This was an emotional event, a roller coaster of belly laughs, tears, and cheers. The prevailing sentiment was: We love Dutch — no golfer ever earned more affection than Dutch. We wanted to do something that would benefit him for the rest of his life.

Bing Crosby wrote Dutch that he was planning to attend the dinner, saying, "I know it will be great fun."

There was one vacant chair that evening, the one that Bing would have occupied had he not died two weeks previously in Madrid, Spain, after playing an excellent round of golf. Dutch had always been a favorite golf partner of Bing's, "even though Dutch couldn't sing worth a lick." Bob Hope had tears in his eyes as he spoke at the dinner about Bing. "My friend, Bing, was supposed to be here tonight — he was going to come out swingin'. I know he's watching us tonight. He was in love with you, Dutch, 'cause you're a beautiful guy."

Even the invocation by the Reverend Monsignor Hoflich of St. Louis had a bit of humor, "...I am sure that when Dutch speaks to you, he begins by saying Mr. Lord. Amen."

After announcements and introductions by the Master of Ceremonies, Dutch was called upon to present the first annual Dutch Harrison Stroke Average Championship trophy to the junior golfer with the lowest average in the Gateway District of the PGA. Sixteen-year-old Jay Delsing came to the speaker's table to receive the award.

Dutch said, "This gentleman looks awful young to be takin' these kind of prizes. This is a beautiful trophy — an' I want to present it to you."

Shirley Harrison moved the throng with this tribute:

"All of you know that I love Dutch Harrison and it is a very gratifying feeling to know that so many other people love him too. I want to say thanks to all the people who've worked so hard to make this day possible. I won't even attempt to name you all because I'm sure to miss somebody. However, I could not let this evening end without specifically thanking four people.

"First are the two Van Norman boys, Barry and Scott. For the past six months they have had to contend with an invasion of their home and privacy by hordes of women, and worse that they have often been deprived of the attention of their mother because she was either at a meeting of the Dutch Harrison Committee, on the phone about the Dutch Harrison event, or so blasted tired because of working day and night that she couldn't hold her head up. Dutch and I say thank you, Barry and Scott.

"The third is Wilma's husband, Warren. He came home from work each night, not to a nice quiet home and dinner, as he had every right to expect, but again to a houseful of women working diligently and an exhausted, busy wife, and very often no dinner and no prospects of any unless he grabbed the boys and took the three of them out to eat. He not only put up with this, but constantly provided encouragement and support. He truly deserves a medal for service above and beyond. Thanks Van.

"By this time, it's obvious who that fourth person is. Wilma Van Norman. Almost a year ago, Wilma had a dream. That dream was to have a testimonial for Dutch. And she went to work to gain the support of many people, some of whom had doubts, but her optimism and determination were contagious. More and more people became caught up in her enthusiasm. What we have all participated in today is the result of that dream. Without her, it couldn't have happened. It's difficult to adequately say thank you to someone who has given so much of herself, so I'll only say thank you and hope Wilma knows that it's said with my whole heart. Just one last word. I suggest that all of you, when you go home tonight, pray that Wilma Van Norman doesn't dream that she will be dictator of the world."

Doug Sanders thanked God that Wilma was at the dinner. "I have a lovely wife and she never questions anything I do, but 351 phone calls in one month — that was too much. So I had to bring my wife tonight. Honey, you see there is a Wilma, right?"

Bob Hope complimented Wilma on her wonderful job, then kidded her about her phone calls.

"She phoned me eight or nine months before and asked me if I would come and do a dinner for Dutch. I told her, 'Yeah, if we can get a date set.' She'd phone me every month, then every week, then daily. This last month I've had to go through her office to get an outside line from my house! There's no way I could have escaped this date," Bob kidded.

Doug Sanders brought down the house with his colorful stories, but Bob Hope was equal to the challenge of funny lines.

Honorary Chairman Symington noted in his introduction of Hope, "There is only one Bob Hope. He's given more happiness to more people than anybody who ever lived."

Bob Hope spoke from his heart and funny bone about his good friend, Mr. Dutch, "I wouldn't have missed this. I was told to either show up or send a check, so here I am. Just being here with Dutch is something — just playing together. He means so much to me — and there's a lot of love in this room for him, I'll tell you that."

Dutch was deeply moved by the entire program.

When called upon, the "Man of the Day" spoke extemporaneously in his usual humble manner, "I want to thank you Mr. Hope an' I want to thank every one of you wonderful people out here...I just can't hardly believe it myself. Ya know, I really appreciate this wonderful thing that y'all have done for me, like Doug Sanders, Tommy Bolt, Lew Worsham, Mr. Hope, an' all the wonderful people an' Mr. (Al) Hayes lettin' us play that great course. I just really don't hardly know what to say, I just appreciate it so much. I think it's a wonderful thing when you can have so many great people talk for ya like Mr. Hope an' like all of the people around here. I really appreciate each an' every one of y'all — for all of the most wonderful things you've done for me. An' I want to thank Missus Van an' Mr. Van. They were so wonderful. They didn't get discouraged in anythin'...

"Never in my life was I ever so honored. I really mean that, 'cause I think I was lucky to get away from the farm and bein' a cotton picker. But to think now where I am...it's a long way from the cotton fields of Arkansas to this day — bein' honored by all of my friends. I will never forget this special dinner...I've always said I'm as rich as any man in the world, 'cause I measure wealth by my friends — golf has given me this opportunity...I think one of my finest friends who's always been nice to me — he's wanted to kick my pants a couple of times but he never did — is Mr. Hayes. I certainly enjoyed playin' with him an' Mr. Hope today and so many — and I want to thank each an' every one of y'all so very, very much..."

One of Dutch's greatest thrills that night came from Bob Hope and the entire crowd singing these words to him:

Thanks for the Memory, of
This salute to Dutch, a
Guy we love so much, a
Dinner for a winner with a
Master's putting touch,
How lovely it was!

Thanks for the Memory, an
Autumn afternoon, with a
Foursome quite in tune, a
Day with friends pays dividends
And brings some bread in, too
How lovely it was!

Dutch, many's the time you have feasted,
And many's the time you have fasted,
Through the years our friendship has lasted,
And you're still going strong,
Swinging smooth, hitting long!

And, thanks for the Memory, we've
Had a lot of fun, a
Ball for everyone, a chance to heed
A friend in need, Whose
Smile has never gone,
How lovely it was!

(Words by Warren Van Norman)

Farewell

"You've got to accentuate the positive,
Eliminate the negative,
Latch on to the affirmative,
Don't mess with Mr. In-between."

from "Ac-Cent-Tchu-Ate the Positive"
by Johnny Mercer

A heart attack in March 1979 signaled the beginning of the end of Dutch's spectacular career. He would be hospitalized intermittently over the next three years for numerous problems related to congestive heart failure and diabetic kidneys. During the intervals at home, Shirley busied herself caring for him and administering insulin for the diabetes.

Dutch was too ill to attend the funeral of stepson Raymond, whose fatal heart attack in July 1980 left behind his wife, Helen, and seven children between the ages of 17 and 28. At 51, Raymond was such a popular figure in Hawaii that more than 1,000 paid tribute at the memorial service. It was held in Maui where Raymond had lived since 1971 as a successful businessman and golfer.

In April 1981, Dr. Koehler told Shirley that Dutch's heart condition was deteriorating rapidly. By that August, severe circulatory problems resulted in two surgeries on his left foot. When gangrene set in, one hospital surgeon wanted to amputate the entire left leg. Dutch was transferred to another hospital for vascular surgery to circumvent the amputation. During this time he was despondent, but did not abandon hope.

"Gettin' old isn't easy. It's hard to accept. I guess it's even tougher when you've been an athlete all your life. But I have to accept it. As you get older the courses get tougher an' the steps get steeper," he remarked.

Recovery was questionable, but following the surgeries his health was sufficient to allow him a trip with Shirley to the Phoenix and Palm Springs areas in early 1982. Dutch was invited as an honored guest to the Vintage Invitational in Indian Wells, California in March of that year. During evening festivities he received a standing ovation in grand fashion after Tennessee Ernie Ford delivered a stirring, impromptu tribute that brought the audience to their feet in applause.

Ten days after his return to St. Louis on March 30, Dutch entered Missouri Baptist Hospital again. He was in and out of the hospital through April and May.

Last Hurrah

An alarming incident occurred on May 23 while Dutch was a guest of honor at the Hale Irwin Children's Hospital Golf Tournament held at Old Warson Country Club. He had received his last hurrah from the throng attending the golf clinic that morning. As Dutch left the grounds in front of the crowd to have lunch with T.D. Morris, Hale Irwin and other professional golfers, he insisted in his gentlemanly manner that Shirley precede him down a few low steps from the practice area. Without her guidance, his size-12 shoe caught between two parked golf carts. He lost his balance and fell. Deeply shaken, Dutch was rushed to a hospital. Everyone breathed a sigh of relief when they learned he had suffered only minor cuts and abrasions.

He was again hospitalized shortly thereafter. He wanted very much to return to Little Rock and visit his family and kept vowing, "As soon as I get to feelin' better, I'll wander down there an' surprise 'em." But his physical deterioration continued, and on June 19, 1982 Dutch called his last shot.

After a beautiful memorial service on the sunny afternoon of June 22, 1982, the Arkansas Traveler was laid to rest beside Thelma Akana Harrison in Hiram Cemetery, golf club in hand. His family requested that contributions be made to the Chick Evans college scholarship fund for caddies.

Remembering Dutch

E.J. "Dutch" Harrison: 1910-1982

I am with you, wandering through Memory Lane;
Living the years, laughter and tears, over again.

from "Memory Lane"
by B.G. De Sylva

The Arkansas Traveler parred through his course in life and parred out at age 72. From a boy who had enormous difficulty expressing himself, Dutch gradually learned to embrace the English language so affectionately he added a new dimension to it. He is remembered almost as much for his words as his deeds. He was unique in his commonality, a loving, caring person who had a reverence for all living things. The world was drawn to him like metal to a magnet. As Bob Hamilton and Herman Keiser both said, "They broke the mold when they made Dutch."

Dutch didn't alter his easy, slow pace nor his matching drawl. The only time he rushed anything was to bet on a horse. Joe Dey witnessed one of the few times Dutch was seen running. "I remember him clattering through the airport in his golf shoes and golf togs, carrying his golf bag over his shoulder, golf cap in one hand and ticket in the other."

Dutch's philosophy of tempo was that of Winston Churchill: "You never run when you can walk. Never walk when you can sit. And never sit when you can lie down."

Glory

Dutch's golf career was not a sudden burst of fire that flamed brightly and fizzled quickly. The Arkansas Traveler began his odyssey when Model A's were sputtering over one-way bridges and dirt roads, and concluded his journey on interstate highways and in jet planes. He spanned six decades of winning tournaments, beginning in the 1920s and ending in the 1970s. He won 30 significant tournaments, including the Canadian Open, the Western Open, the "Australian Cup" of that day, and qualified 25 times for the U.S. Open, narrowly missing victories in both the Philadelphia event in 1950 and the Denver in 1960. In 1947, 1949, 1951, and 1953 he was elected to the Ryder Cup, the most prestigious golf group of that era. In 1954 he was awarded the Vardon Trophy for lowest average score of the year, and in 1962 he was elected to the PGA Hall of Fame. The Ol' Traveler was internationally known for his many dramatic clutch performances and those "unbelievable shots and rounds."

When Dutch nearly won the U.S. Open at age 50 and then won five out of six National Senior Opens, people wondered if he had discovered the Fountain of Youth. One fan suggested he bottle the water he was drinking and sell it to senior citizens everywhere. And there were still others who believed that each of his three wives successively provided some of the basic ingredients that contributed to his longevity. Dutch maintained that playing golf ensured there was no time to get old.

Sportsmanship and Tributes

Dutch was impressed with the veracity and sportsmanship of modern-day tour golfers. "That aspect gives me so much pleasure — the players are so upright, despite all the money that's at stake. In the old days I'd see tour players mark their ball, then replace it in advance of where it had been. I never said anythin' to them in front of anyone, but I'd take them aside later an' caution them not to do it again an' they'd straighten out."

Throughout his lifetime, Dutch earned the respect of nearly everyone in the golfing community. He was saluted by the unknowns, who marvelled at his golfing ability; by the amateurs, who envied his skill and who studied under him; and by well-known professionals who admired him not only for his performance on the course, but for his incredibly consistent personal warmth, fairness, and sincerity. A selection of their tributes follows:

Trini Alvarez (Head professional at El Rio Golf Course, Arizona) said, "I have never met a kinder person. Dutch went out of his way to help poor caddies like me. When I was a slip of a lad, I lost all of my caddie earnings at what was then El Rio Country Club. Dutch saw me in tears and came over to see what happened. I told him I had lost $14 on the driving range. He pretended he had found it and handed me a $20 bill. Dutch always looked after the poor people in Tucson and set a wonderful example for me."

Ellie Akana (David's wife) declared, "Dutch was a man's man, but a very gentle man, a rare combination."

Andy Anderson (Tour pro, dubbed the "Babe Ruth" of Golf) put his feelings this way, "If Dutch's heart was the size of a peanut, he'd have been the best player in the world."

Patty Berg (Member of LPGA Hall of Fame, PGA Hall of Fame and World Golf Hall of Fame) said, "Dutch and I, while representing Wilson Sporting Goods and Joe Jemsek's St. Andrews course at the same time, played exhibitions together. Dutch was a super person and I'm proud to have had such a wonderful friend. With that Arkansas drawl and mode of speech, he was very entertaining. He was always full of fun and he never said an unkind word about anyone. What a great shotmaker and teacher he was. He knew golf from A to Z."

Al Besselink (Tour champion and good friend of Dutch) said, "Everywhere Dutch went there was a crowd of people who were his good friends. He'd give me the shirt off his back — and he did."

Tommy Bolt (Top PGA champion in the 1950s and 1960s) remarked, "I marvelled at Dutch — what an easy tempo. Ol' Dutch could charm the skin off a snake, but he was too nice to have that killer instinct in competition. He would have been the greatest golfer of them all if he had been able to concentrate on golf more. You couldn't count the people he did favors for on the tour. They never hesitated to come to Dutch for favors, and he never turned one of them down when he could help."

Cal Brown (Honored sportswriter) remembered, "Dutch had a peculiar attitude toward people. He liked them. His butter would melt even the coldest fish. To rile Dutch, you had to prove you didn't like puppy dogs, that Santa Claus was a myth, that golf wasn't the grandest game in the whole of the outdoors, or perhaps, that you frowned on an occasional game of chance."

Kyle Burton (Former head professional at Olympic Club and Vintage Club, Indian Wells, California) said, "I never knew of a person who said a derogatory word about him. He had sophisticated smarts in a hillbilly mode of expression. I admired Mr. Dutch very much — he was liked and respected by everyone."

Bing Crosby (Entertainer supreme, tournament pioneer) declared, "Dutch was one of the real important men in the development of professional golf in the United States. His humor, good spirits and genial attitude contributed to everyone's enjoyment of the game."

Tim Crowley (Protegé of Dutch at Forest Hills) said, "I loved Dutch, and so did everyone that really knew him. I know of only one other person (my father) that enjoyed as much love and respect from his peers as Dutch."

George T. Davis (Former Sports Editor of the *Los Angeles Herald and Express*) wrote in 1956, "If a popularity poll were held among golfers, fans, and the press to establish the best-liked player of them all, I think you'd find the ol' Arkansas Traveler, Dutch Harrison, right up there at the top of the list."

Gardner Dickinson (PGA champion in the 1950s through the early 1970s) recalled, "We were all crazy about Dutch. He not only helped me with my golf but he helped a lot of youngsters. He set an example for younger pros in handling pressure situations, in sportsmanship and getting the most out of life. To Dutch the tour was like a family outing and he was always pulling for his opponents to do better. When you suffered through a couple of bad holes, he would say, 'C'mon, little buddy. Let's get it goin' again.'

"I remember he counseled me when I was negotiating with Wilson Sporting Goods. He convinced me I was worth twice what they were offering and I finally signed for that figure. Oh, he might hustle you, but he'd never cheat anybody. With Dutch it was easy come, easy go."

Chick Evans (Famous amateur golfer and U.S. Open Champion) said simply, "Dutch exemplified what a real professional should be."

Tennessee Ernie Ford (Celebrated entertainer and good friend of Dutch) remembered, "As an amateur player and lover of the game of golf, some of my warmest moments and hours were spent with Dutch. He endeared himself to people around the world with his down-home wit and great golf swing.

"So Dutch, I know you can hear me when I say, 'My prayerful wish is to one day meet again on a green that is always true, a fairway that is always green, and sand traps that are always raked, and hear you say to me once again, 'Time to tee it up, Mr. Ernie... an' please, Mr. Ernie, try to keep the club head on the ball as long as possible.'"

Bob Goalby (Master's champion, noted telecaster and Senior Tour Advisor) said, "If the world had more Dutch Harrisons in it, it would be a lot better place to live.

Dutch was the most friendly guy in the whole world. He never made an enemy. He gave me golf lessons and never charged me. Dutch was always trying to help everyone who liked golf.

"Guys like Dutch who were on the early tours had to hustle a bit to make ends meet. He was a sweet-talkin' guy, a bit coy like he was romancing somebody — never a con artist."

Stan Grossman (USGA Committeeman) recalled, "Dutch treated people in the entertainment field and the athletic and business worlds the same as he treated the working man, waiter, cook or shoeshine boy, all with the same respect and dignity. He was the most gentle man I have ever known. And never in all my years with him did I ever see him really angry."

Ralph Guldahl (Champion pro golfer of the 1930s; won consecutive U.S. Opens) emphasized, "We all liked Dutch. He was such a unique person. I always wanted to do a book on Dutch. He could charm a pearl out of an oyster."

W. Alfred Hayes, Sr. (Civic leader and builder of the Old Warson Country Club, St. Louis) said, "Old Warson Country Club loved Dutch Harrison. We loved him in the beginning, we love him now and we'll always love him. I've known lots of good golfers and lots of wonderful gentlemen, but I've never known a better combination of gentleman-golfer than Dutch Harrison. He believed that golf is a gentleman's game and everything associated with it should be conducted accordingly."

Ben Hogan (King of the pros in the 1940s and early 1950s) remarked, "Dutch was a good friend who knew everybody — he was a very pleasant person. He was a heckuva good golfer, and I might say he didn't win as much as he should have won. I thought he was a lot better player than his record showed — he should have won more of the major tournaments."

Betty Jameson (Texan child prodigy and LPGA champion) explained, "As great a golfer as Dutch was — and he was such a great golfer — I think of him as a superb human being. He was a beautiful person. I always had the feeling he was the Original Arkansas Traveler. His homespun humor, manner and character were like another original, the greatly beloved Will Rogers."

Otto Kohl (Professional golfer) recalled, "Dutch really gave me the incentive to make something of myself and graduate from caddie to pro. He taught me more than anyone about golf and real life. I think he helped more young pros get started than any other professional. I wished that I had been caddying for him at the U.S. Open in Merion, Pennsylvania when he lost by one stroke. I would have had him in first place."

Dick Kohlmann (Well-known St. Louis pro) said, "Dutch was an all-time great golfer possessing extraordinary skill at his chosen profession. He was not only big in stature but big in heart. I was one to be blessed with his good nature and congeniality as a good friend. His achievements brought joy and happiness to thousands who only knew "Mr. Dutch" as a person of great capabilities, inside and out. Dutch worked hard to preserve the integrity and tradition of the game of golf. His pathway is an inspiration that won't be forgotten."

Charlie Lacy (Head pro at Rancho Municipal in Los Angeles) remarked, "I've played in tournaments with Dutch for more years than I care to remember, and I always find him actually rooting for the other fellow. Golf is a sport with the ol' Traveler. Sure, he wants to win, and he wins his share, but he wants it to be by his own shots and not by the other fellow's errors...(he's) a man who treats others as he would be treated himself."

Palmer Lawrence (PGA tour professional) said, "Dutch was more than a legend of golf and I cherished knowing him. He always tried to help us younger golfers. At a tournament in Tucson I was surprised to find he even knew me. He came over to me and said, 'Mr. Palmer, I bought a ticket on you. I want you to do good for me now. Be relaxed out there. Take your time. Don't rush it. Don't try to do things you can't do.' He truly helped my game that day. No other player ever gave me confidence like that."

Lawson Little (Former U.S. Open Champion; U.S. and British Amateur Champion) reflected, "Dutch's infectious personality made everybody in the Hawaiian Islands love him, just as it did when I first got to know him in the Army. He had the generals at his beck and call — flying him to tournaments in B-17s."

Cary Middlecoff (Famed U.S. Open and Masters Champion) said, "I happened to be one of those fresh pigeons who first met Dutch in 1940-41 during a practice round before a tournament in Little Rock. Dutch downplayed his talent and disarmed all of us amateurs with his engaging jive. He proceeded to shoot a nifty 65 to win the two-dollar nassau. I didn't know then he was the best two-dollar nassau player in the world. His golf was outstanding, but what impressed me most was how much fun he was to be around. He didn't have a mean bone in his body. One hour after I met him I felt like he was an old friend. We remained close buddies ever after."

T.D. Morris (PGA professional) remembered, "One of the greatest things that ever happened to me was to go to work as caddie master for Dutch Harrison. I came from a poor family. Dutch took me under his wing and was a second father to me. He trained me and educated me. He literally raised me. He stimulated me to become a pro, but he taught me so much more about life. Everything I am and have today as a professional golfer I owe to Dutch Harrison.

"He had the best disposition on the golf course of any player I've ever seen. He always made you feel at ease."

Arnold Palmer (Top Honoree in Golf and King of Golfing Charisma) remarked, "Dutch was one of the real artists of the game and did so much for the tour. He was a good friend of mine and helped me a lot."

John Raitt (One of Dutch's favorite celebrities) said, "To Mr. Dutch I was his singin' cousin, Big John. He was my only golf teacher and such a good one. His friendship meant the world to me and my admiration of him as a person knows no bounds."

Henry Ransom (A true legend of pro golf and accomplished golf coach) said, "Dutch was my friend and a good one. He reminded me of my real friendly big Airedale dog — a lovable guy."

Johnny Revolta (Tour leader and teacher extraordinaire) recalled, "Dutch was unique in being able to perform so well two different roles: serving the amateur player in the pro shop and providing showcase tournament entertainment. He was a true and loyal friend."

Chi Chi Rodriguez (Champion pro golfer and golf humanitarian) said, "Dutch was the greatest shotmaker of all time. There may have been a greater golfer, but there was never a finer gentleman."

Dr. Dean Sauer, M.D. (Dutch's physician while at Old Warson) remembered his friend, "There is only one incomparable Dutch in golf's long history. He was deep in the affection of all of us who knew him. His great heart, courage and spirit, coupled with a matchless athletic skill will always be an inspiration to me. Dutch's gratitude for the smallest favor was unbelievable. No one ever matched his generosity. Now that he is in eternity, we truly know how fully he lived the old proverb, 'The only thing the hand can hold in death is that which it has given in life.'"

Randolph Scott (Esteemed movie actor) said, "I have fond memories of Dutch — such as at the El Rio Country Club, and the Rocky Mountain Oyster Club (Tucson). Dutch always slayed them with his scintillating wit. Amateur golfers came from afar to play with Dutch. What a wonderful friend he was."

Charlie Sifford (An early golf legend) spoke plainly, "A helluva man. One of the greatest men I ever met. A true gentleman. I enjoyed teaching Dutch and Porky Oliver how to shoot dice in Fort Wayne, Indiana."

Sam Snead (the "best golfer" Dutch ever met) said, "There will never be another Dutch. I had many outings with him and we had a lot of fun together. He was a good friend and I sure miss him. The Arkansas Traveler is a fitting name for Dutch. He's somewhere in Heaven plucking a pigeon for a two-dollar nassau."

Frank Stranahan (Top amateur player of his day and winner of many pro tournaments) said, "I admired Dutch greatly and always enjoyed playing with him. He encouraged and helped me with my game. The week after he presented me with his Wilson club (wedge) I won the Kansas City Open."

Bob Toski (A tour champion and renowned teacher and goodwill ambassador of golf) remarked, "Dutch has always been one of my favorite people, and I have many kind and happy memories of him when I was first on the tour. He was such a gentle and kind man. I don't think I ever heard Dutch Harrison raise his voice or get mad at anybody. I'm also indebted to him for helping build my character as a person. He was such a good storyteller and entertainer. I miss Dutch because he was so much fun. After a golf round if I came into the locker room and had shot 80, he'd say, 'Where'd you make all your birdies?' And he didn't have a weakness in his own game."

Lee Trevino (An all-pro since 1968, Hall of Famer, Superstar) said, "Dutch was an inspiration. A lot of good people don't realize how good Dutch Harrison really was as a golfer. He was like Bobby Jones and Ben Hogan, an important stepping stone in the development of professional golf. I certainly enjoyed Dutch."

Harvie Ward (Two-time former National Amateur Champion) remarked, "Dutch as a Senior Golfer was better than most of the young boys on the tour. A lot of that was because of temperament. His easy-going approach was instrumental. He enjoyed playing golf as much as anyone I ever knew."

Roger Williams (former Head Professional, Forest Hills, St. Louis area) said, "With all of his golf accomplishments, Dutch was better known for just one thing:

his love for his fellow man. Will Rogers said, 'I never met a man I didn't like.' Dutch said it in his own way, 'I never met a stranger.' You always felt when you were introduced to Dutch that he had known you for years. Some of the current PGA Tour stars have won millions in cash. Dutch won millions in friends."

Warren and Wilma Van Norman (St. Louis confidants of Dutch) both remembered their dear friend, "Great as Dutch was in his professional field — and he was a golfing legend — we will remember him as a marvelous human being. You would describe his personal qualities by making a list of all those things you would hope to find in your own parent, or your own child, or that you would hope others would find in you."

Christopher Morley once said, "There is only one success — to be able to spend your life in your own way." Dutch essentially achieved this and lived the kind of life that many only dream about. "My work is my sunshine," he would say.

The Bob Hope Testimonial was just one of the golden moments in the rich lifetime of the Arkansas Traveler. Though Dutch had no tangible fortune, he possessed copious amounts of spiritual wealth and gave it freely to all those who shared time with him.

He lived the sage adage, "To keep it, you must give it away." His smile and gentle Southern ways were imprinted on everyone he greeted. To remember Dutch is to be filled with a sense of serenity, a sudden tenderness, and a smile. Somewhere, Mr. Dutch is still travelin', golf club in hand.

Unbelievable
Shots
and
Rounds

"I don't mind playing anyone head-to-head except Dutch Harrison. He hits some shots you can't believe," said Sam Snead. "Golf balls just seem to act kindly for ol' Dutch."

Tommy Bolt concurred that Dutch's skill was unsurpassed:

"Dutch was the Michelangelo of the shotmakers in golf. His artistry with a club was a thrill to behold. If one golfer were chosen to play a difficult shot under trying circumstances, many pros would have chosen Dutch Harrison. Some of his shots seemed to defy the laws of physics."

Escape Shots

Pro Mason Rudolph asserted, "If the number of golf clubs had been limited to seven, everyone would be betting on Dutch, because he had more shots with fewer clubs than anyone."

Not many single shots are commemorated with a plaque, like the shot Dutch made on the sixth hole of the

Pecan Valley Golf Course, San Antonio in August, 1963.

Harold Blaylock tells the story, "For the grand opening of the golf course, we invited four well-known professionals, Jimmy Demaret, Miller Barber, Byron Nelson and Dutch, to play in the dedicative exhibition. On this 600-yard, par-5, Dutch's second shot carried behind an oak tree. The ball rested in heavy grass two feet from the tree. Dutch opened up the face of his 8-iron. He magically imparted spin to that ball so that it followed a curving arc — something like a wind-blown lazy pop fly. It looked like it was going out of bounds but gradually curved toward the green where it wound up 8 feet from the hole. After that shot, Byron Nelson remarked, 'That shot carried out of bounds for 5 minutes before coming back to the green.'

"It had more air time than Lindbergh. The gallery had never seen a shot like that before and they still talk about it at the Pecan Valley Club. I'll always remember the flight of that ball, almost hanging in space out of bounds, then curving toward the hole as if it was on automatic pilot. Only Dutch could have executed a miraculous shot like that. We placed a plaque on the oak tree that blocked Dutch's path to the green and it's still there today."

Paul Runyan and Ellsworth Vines tell about a shot that Dutch did better than anyone else and is one of his finest legacies. Dutch used it from heavy rough when he needed to loft the ball over a bunker onto the green and then stop it quickly.

Ellsworth Vines noted how Dutch could make his ball stop close to the pin and others could not, "I asked Dutch to help me add that shot to my repertoire one day at Brentwood Country Club in Los Angeles. He was so marvelous with the shot, lifting the ball and dropping it so softly. He spent about a half hour with me. I must have hit over 50 balls, but I never could duplicate that shot."

Paul Runyan was also impressed with this stroke. He said, "I finally figured out that Dutch did it by using a very tight grip and transmitting his raw power from his shoulders and arms to the club, allowing the club to tear through the grass and maintain full control of the ball. Few others could duplicate the combination of essentials needed for this shot."

Chick Harbert exalted, "Dutch was the only one that could play the pitch-and-run on hard greens. Some of the greens were so slick and smooth that they appeared to be ironed. Dutch would pitch and run so superbly. He could also invent some amazing escape shots."

One famous escape shot was captured on the TV World Series of Golf. Dutch served not only as a commentator on the show, but also as a contestant. In a match at Cypress Point, he drove his ball into the heavy rough behind a cluster of trees, leaving a 180-190 yard shot to the green.

Bob Crosby, microphone in hand, asked Dutch, "What are you going to do here?" Dutch's expressive hands moved into motion as he described his strategy to the TV audience. "Mr. Bob," Dutch drawled, "I think I can take this lil' 2-iron an' wagon-train the ball through the trees. It's been rainin' hard so the ball will go hoppin' 'cross the wet sand of the traps near the green an' roll up toward the flag."

Dutch did exactly that, thus enabling him to drop a 10-foot putt for a birdie.

Important Shots

When asked in 1944 what his most important shot was in his career, Dutch answered, "The shot I liked best was a chip-shot on the last hole of the 1939 Oakland Open in California. It was a par-5 hole an' I had to get a 4 to tie Dick Metz. My second shot failed to reach the green. From the rough, I had the pitch to a green that sloped sharply away from me. I played it so it would be detained by the heavy grass at the apron an' it ran down to within 4 feet from the hole."

"Dick Metz recalls that Dutch was able to tie him for

the championship with that last putt, "I think he learned to chip so well because of the early sand greens, and later the grass greens that were in poor condition. Often he would take his ball from the middle of the green to the edge of the green and chip it close to the hole. When playing in heavy rain, he might elect to chip from the fringe rather than putt. These circumstances probably helped him to acquire his delicate touch in chipping."

Another favorite shot was one at the Azalea City Open held at Mobile Country Club, Springhill, Alabama. On the 17th green, Dutch received a bad break when his second shot struck a spectator at the right side of the green and ricocheted 50 feet into the woods. The situation looked hopeless when he found his ball with a bad lie in uncut grass beneath the trees. The ball was 100 feet from the cup. Dutch executed one of his finest recovery shots that struck the pin and fell dead next to the hole.

"My wedge was my snake killer. It sure got me out of a lot of trouble an' when I was within wedge distance of the green an' not in 'jail' (a hazard), I always had confidence I could make a birdie," he declared.

During the famous Bobby Locke exhibition match at Tulsa Country Club in 1947, Dutch teed off on a par-4 hole and smoked a driver "straight as a string."

Skee Riegel, the 1947 U.S. Amateur Champion, who was playing in the foursome, knew the course well and asked Dutch, "Did you like that drive?"

Dutch responded, "I never hit it better in my life."

Riegel smiled and said, "Okay, I'll bet $20 against you on this hole."

Riegel thought Dutch had hit the ball so far it probably reached the water some 100 yards in front of the green. As the players reached their second shots, Riegel was chuckling to himself — he spied Dutch's ball in the water.

After surveying all possibilities, the Dutchman selected his wedge, waded in the water, and calmly splashed the ball out of the water. It landed two feet from the pin for an easy birdie. Riegel negotiated a par and handed Dutch a $20 bill that had seen better days.

"The great golfer plays with his hands," Dutch declared. "I can practice a long time an' not develop callouses. That's because I do not grip the club tightly. Ya can tell a lot about a golfer by looking at his hands. When he sits down an' lays his hands flat on the table, that's your winner. Because if his palms are straight down, that means his hands are relaxed. And if his hands are relaxed, that means his whole body is relaxed. There's no way for the body to be tense if the hands are relaxed. When I see a golf opponent with a fist clenched, I know he's not relaxed an' I think to myself, 'I can beat him.'"

Dutch originated the expression "I hit it quail high," meaning that he could knock it extremely low when playing into the wind or out from underneath the branches of a tree. At age 59, Dutch was qualifying for the U.S. Open in St. Louis when he found his ball underneath a tree on the last hole.

Stan Grossman was caddying for Dutch and encouraged him to just chip back onto the fairway, "You can be medalist, Dutch, by just playing it safe."

Dutch said, "Mr. Gross, do you see all those people up around that 18th hole? Well, I'm going to show them a little class. I'm going to take this 3-iron an' I'm going to hit it quail high, then it's going to rise over that bunker to the green."

"Dutch hit it perfectly and it wound up on the fringe of the green," said Stan.

"All the people were clapping when he got to the green. They really appreciated that difficult shot. I remember another 18th hole approach shot he made in Florida that wound up 6 to 8 inches from the hole. When Dutch went to mark his ball, he noted the silent crowd around the green and smilingly said, 'Are all you people handcuffed? How 'bout givin' the man a hand?'

"Everybody broke up after that and became a supportive crowd."

In the 1947 Hawaiian Open, Dutch executed a wedge shot that left everyone gasping. It carried some 130 yards over some high trees and stopped cold beside the pin on a hard and fast green.

Dutch's playing competitors, pro Harry Cooper and amateur Arthur Armstrong, looked at each other in shock and Harry said, "How in the world can that guy stop a ball on a dime with these fast greens?"

Arthur replied, "I can't understand it either."

After the tournament Dutch presented his Wilson pitching wedge to Arthur and said, "With the grooves I've deepened in the face of this club, it's agin' the rules to use this in PGA Tournaments. The club is yours."

Many's the golfer who rued betting against Dutch with wedge in hand. After Wilbur Johnson hit a 9-iron about two feet from the cup on his second shot, he exclaimed to Dutch, "Now put one closer than that." Without hesitation, Dutch asked, "What are the odds?"

"I'll lay you 10 to 1," Wilbur responded without thinking. As Dutch zeroed his wedge shot closer to the pin, Wilbur cringed. "That was the easiest $10 the Dutchman ever made."

Arthur Armstrong remembered one pro-am tournament in which Dutch finessed some unusual chip shots, "The golf course in Sacramento had standing water from a downpour. When Dutch reached the green, he'd carry his ball off the green twice as far from the hole as his ball originally was and chip dead to the pin every time. Our foursome was stunned to see him knocking it next to the hole when they couldn't putt from ten feet as close."

One of Dutch's favorite recovery shots was with a putter and gave spectators a thrill in 1951.

"I was playin' the famous par-3, 16th hole at Cypress Point an' standin' on the edge of a cliff 80 feet above the ocean," Dutch said. "My ball was in that wiry ice plant that surrounds the green. If I'd hit the ball from the right-handed stance, I would have fallen down the cliff an' killed myself. So I turned my putter around an' hit from the left side, an' got the ball close to the hole for a par. The wind was so hard I thought I'd be blown out to sea. Bob Hope hit the nail on the head when he said this course has the looks of Christie Brinkley an' the tenderness of Tokyo Rose.

"I was never a very good mudder, but I never had it as bad as Sam Snead did when we played together in the goo at Breckenridge (San Antonio). That was one wet Texas Open. Sam hit a short approach shot an' the ball stuck to the divot that stayed caked onto his club. He asked, 'What do I do now?'

"I told him, 'Run over to the hole an' shake your club head real hard.'

"That sticky gumbo would bog a buzzard's shadow."

An admirer of Dutch's putting was Ky Laffoon, brilliant but erratic tour pro from Oklahoma, of Irish-French-Cherokee descent. He was known to punish a misbehaving putter by dragging it along the highway behind his car.

After finishing out of the money in the Montgomery Invitational in 1945, he said to Dutch, "Let's take some time off. The way I played in this tournament, I'm going back to the Reservation and I'd like you (with your putting touch) to ride in the back seat and hold my putter."

Dutch recalled, "Somethin' musta worked, 'cause he won the Montgomery Invitational the followin' year with some wonderful puttin'. Ky an' I had alotta fun."

"Dutch was an exceptional putter," claimed Wilbur Johnson. "He one-putted nine holes in a row at the 1939 Miami Open — and many were lengthy putts."

Frank Stiedle, one of the longest off the tee in pre-World War II days, remembers, "I could often beat Dutch tee to green, but ol' Dutch could beat anybody on the greens. I'll always place my money on Dutch as a putter."

Jack Berkley of Old Warson spoke of Dutch as one of golf's great putters, "Dutch was a fantastic putter. At Old Warson he looked like he hooked every putt he hit.

I don't know how he did it. Some say he learned from Bobby Locke who Dutch thought was the best putter of them all. He'd talk about 'knee knockers' and puttin-'itus,' a malady of tensed hands that comes with old age, and he'd say, 'Wristy putters will eat cold cereal.'

"He never suffered these afflictions like other pros. He'd teach everybody to 'hold the putter like a marsh-mallow.' At his prime, his putts caught the hole like a falcon sweeping down on a rabbit."

When Dutch sank a long putt to win a tournament, it was vintage Harrison: "That long putt I made was the kind ya sorta close your eyes on an' swing. When I got up enough nerve to peek I couldn't see the ball an' I thought, 'Looka here! What's happened?'"

Or he would say, "I got lucky on the greens. My puttin' was like a blind pig pickin' acorns."

Sneaky Long

When Dutch would drive from the tee, he concentrated on keeping the ball in play and consequently was short of the drives by the longest hitters.

"I'd give up ten yards to keep it on the fairway. Watch the guys who try to kill the ball. They'll wind up in the rough." His byword was, "Don't over-swing. Just hit it straight as a string."

Nevertheless, Jay Hebert recalled what a large arc Dutch could produce in his swing, "Dutch was 'sneaky long.' By increasing his arc on par-5 holes he could outdrive just about anyone in order to reach the green in two. He could really let it out."

Another observer said, "Dutch could outdrive anybody he wanted to on those long holes. 'Swish' went the club and the impact sounded like a sledgehammer hitting a block of concrete. The ball whistled like a German buzz bomb. He could hit it a ton — winding up about 60 yards ahead of the big hitters."

Ellsworth Vines recollects Dutch's drives at the Western Open in 1950 (Brentwood Country Club, Los

Angeles). "When we came to the longest par-5 hole, the spectators were still oohing and aahing over Sam Snead's prodigious poke that permitted him to reach the green in two. After Dutch heard this, he volunteered, 'That's not so great. I can do that.'

"And he did. He could be as long as he wanted to be — over 300 yards when he was at his peak."

Wilbur Johnson recalls, "On many par-4 holes, Dutch used only a driver and a putter. Countless times he drove the 320-yard par-4 at the Riverside Golf Course in Little Rock with a driver, even driving over the green on windy days. As he became older, he'd say, 'I can't keep up with you flat-bellies.'

"Then he'd extend himself and outdistance them all. He could take that swing and make it look so easy, yet get so much power into it."

Renowned sportswriter Jim Murray of the *Los Angeles Times* described the Dutch Harrison swing as "a thing so soft you could spread it on bread — and so effective he could have broken par swinging a rake, a stove poker or even a stove. Harrison doesn't hit a golf ball, he caresses it. The ball usually returns the favor."

Dutch learned to minimize mistakes on the golf course by keeping the ball in play away from hazards and out of bounds. He could maneuver the ball at will, hitting high "rainmakin'" drives when he had the wind with him, and low "wind cheaters" when he was shooting into the wind. He would work the ball from left to right or right to left as needed. He would say to himself, "Don't crush it, because you might rush it; rocket it, an' I don't pocket it."

Greatest Day in Golf

One of his finest rounds of golf was the final round of the 1937 Nassau Open Tournament in Nassau, Bahamas. Horton Smith called it "the greatest round of golf I ever saw." Although Dutch won three small tournaments in 1937, this round was the apex of his career to that point. In an interview a decade later with D. L. Darsie, Dutch described this last round as "my greatest day in golf."

"Up to that time I never really clicked on the golf tour. In 1936 I played the winter circuit without earnin' enough to pay my expenses. I knew the 'big boys' to speak to, but none of them considered me in the same league with them. I didn't myself.

"I played well enough through the first three rounds of the Nassau Open to place me among the top 20 to 25 players as the final round came up. Because of my good showin', they put me in a feature threesome with Horton Smith an' Sam Byrd. They were two of the 'hotshots' I had been readin' about an' watchin' with envious eyes.

"Now, at last, I had the chance to play with 'em. It was my big opportunity an' I went into this last round fiercely determined to win a share of the prize money or know the reason why not.

"At the same time I was nervous. I feared I might blow up under fire. I knew that I could play some good golf, but I also knew that I could play some all-fired bad golf. This time it was strictly up to me. I didn't want to wreck the chances of Mr. Horton an' Mr. Byrd, but neither did I want to be blowin' the chances of one Dutch Harrison.

"So I was fidgety as we came up to the first tee. But the course was not too long an' was well-suited to my game. I tried to forget that 20 of the best professional golfers in the world stood between me an' first money — an' that I had missed my chance many times in the past. I put my mind to work at the very first tee, concentratin' on swingin' smoothly an' hittin' that first drive as well as I could hit a ball. My concentration paid dividends. The drive was straight an' I laid my next shot so close to the hole that a blind man could have dropped a putt for a birdie. I wasn't blind — I dropped the putt an' I was off to the races.

"My nervousness disappeared an' my confidence rose. I didn't worry anymore about hurtin' the scorin' chances of Mr. Horton an' Mr. Byrd. I thought about nothin' but Dutch Harrison an' how I was going to concentrate on every single shot in that round.

"When I hit the half-way point in 32 strokes, I had arrived in golf. I was no longer an upstart. I was in the first ten with nine holes to go. On that last nine, it would have been so easy to blow the works through carelessness or overconfidence. So I deliberately tried to think only of the shot I was playin', to make the best shot I could play, an' to put it so close to the flag I couldn't miss the putt.

"It paid off. I came home in 32, givin' me a final round score of 64. I moved up to the front only two strokes behind Sam Snead's winnin' total of 276. I had hit pay dirt. It was my first really good showin' in a big tournament an' broke the ice for me besides settin' a course record."

Lowest Competitive Scores

"In 1945 when I was still a Sergeant in the Army, I won the Decatur Open Championship."

Major McCallister, who Dutch served under at Wright Field, related that Dutch had presented him with his first prize of $1,000, because the Major had done so much for him while in the Army.

"I'm real proud of my final round in that tournament," Dutch said. "I started three strokes ahead of Mr. John Revolta, but he shot a 62 on that final round for a course record. Mr. John was a friendly, likable chap an' he had helped me cure my hook back in the 1930s. Well, he shot the daylights out of the course that last day — scored 30 on the first nine. Then he sends word back to me on the first tee about his record score. In the early days there were no walkie-talkies to relay scores of opponents. Mr. John was tryin' to apply a little pressure before I even started. After he shot 32 on the last nine, he was pretty confident he had the tournament in the bag. But I kept workin' an' almost equaled his 62 with a 63. That day in golf almost equaled my lowest competitive scores of 61 in the Texas Open in 1961 an' 61 in 1953 at the Hobbs Golf Club in Hobbs, New Mexico when I walked away with all that bettin' loot.

"Playin' in bad weather always bothered me. In some of those Bing Crosbys outta Monterey it was colder than a well-driller's fanny in the Klondike, an' I'd have trouble grippin' the club. I played in Toronto in a windbreaker, in Portland in a rainsuit, an' in Monterey in a heavy jacket. I even played in snow once in the Texas Open. They really have some log-rollin' an' toad-chokin' storms down there. But the worst weather was when that thunder sounded like the tater wagon rollin' round the heavens an' ol' St. Elmo's fire danced around. The golf course was the last place you wanted to be, an' I sure had some close calls."

Pulling a "Dutch Harrison"

A new arrival on the pro tour received his "new-kid-on-the-block" indoctrination from Dutch. It became common to hear golf professionals and amateurs say during a match, "Don't pull a 'Dutch Harrison' on me."

They would be referring to a shot that became as famous as Dutch himself. Friends told about the wonderful way he took what appeared to be his beautiful, powerful swing, but by cutting across the ball to feather it, he camouflaged the lesser power transmitted to the ball. He'd squint his eye at those fellows who were shading the unwritten rules of golf by looking into his bag to copy the club he had used.

The earliest report of Dutch's feather shot was by an assistant professional at Little Rock Country Club. Dutch had just returned from tour in the late 1930s and was playing a round with the assistant who had what would normally be an iron shot. Dutch showed him how to take his 2-wood and cut across the ball in order to reduce the distance of the shot. To the amazement of the assistant pro, Dutch put the shot right on the green.

Doug Sanders maintained, "Dutch was the daddy fox of them all. He would take that big old swing and you could never tell if he hit it hard. I remember when we had a match with Bo Wininger and Bobby French. It was the ninth hole, a par-3 for all the money. Dutch took his normal swing and that ball took off straight for the hole and couldn't have stopped more than an inch or two from the hole. Dutch turned and stuck that 1-iron right in their face and said, 'Boy, I keeled that one, I really keeled that one.'

"So Bo Wininger takes a 2-iron and the people behind the green just gawk as that shot goes over their heads. I had a 3-iron in my hand and was almost ready to hit a 4-iron when Dutch comes over after his shot and says, 'What are you doin'? Are you goin' to make a hole in one?'

"I said, 'No.'

"Dutch said, 'Well, put that club back in the bag an' don't show them anything.' Fortunately, I didn't have to shoot because our ball was so close to the pin.

"In one practice round we drove our golf balls side by side and I asked Dutch what he was going to hit next.

"He says, 'You hit a 6-iron, I'm goin' to hit a 4-iron.'

"I said okay and we both put our shots on the green. Two holes later our balls are side by side again.

"I asked, 'Dutch, what are you going to hit?'

"He says, 'I'm going to hit a 6, but you better hit a 4 this time.'

"'Wait a minute, Dutch. Two holes back you said'...and he breaks in and says, 'I'm going to turn on this one a little more.'

"You could never tell. One time he'd hit a 4-iron 160 yards and next time he'd hit it 185 yards and the next time he'd hit it 205 yards. You could never tell in his swing if there was any difference. He had all the shots with every club."

Dutch finessed most of the golf professionals until they would stop looking in his bag and asking what club he had used. Ken Venturi was pitted against Dutch in a

Challenge Tournament televised from the Monterey Country Club. They came to a par-3 hole and Dutch pulled out a 6-iron, mentioning to Ken that he really needed to impact this one. Ken took out a 6-iron and flew the green.

"That was the last time I ever looked in another person's bag," Ken admitted.

Dow Finsterwald, PGA champion, learned a similar lesson from Dutch at the Motor City Open in 1952. He also watched Dutch, then airmailed the green by 30 yards.

Lionel Herbert, another PGA champion, recalls playing with Dutch and Lloyd Mangrum the last day of the Phoenix Open, "I was awed being paired with the tournament leaders — they had so much road knowledge. We came to the eighth hole, a long par-3.

"Dutch takes out his 3-wood, puts the ball on the green and says, 'I hit the stuffin's outta that one.'

"So I hit my 4-wood. The gallery in back of the green never had to move as my ball soared over their heads. That was the first and last time ol' Dutch pulled that fake shot on me."

Dutch finished with a 67 to place second to Lloyd Mangrum in this 1952 tournament, his last before becoming head pro at Ardmore.

Golf champion David Marr recalled that his second year in tournament play was 1958 at the Bing Crosby. The seventh hole was about 100 yards. Dutch took out a 5-iron and hit a soft shot to the green in front of the ocean.

"I had heard stories about Dutch, so I took out the club I had planned to use, a 7-iron, and hit it within 1 foot of the hole. I looked up at Dutch and he just grinned. From then on, he never tried to finesse me."

The wily fox used his bag of tricks to qualify for his last U.S. Open. Kimo was caddying for Dutch and tells the story, "Joe Jimenez and Dutch tied for the last qualifying position at Old Warson, St. Louis. On the first playoff hole, a par-3, Dutch used his 5-iron instead of 8-

iron and eased the ball on the green. Joe took an 8-iron and really jumped on it, pulling it into the woods so that Dutch won the hole and the play-off."

Dutch had fun teaching amateurs and pros not to peek at the club selection of other players. He was like Brer Rabbit of Uncle Remus, as many of the top golfers fell for his trickery, not just once, but a multitude of times. Dutch was playing with Tommy Bolt in the Doral Open in Florida in 1963. It was the ninth hole, a par-3. Several threesomes were finished and waiting at the tee. Dutch played a wood shot that landed in the middle of the green. Tommy Bolt took out a wood, then decided on a 2-iron and hit it far over the green.

Everyone doubled over in laughter as Tommy said, "How did I ever fall for this again?"'

When someone selected the same club Dutch had used, and watched with dismay as his ball soared over the green, Dutch would roll his eyes and say, "My, my, Mr. Henry, that ball o' yours sure did have extree pep. Cain't understand it. You best call the manufacturer. Well, I guess you owe me a hundred. That's a durn shame." (From Al Barkow's *Golf's Golden Grind*)

Dutch's artistry during spontaneous clinics certainly belied his aging bones and still made onlookers take notice in the 1970s. Sportswriter Bob Allison witnessed a late afternoon clinic in the chilly winter air of Phoenix. Dutch was demonstrating shots with his old "99 wedge" to budding stars Paul and Tom Purtzer.

As Dutch neatly thumped one ball after another out of a bunker to within spitting distance of the hole, he said, "If you gonna hit 1,000 practice shots, you oughta (thump!) hit about 800 of 'em (thump!) close to the green before you (thump!) go out there an' beat your brains out with the drive (thump!). You gotta (thump!) make that li'l ol' dude talk to you on a (thump!) shot like this. You gotta (thump!) get that action on it. You ain't gonna (thump!) beat anybody unless you can do that."

Then from behind the bunker, "The guys today don't try to learn the little lob shots anymore," as he spun a few high pitches over the sand to stop dead to the pin despite a steeply sloping green.

Next a few 9-irons from 30 to 40 yards in front of the green finished stiff to the pin. Allison remembers the Purtzer's eyes bugging as the two exclaimed almost in unison, "Unbelievable!"

Sources and References

Persons

Akana, David and Ellie
Akana, Dutch Harrison
Akana, Helen Dillon
Akana, Joe
Akana, Kekuhaupio
Akana, Nalani
Alexander, Skip
Allen, Bob and Edith
Alvarez, Trini
Anderson, Andy
Anderton, Mrs. Frank
Arcaro, Eddie
Archer, George
Armstrong, Arthur
Barber, Jerry
Barber, Miller
Bass, Bill
Beman, Deane
Bennedek, Martha
Berg, Patty
Berkley, Jack
Besselink, Al
Billingsley, Carolyn
Blaisdell, Richard K., M.D.
Blaylock, Harold
Blomquist, Ralph
Bolt, Tommy
Brown, Cal
Brown, Hugh
Broyles, Frank
Bryant, Bill
Bryant, Jean A.
Bulla, Johnny
Burke, Jack, Jr.
Burton, Kyle
Campbell, Glen
Carter, Reese

Chong, Kahala Akana
Coe, Charlie
Consolver, Ted
Crenshaw, Ben
Crosby, Bob
Crowley, Ed
Crowley, Timothy
Cusik, Johnny
Dahl, Marv and Shirley
Darragh, Ted
Davis, George T.
De Vicenzo, Roberto
Delgado-Ringor, Annie
Delmar, Mrs. Jack
Demaret, Jimmy
Dey, Joe
Dickinson, Gardner
Dobereiner, Peter
Dowell, Walter A.
Doyle, Scorpy
Eliaser, Dr. Maurice, Jr.
Fairfield, Don
Faye, Alice
Fazio, George
Ferree, Jim
Fetchik, Mike
Finsterwald, Dow
Fleck, Jack
Fleming, Pete
Ford, Doug
Fraley, Oscar
French, Colonel
Furgol, Marty
Gallagher, Jack
Goalby, Bob
Grizzelle, Lucille
Grossman, Stan
Grout, Jack
Guldahl, Ralph

Haas, Fred, Jr.
Hamilton, Bob and June
Hamilton, John
Hamilton, Everett
Harbert, Chick
Harris, Lebron
Harris, Phil
Harrison, E. J. "Dutch"
Harrison, Emma
Harrison, Kimo and Molly
Harrison, Shirley
Hawkins, Fred
Hayes, W. Alfred, Sr.
Heafner, Paige and Vance
Hebert, Jay
Hebert, Lionel
Henry, Bill
Hickey, John
Highfill, Wilma
Hines, Jimmy
Hogan, Ben
Hull, Jack and Sue
Isom, Charlie
Jacobs, Tommy
Jameson, Betty
Jemsek, Frank
Jemsek, Joe
Jimenez, Joe
Johnson, Mrs. William "Teddy"
Johnson, Wilbur
Kauaihilo, Anne (sister of
    Thelma)
Keiser, Herman
Kirwin, Florence (sister of
    Thelma)
Keyes, George
Koehler, Dr. George
Kohl, Otto
Kohlmann, Dick
Kretlow, Lou
Kroll, Dick
Lacy, Charlie
Lawrence, Palmer
Leon, Dave
Lewis, Charles F., Jr.

Littler, Gene
Locke, Bobby
Loudermilk, Hardy
Mapes, Charlie
Marr, David
Maxwell, Billy
McCrotty, John
McDonnell, William
Menkus, David
Metz, Dick
Middlecoff, Cary
Miller, Del
Moeller, Larry
Monteyro, Lt. Col. Romeo M.
Morris, T.D.
Mullins, Moon
Murdoch, Joe
Murphy, Don
Nagle, Kel
Nicklaus, Jack
Nuelle, Bob
O'Connell, Jack
Osment, Barney
Palmer, Arnold
Payne, Jim
Penick, Harvey
Penna, Toney
Picard, Henry
Pilcher, Dan
Player, Gary
Pounders, Leon
Price, R.G.
Raitt, John
Ransom, Henry
Revolta, Johnny
Reynolds, Johnny
Roarke, Cecil
Rodriguez, Chi Chi
Rosburg, Bob
Ross, J.M.
Roussin, Steve
Rubin, Larry
Rudolph, Mason
Runyan, Paul
Sanders, Doug

Sauer, Dr. Dean
Scott, Randolph
Sharlau, Herman
Shaw, Bob
Sifford, Charlie
Sikes, Danny
Sikes, R.J
Skidmore, William
Snead, Sam
Spray, Richard
Stiedle, Frank
Stranahan, Frank
Swanson, John
Switzer, Joe
Tabor, Ed
Thomson, Peter
Toler, Earl
Toski, Bob
Trevino, Lee
Tucker, Forrest
Ukauka, Jimmy
Van Norman, Wilma and Warren
Venturi, Ken
Vines, Ellsworth
Vossler, Ernie
Wade, Charles "Monk"
Warters, Jim
Watkins, Everett J.
Welk, Lawrence
Weslock, Nick
White, Charlie
Whittaker, Paul
Wiesenthal, Harold
Williams, Andy
Williams, Roger
Wofford, Peter
Worsham, Lew

Newspapers

Albany Times Union
Arkansas Gazette/Democrat (Orville Henry)
Atlanta Journal (Furman Bisher)
Beaumont Enterprise
Beaumont Journal
Chicago Tribune
Chicago Daily News
Chicago Herald American
Cincinnati Post-Enquirer (Pat Harmon)
Cleveland News
Columbia Tribune (Greg Harvey)
Dayton Daily News
Denver Post
Florida Golfer
Fort Worth Star Telegram
Greensboro Daily News
Harrisburg Patriot
Harrisburg Telegraph
Honolulu Advertiser and Star-Bulletin (Bill Gee, Bill Kwon)
Houston Post (Jack Gallagher)
Kansas City Star
Los Angeles Examiner
Los Angeles Herald and Express
Los Angeles Times (Jim Murray, Shav Glick)
Miami Herald
Milwaukee Journal
Minneapolis Journal
Minneapolis Tribune
Nashville Banner
New Orleans Times
Oakland Post-Inquirer
Oakland Tribune
Odessa American
Phoenix Gazette (Bob Allison)
Quincy Herald-Whig (Chuck Brady, Johnny Nelson)

San Antonio Evening News
San Antonio Express
San Antonio Light (Harold Scherwitz)
San Diego Union
San Francisco Chronicle
San Francisco Examiner
Schenactady Union-Star (Bill Arsenault)
St. Louis Globe-Democrat (Robert L. Burnes, Bill Beck)
St. Paul Dispatch
St. Paul Pioneer Press
St. Petersburg Evening Independent
Toledo Blade
Toledo Times
United Press International
Wichita Beacon News
Wichita Eagle
York Dispatch
York Gazette and Daily

Booklets and Record Books

Dutch Harrison Book Committee, Bob Hope Pro-Am Dinner (various articles, photographs, correspondence)
Members Handbook, Country Club of Little Rock
Official PGA Tournament Record Books Of Time Remembered — A History of West Shore Country Club,
Camp Hill Senior Tour Books
TPA Tour Books
United States Golf Association Record Books
Wilson Sporting Goods, Wilson Information for Press and Radio

Libraries and Museums

Flagler, Henry Morrison Museum ("Whitehall")
Golf House Library and Museum
Little Rock Library
Memorial Library, York, Pennsylvania
Miller, Ralph W., Golf Library, City of Industry, California
National News Library, London
North Palm Beach, Florida
PGA Hall of Fame, Library and Museum

Golf Clubs and Associations

Bellerive Country Club
Country Club of York
Dornick Hills Country Club
El Rio Golf Course
Forest Hills Golf and Country Club
Ganton Golf Club
Little Rock Country Club
Oak Hills Country Club
Olympic Club
Old Warson Country Club
Pebble Beach Country Club
Pecan Valley Golf Course
Portland Golf Club
Professional Golfers Association of America (PGA)
Riviera Country Club
Seminole Golf Club
United States Golf Association
Vintage Club
Wack Wack Golf and Country Club
Waialae Country Club
West Shore Country Club

Selected References

Armour, Richard. 1962. *Golf is a Four Letter Word*. Hammond, Hammond & Company, London, 123p.

Barkow, Al. 1974. *Golf's Golden Grind—The History of the Tour*. Harcourt/Brace/Jovanovich, 310p.

Bartlett, Michael. 1973. *Bartlett's World Golf Encyclopedia*. Bantam Books, Inc., 486p.

Bates, Daisy. 1987. *The Long Shadow of Little Rock*. University of Arkansas Press, p. 188

Bolt, Tommy, with W.C. Griffith. 1969. *How to Keep Your Temper on the Golf Course*. David McKay Company, Inc., 145p.

Darsie, D.L. 1950. *My Greatest Day in Golf*. A. S. Barnes & Co. Inc., pp. 64-68.

Demaret, Jimmy. 1954. *My Partner, Ben Hogan*. McGraw Hill, 214p.

Dobereiner, Peter. 1981. *The World of Golf*. Atheneum, 287 p.

Gibson, Nevin H. 1968. *A Pictorial History of Golf*. A.S. Barnes and Company, Inc., 237p.

Gleason, Dan. 1976. *The Great, The Grand and The Also-Ran—Rabbits and Champions on Pro-Golf Tour*. Random House, 238p.

Hagen, Walter, with Margaret Seaton Heck. 1957. *The Walter Hagen Story*. William Heinemann Ltd., Great Britain, 299p.

Hitch, T.K. and Kuramoto, M.I. *Waialae Country Club, The First Half Century*. 1981, Waialae Country Club, 220p.

Jenkins, Dan. 1970. *The Dogged Victims of Inexorable Fate*. Berkley Publishing Corporation, 286p.

McCormack, Mark H. 1967. *Arnie—The Evolution of a Legend*. Simon and Schuster, 318p.

Nicklaus, Jack, with Herbert Warren Wind. 1969. *The Greatest Game of All*. Simon and Schuster, 416p.

Nicklaus, Jack, with Ken Bowden. 1978. *On and Off the Fairway*. Simon and Schuster, 256p.

Peterson, B. B. 1984. *Notable Women of Hawaii*. University of Hawaii Press, 427p.

Randolph, Vance. 1947. *Ozark Superstitions*. Dover Publications, Inc. New York, 367p.

Rice, Grantland. 1954. *The Tumult and the Shouting*. A. S. Barnes and Company, Inc., 368p.

Seitz, Nick. 1982. CBS Golf Spot, Golf Digest/Tennis Inc., 182p.

Steel, Donald and Ryde, Peter. (American Advisory Editor: Herbert Warren Wind), 1975. *The Encyclopedia of Golf*. Viking Press, Inc., p. 171, 480 p.

Ward-Thomas, Pat. 1976. *The World Atlas of Golf*. Mitchell Beazley Publishers Limited, London, 280 p.

Wind, Herbert Warren. 1948. *The Story of American Golf*. Farrar, Straus and Company, New York, 502p.